A World of Grace

AN INTRODUCTION
TO THE THEMES AND FOUNDATIONS
OF KARL RAHNER'S THEOLOGY

A World of Grace

Edited by
LEO J. O'DONOVAN

A Crossroad Book
THE SEABURY PRESS · NEW YORK

1980
The Seabury Press
815 Second Avenue
New York, N.Y. 10017

Printed in the United States of America

Library of Congress Cataloging in Publication Data

Main entry under title:

A World of grace.
"A Crossroad book."
Bibliography: p. 185
1. Rahner, Karl, 1904–   —Addresses, essays,
lectures.   I. O'Donovan, Leo J.
BX4705.R287W67   230'.2'0924   79-25588
ISBN 0-8164-0212-4   ISBN 0-8164-2006-8 pbk.

Contents

Preface

WE live in a world that is growing at the same time ever closer and yet further apart. On the one hand there are astonishing new technologies for communication and travel, for industry and leisure. We can dial a business call direct to another continent. On American television we can see a baby being born tomorrow in Japan. Raw materials once imported by clipper ships are now delivered by Greek supertankers. We have grown accustomed to seeing pictures beamed to us from the moon and from still more distant realms of outer space. But, on the other hand, it often appears that we have not been brought closer together by these achievements: they remind us instead of our distance from one another. Global suspicions are aggravated rather than quieted during nuclear disarmament talks. Multinational corporations seem more a threat to free political process than an encouragement to commercial cooperation. Developing countries are not less but more exploited in their relations with richer nations, and we speak now not only of the Third World but also, ruefully, of the Fourth. Whether inner or outer, our pictures of ourselves can seldom be clearly focussed. Thus we live not only amidst an ever increasing pluralism but, as a prominent American theologian has said, in an insistently conflictual pluralism.

How easily, then, it may seem presumptuous to present a collection of theological essays entitled *A World of Grace*. Can we really speak of *a* world today, much less of a *gracious* world? Does it not seem time for the traditional pretensions of theology to retire from the scene, yielding to the many critics who have insisted over the past century and a half that the God of the past is, in our time, at best absent and at worst dead? Some classical ways of speaking about the human condition—-literature, history, philosophy, politics—may still make a certain sense. Newer disciplines—economics, biology, sociology, depth psychology—have added invaluable further perspectives, often in a way openly antagonistic to religion. But is there a future for theology as such in our conversations and our work to make something more human of our world? What part can it possibly play in the drama of our search for ourselves, on the campuses of our universities, in the market place, or in our political process?

The man whose thought our volume introduces does not intend to propose grand answers to such questions. He does not think that the pluralism of human experience in its changing forms can be neatly systematized. He welcomes new ventures in understanding the world in which we live, from the many disciplines already developed as well as from others yet to be discovered. He knows that conflict is an ineluctable part of human history, and he even has theological grounds for expecting it to increase rather than decrease in the future. Our problems, as well as our limited successes, are not so much a situation he regrets as one he recognizes. As a theologian he finds himself called to see how the human situation opens out beyond itself, not simply to limit it to earlier perspectives. That the question of God has been raised with new urgency in our time is as clear to him as that we human beings have become increasingly more puzzling to ourselves. The question of God, after all, who God is and what God means for the world, has always been the defining issue of theology. But it has always been accompanied in one way or another by the question of humanity, who we are and what we mean for the world. And for Karl Rahner the two questions and their always partial answers must continually walk together: We can only seek God as we seek true humanity, we can only find truth about ourselves as we find truth about God.

This fundamental incarnational principle, this good news that God and humanity can only be found together, has guided Karl Rahner's life and thought from the beginning. Born on March 5, 1904, in the beautiful Black Forest city of Freiburg, Rahner cherishes the family piety—"not at all a sanctimonious one," as he has said—that nourished his faith. When he entered the Society of Jesus in 1922, three years after his older brother Hugo, who was himself to become a famous patristics scholar, that faith was nurtured in a new way by the spirit of Ignatius of Loyola, a figure who stood astride both the late medieval world and the emerging modern one. Ignatius' viewpoint, with its emphasis at once on the glory of God and the scope of human decision, has had an incalculable influence on Rahner's own. Together with other classical authors on Christian living, Ignatius combines a sense both of historical risk and of amazing grace. A world is waiting to be won, but the adventure is a cause we have not so much discovered ourselves as joined upon invitation. It is this conviction of serving in the company of Christ for a world as replete with division and discord as it is with promise and peace that has grown in the man Karl Rahner through his fifty-seven years as a Jesuit.

A living and moving center, however, is one that welcomes reflection and criticism. Rahner's philosophical and theological studies—at Feldkirch in Austria (1924–25) and Pullach, near Munich (1925–27); at Valkenburg in Holland (1929–33); then at the University of Freiburg (1934–36)—developed his formidable analytic and speculative skills, and also the historical sense which he fostered during his early years of teaching, especially through his courses on penance and grace. He had begun lecturing at the theological faculty of the University of Innsbruck in 1937. When it was closed by the Nazis in 1939, he left for pastoral work in Vienna. For several straitened years after World War II he taught theology again at Pullach. When the faculty at Innsbruck reopened, he returned there in 1948 and began to emerge in the next decade as one of Europe's leading theologians.

In a remarkable way his thought combined depth and sensitivity, witness to Christian tradition and awareness of faith's new situation, a powerful appreciation of human suffering and an unvanquished hope for its redemption. He became at once a theologian among theologians and a pastor among pastors. His importance was underlined by his role as an expert at Vatican Council II, both in its preparatory stages and during the Council sessions themselves. In 1964, a year before the Council's end, he succeeded Romano Guardini in the chair of Christian Worldview at the University of Munich. There he remained until 1967, when he became professor of dogmatic theology at the University of Münster until his retirement in 1971. In the active years since, residing again in Munich, he has continued to lecture and to write, bringing the number of publications which have appeared under his name in various languages to a current total of over 3,500 items. In so many of them one notices how his reflective theology lives from his experiential faith. Only by reaching beyond ourselves can we come to our true selves; only by opening ourselves to the holy mystery at the center of our lives can we become open to those lives in all their historical variety and promise.

This body of work, immense in both depth and breadth, was not produced, however, according to some preconceived scheme or method. Rahner's theology has appeared chiefly in the form of occasional essays addressed to what he considered pressing issues in the life of the Christian community. Frequently he is described as using a transcendental method, but this evaluation disregards his frequent insistence that one can do justice to a theological question only by combining a historical investigation of actual experience with a transcendental reflection on the conditions of its possibility. There is often more history in his very choice of topics than many critics recognize. Above all, there is always the emphasis that adequate treatment of any question must include fuller historical analysis. To a considerable extent, the critical method of current political and liberation theologies are producing just that necessary historical embodiment. But Rahner seems correct in arguing that we cannot return to historical experience, the great imperative for twentieth century Christian theology, unless we have an interpretative sense with which to read history. There are no facts, whether of oppression or of liberation, without the commitment which interprets them.

This polarity of historical concreteness and historical openness gives Rahner's thought great flexibility, richness—and incompleteness. But he has never claimed more. To raise a significant question of faith in its new historical situation and to frame a part of the answer, to reflect systematically but without any pretension towards complete system, this has sufficed for him as a modern theologian, and it suffices for most of his readers. Perhaps in the arts we are more familiar with the phenomenon of satisfying incompleteness—Michelangelo's increasingly fragmentary Pietàs, Mozart's unfinished Requiem, Cézanne's late canvasses. But in theology it seems especially appropriate to speak whatever words about God are given us for our time—and to take their very partiality as some small evidence of how great the mystery is and how limited our understanding, how full the possibility of God's humanity may be and yet how impoverished our own cooperation with it. Whoever is called to the service of the Kingdom today can only be called from the world as it is, a broken world of divided consciousness and alienated societies. In a deeper sense than he knew, Gerard Manley Hopkins spoke so well for the contemporary Christian when he wrote of Christ: "For I greet him the days I meet him, and bless when I understand."

A Note on Using This Book

This collection of essays can be no less fragmentary and incomplete. We hope nevertheless to provide interested readers with helpful introductions not only to Rahner's style and language but also to the major themes and fundamental principles of his theology. We are convinced that his thought is of enduring value for those who believe, for those who struggle with belief, and also for those who simply respect the belief of others. An introduction in accessible language, written on the American scene, and drawing on collaborative expertise seems in fact overdue. Our book, furthermore, may be used in several ways.

On the one hand it can be read as a current introduction to Rahner, supported by selected readings from his theology, much of which has been so expertly anthologized in Gerald McCool's *A Rahner Reader* (New York: Seabury, 1975). With each of our chapters read in turn as a first survey of a topic, readers might then approach some key Rahnerian essays, chosen perhaps for their systematic importance, or else for their suggestiveness for contemporary spirituality, or even from a still more practically pastoral perspective.

Another possible use of our book, however, is in relation to Rahner's masterful *Foundations of Christian Faith: An Introduction to the Idea of Christianity* (New York: Seabury, 1978). The sequence of our own chapter topics is designed as a running introduction to *Foundations,* with an essay devoted to each of the topics there, and in the same order. Because of the length and importance of Rahner's treatment of Jesus Christ, we have provided two essays on Christology (chapters 7 and 8), the first emphasizing Rahner's later, more historically accented approach, the second examining his now classic claims on how Jesus of Nazareth may in fact be recognized as the Christ of God. To highlight the inherently practical and ethical dimension of this theology, an essay has been added (chapter 12) to reflect on Rahner's contribution to contemporary and future Christian ethics. All our essays necessarily involve personal interpretation of Rahner's work; no one has taught us better than he how useless, and even wrong, sheer repetition can be. But all our authors have also cooperated in a symposium on Rahner's thought which met under the auspices of the American Academy of Religion each year between 1974 and 1978, and we believe our readings are consistent and mutually corroborative.

Although Rahner himself came to reflect on his theological method only relatively late in his career, he has always been a highly systematic thinker. *Foundations* opens with an Introduction on method, and we too begin there, with an essay by William V. Dych, S.J., who has so expertly translated *Foundations*. (Readers who prefer to postpone questions of method may wish to read this chapter last rather than first; such questions are often more interesting after one has seen how a method is actually used. However, students of *Foundations* itself should certainly examine Rahner's introductory reflections with special care). Anne Carr, B.V.M., from the Divinity School of the University of Chicago, then introduces Rahner's crucial views on the human person. Michael J. Buckley, S.J., of the Jesuit School of Theology at Berkeley, considers next the absolute mystery toward which all human life is directed. Guilt and sin as disruptions of the human situation before God are discussed by Brian O. McDermott, S.J., of Weston School of Theology.

In the essays that follow, the universal offer of grace as God's own life is examined by John P. Galvin of St. John's Seminary in Brighton, Massachusetts, and the revelatory history of the effects of grace is explored by Thomas F. O'Meara, O.P., currently Vice President of the Catholic Theological Society of America. The central section of *Foundations* comprises a discussion of Jesus Christ; our two essays on this topic are by J. Peter Schineller, S.J., of the Jesuit School of Theology in Chicago, and Otto H. Hentz, S.J., of Georgetown University. Michael A. Fahey, S.J., of Concordia University in Montreal reflects on Christianity as Church, while John Carmody of Wichita State University analyzes Rahner's approach to Christian life and the sacraments. William Thompson of Carroll College in Helena, Montana, studies the realism of Christian hope. Finally, Rahner's ethics of faith is discussed by James F. Bresnahan, S.J., of the Jesuit School of Theology in Chicago.

Not all of Rahner's theology by any means is presented here. Much more might be said about topics such as God as trinity, Christian spirituality, the nature of pastoral theology, the Church's relations with secular society. But just as *Foundations of Christian Faith* does not intend to be a *Summa* of Rahner's thought but an introduction to the experience of faith from one clearly defined perspective, so our own introduction to his theology has aimed simply at presenting his major themes and their foundations.

We have also tried to promote understanding and study of the text in a number of ways. Each chapter includes, or is followed by, questions for discussion. Likewise, each author has made several suggestions for possible further readings in which Rahner treats other aspects of the topic at hand. The readings are recommended in order of relative accessibility, and with a brief introductory comment in each case. Full bibliographical references will be found on pages 185–86. We have also jointly compiled a glossary of some basic terms that Rahner and his commentators frequently employ. Such a glossary raises as many technical questions as it settles, of course, but we hope it may still be helpful to readers who are orienting themselves in Rahner's thought.

Finally, we want to recommend that you use your own imagination as much as possible while you are reading these chapters. Examples from your own life or social situation should be explored to test the validity of insights proposed here. At different stages of your reading it would undoubtedly be revealing to compose a brief expression of your own Christian faith, comparing your accents and emphases with Rahner's own. He has often asserted our need today for such "short formulas of faith," and *Foundations* closes with an epilogue on the significance of these brief creedal statements. Such an exercise can be as simple as it is serious, if one recalls that faith, and theology's reflection on it, is concerned not with an exotic margin of our lives but with their central and abiding mystery.

It has been a special pleasure for the authors who have worked together on this volume to do so in the seventy-fifth year of the man whose thought it discusses. His influence on all of us has been salutary in so many ways, and has so encouraged our own personal and communal hope for a world of grace, that we can only wish some similar invigoration of faith for our readers. But true praise needs few superlatives. It looks instead to describe as exactly as possible what it appreciates, with the joy of that appreciation. To praise truly is to recognize the connection between an enhancement of our lives and the one who is responsible for it. It is to see deeper into the mystery of a gift, and discover something more about the giver. Praise is the opening of hearts whose very openness is gift. It can be grateful, even in a broken world, whenever it recognizes a need for healing. It can be hopeful, against all hope, whenever new questions about human possibility are awakened for it. Here we shall have truly praised Karl Rahner at the age of seventy-five whenever a reader joins with him in thinking about the human question that is also God's: "What is the human, O Lord, that you are mindful of it?"

Leo J. O'Donovan, S.J.

Cambridge, Massachusetts

A World of Grace

1

Theology in a New Key

WILLIAM V. DYCH

To appreciate Karl Rahner's theological method we must understand where in human experience he finds a starting point for theology. This leads us to an overview of how he sees the situation of the human person before God. It also addresses the relation between the reflection on human experience found in philosophical thought and the reflection on lived faith conducted by theology.

ALL scientific inquiry, however advanced and complex it becomes, has its deepest roots in the simple human reality of curiosity and wonder, in what Aristotle long ago called our common "desire to know." This desire reaches the level of scientific inquiry when our curiosity and wonder come to expression in specific questions about specific realities, and when the inquirer has found an adequate method to conduct his search and an adequate language to express his findings. Genuine search must be motivated by genuine wonder; genuine wonder must hit upon the right questions and the right method if it is to lead to knowledge and truth. Theology, like other sciences, begins with wonder; it differs from them in the kinds of questions it asks. But theologians can also differ among themselves not only in their answers, but also in how they pose their questions and how they go about answering them. To understand the method of Karl Rahner's theology, then, we must look first not to the nature of his answers, but to the nature of his questions.

In our contemporary culture, however, the legitimacy of theological questions is not something which can be taken for granted, for it is questioned on two very different fronts. In the world of contemporary philosophy and science, theology is often afforded space on the univer-

sity campus, but not really a home. For many, if not most, it is not really a respected partner in the work of the university. Some dismiss it as
a relic of the past, a fossil from a bygone age, while others see it not as
an affair of the mind and its search for knowledge and truth, but as an
affair of the heart and feelings, a private affair of the individual and his
needs or wishes or hopes. But on this front, too, theology does not
always find an eager public. Many people who are trying to live their
everyday lives as believers and as Christians, or at least would like to,
find very little in theology to help them. Many an average person finds
theology as heartless as the intellectuals find it headless. This truncated
specimen has, indeed, survived, but are theology's questions really of
interest to anyone today except theologians? Why theology, then?

Faced with this situation, Karl Rahner is deeply enough involved in
the intellectual life of his times to appreciate the validity of the criticism
on the first front, and at the same time deeply enough involved in the
life of Christian faith to be equally sensitive to the criticism on the
other. Together they presented him with a twofold task, and he ap-
proached it with a principle that was to guide his theological method
throughout. The task was, first, to make theology intellectually respectable in the modern world by honestly confronting the difficulties posed
by modern philosophy and science, and, second, to place theology at
the service of the larger concerns of Christian faith and life. The principle governing both is that they must be done together, that the success
of one depends on the success of the other. For not only is there no contradiction between the life of the intellect and the life of faith, but the
more deeply one thinks the closer one comes to the realities of which
faith speaks. By insisting on and maintaining this unity, two extremes
can be avoided: an unthinking pietism on the one hand, and a false intel-
lectualism on the other. This unity is rooted ultimately in the unity of
the thinking, believing subject, in that wonder which grounds both our
intellectual and our religious search.

We shall try to trace the steps by which this basic purpose is translated into a definite program and a specific method. First, where to
begin? Two traditional starting points seem obvious enough. At the
heart of all religion, as well as of all theology, lies the basic presupposition that there exists a reality which we can know and which we call
"God." But it is to this very heart of the matter that the critiques of
modern philosophy and science strike. For some, God is an unnecessary
or at least an unverifiable hypothesis, for others an illegitimate "projec-

tion" or "illusion," and for others simply unknowable by the canons of modern scientific and philosophical knowledge. God, then, cannot be the starting point or the presupposition for theology, for in the modern world God is not an answer but part of the problem. Should the starting point, then, be what Jesus Christ and the scriptures tell us about God? Modern historical criticism strikes just as deeply at this point. What can we really know of this man, it asks, and what sense can we really make of so much that Christian tradition says about him? Once again, Jesus Christ and the scriptures cannot be the answer, for they, too, have become part of the problem.

Is there a starting point, a presupposition, which can also be examined critically but which at least offers a common ground of discussion for everyone, whether they are believers or unbelievers, educated or uneducated? There is something, Rahner suggests, which touches all of us and to which we all have direct and immediate access: our shared human existence. If human existence and our experience of it can be analyzed to discover categories in which God can be spoken of intelligently and intelligibly by the strictest canons of knowledge and truth, then theology has at least a starting point to begin speaking of God in the contemporary world—no more than that at this point, but also no less. If, second, this same human existence offers a framework in which the history of Jesus and the history of what Christian tradition has said about him makes sense, then theology also has a starting point for speaking about Jesus Christ. And if, third, theology can discover its roots in human existence, then it can also stay close to human life and to all who are seriously trying to live it. In becoming intellectually respectable it need not become purely academic. In judging the success of his attempt, we must listen with one ear to what Karl Rahner is saying about human existence, and with the other, of course, to human existence itself, to my human existence, and then ask: Is he saying something true of me, and true of all of us?

The Primacy of Experience

If we are going to take human existence as the starting point for our theological reflection, we must state a very important principle here at the outset: One must first *be* in existence before one can reflect on it. But can we not take at least that much for granted? Yes and no. A child knows human existence at the level which is possible and appropriate at that age. But a child can neither exist nor know existence in the way

that a person can in the course of a lifetime of making decisions or fail-
ing to make them, of successes and failures, of surprises and disappoint-
ments, of joys and sorrows, and all the other things which make up the
stuff of adult human life, and also the "stuff" of theological reflection.
But at this adult level, too, there are different ways of being or not
being in existence: Has someone ever tried to be faithful to conscience
even when it cost something, perhaps a great deal, or tried to love
someone or something unselfishly, or experienced something good or
beautiful or admirable in others? In all of these situations that person
would have touched human existence and been touched by it in ways
that another might not, and thereby come to know it in a way that the
other cannot.

There is, then, a kind of knowledge we acquire not from without, but
from within existence, by actually being in existence and experiencing
it, and this we call "experiential knowledge." Since it is not conveyed
to us "from outside" by concepts or words or sentences, we also call it
"preconceptual" or "unthematic" knowledge. We can learn about
outer space or molecular physics or the existence of a distant continent
we have never visited from the observations of others communicated to
us by words and concepts, but we know about our own existence "from
inside." Human existence is not a thing which we have, or an object
which we observe, but a process which we do and are; experiential
knowledge is the knowledge we have of ourselves related to a world of
persons and things in the actual living of this relationship. Hence
Rahner calls this kind of knowledge "original" knowledge. It is "original" not in the sense that no one had it before, but in the sense that it
wells up from the origins or depths of our own selves in our lived interaction with the world.

However, since we are not isolated individuals but social beings who
exist with others, this knowledge wells up and reaches the level of
reflection, expression, and communication. To express our experiential
knowledge we must objectify it, in the sense of embodying it in concepts and words which others can hear and understand. Knowledge at
this second level, which we call explicit, thematic, or conceptual knowledge, does not create our relationship to the world but rather gives
expression to it.

Moreover, when we reflect upon experience, objectify it, and express
it, the expression never completely recaptures or is identical with the
original experience. The concepts of hope or joy or sorrow are not the

same thing as the realities themselves. The symbol expresses the symbolized, but is never identical with it. Hence there exists a two-directional relationship between these two levels of the one knowledge: We must reflect and express in order to clarify and understand and communicate, and we must also constantly relate our concepts back to their source, lest they become empty abstractions. Applying to these levels of knowledge our original principle that one must first be in existence before one can reflect on it, we can also say that one must first experience existence before one can speak about it.

The Experience of Transcendence

To understand Karl Rahner's theological method, we must attend in a special way to the aspect of human existence which he calls "transcendental experience." By this he does not mean a separate experience among others but rather an element within all our existence in the world. Since it is unthematic in daily life, theology must reflect upon it. But just because it is unthematic, it can also be easily overlooked. How can we become more aware of what Rahner means?

First of all, we must observe that all of our experience of the world is also simultaneously an experience of the self, not an isolated self, but a self precisely in this world. In knowing something else, we are also aware of ourselves in this process of knowing, not as an explicit object of our attention, but in the sense that knowing is a conscious process or activity. Just as we are aware of ourselves as walking or talking even though we are not explicitly thinking about it, so too we are aware of ourselves in the process of knowing. Knowledge, then, is "two-directional." In knowing an object the subject is aware of itself; knowledge encompasses both the knower and the known. This self-awareness, which is always present in our knowledge, is our capacity for being present to ourselves, and is that basic characteristic which makes human existence spiritual existence. We exist in the world as spiritual beings because our existence is not completely absorbed by or immersed in the world, for we retain and possess ourselves in this capacity for self-presence. This experience of self-presence in the midst of being present to a thousand other things is part of our experience of subjectivity, of being a conscious subject in the midst of the world of objects around us.

Secondly, we must also notice in this experience of subjectivity or personhood that the self we experience is not entirely determined by the world in which it exists. We are, indeed, part of the world and determined by it genetically, environmentally, and in countless other ways; we are very much the product of what is not ourselves. But because we possess this total self, including all its determinations, in our knowledge, we are also responsible for it. We experience ourselves as responsible for ourselves. Our freedom to choose this or that or to do this or that is really and fundamentally a freedom to make a self and choose an identity. And to the extent that we are free, self-conscious subjects we exist beyond the world and its causes and explanations, and in this sense we transcend it. This experience of subjectivity or personhood is the characteristically human mode of existence in the world, of being a spiritual existent in the world.

Where, then, do we come from, if not entirely from the world, and where does our transcendence take us, if the world does not entirely define our limits? All the knowledge we acquire always gives rise to further questions. When pushed far enough all of our clarities trail off into obscurity; the chain of scientific logic hangs loose at both ends. The more we know, the more we realize we don't know, and in this known unknown we have transcended our knowledge. Our freedom, too, ultimately ends in a question: Am I responsible only to myself and within the limits of time, or do I have a value beyond time and am I responsible to someone else? In raising the question we have already transcended the limits of time. Because we are self-conscious and free we experience our hopes, our desires, our loves and life itself as a question: Does it all make sense, does it have any ultimate meaning? This unthematic experience, the transcendental experience, is not just a single experience but an element within *all* experiences. To have experienced this ultimate question, which confronts us at every turn in our lives, is to have experienced the mystery which we are. It is this transcendental experience which Rahner reflects upon as a starting point for speaking of God.

The Philosophical Moment:
Reflecting on General Human Experience

It is ultimately the work of theology to present the Christian interpretation of the human situation we have just described, but to do this adequately an intermediate step is required. For theology claims to be an interpretation of *all* human existence, to be a response to human existence which is *universally* valid. Secondly, it claims that this interpretation and response is reasonable—intellectually justified. Hence it will be the work of philosophy to discover, in the world of individual experiences, certain general structures which necessarily characterize all human existence, and which therefore can constitute the philosophical foundations upon which theology can build. These structures are called "existentials," and we have already considered three of them: self-presence, freedom, and transcendence. We shall be seeing a fourth when Rahner calls grace a "supernatural existential." He sees the first three as philosophical presuppositions for his theological statement about grace.

Philosophy in this approach means, first, reflection upon our experience of human existence in its totality; our experience results in this total question which we are for ourselves. It means, secondly, a reflection which is accessible to anyone, believer or unbeliever, because it is not logically dependent on theology. In actuality, everyone has and lives out some presupposed or implicit view of human existence, and the role of philosophy is to make this explicit. In this sense philosophy does not give us new knowledge about ourselves, but articulates on the level of conceptual discourse what we already know on the experiential level. Otherwise philosophy is empty of experiential content: one must first be in existence before one can philosophize about it. Of the so-called philosophical "proofs" for the existence of God, for example, Rahner says that they are not informing us of a reality we have never touched in experience, but they are articulating our experience on the level of logical, conceptual, public discourse. If God is not present at the beginning of our syllogism, neither is he present at the end.

This approach to philosophy, therefore, is different from any kind of rationalism, which is based on the conviction that we know reality primarily through concepts, through "clear and distinct ideas" which reach their fullness in scientific knowledge. But neither should we go to the other extreme, the position of classical modernism, which sees conceptual and logical discourse as an entirely dispensable process. The philosophical moment is necessary in theology in order that theology have a "public" language, a language that is intellectually justifiable before the public canons of knowledge and truth. By thus enabling theology to speak in and to our contemporary world, philosophy also provides theology with a link to the past. If it is successful, it can provide a contemporary framework of understanding in which to speak of the realities which past ages spoke of in their own frameworks. This work of "translation" is necessary if we are really to understand what past ages have handed down to us, and not just repeat it.

Since human existence is Rahner's starting point in theology, what he needs more specifically from philosophy is a philosophy of human existence, that is, an anthropology. Where does he find the language to express his philosophical anthropology? As a Christian theologian he is working out of the philosophical tradition of the West, which has its roots in Plato and Aristotle and which in the Christian era reaches its high points in Augustine and Aquinas. He is aware of the greatness of this tradition and feels indebted to it, and in no way thinks that in order to exist in the present one has to forget the past. But he is also living in the intellectual milieu of the twentieth century and does not think that the history of philosophy ended with the Middle Ages; he is indebted to his own more recent German philosophical tradition "from Kant to Heidegger," as he says. It is from these two traditions that he is going to draw the philosophical structures for his theology—not in eclectic fashion, taking a little from one and a little from the other, but viewing them as a single tradition. An example of this process of "cross-fertilization" should clarify how it provided him with fresh insights into his Christian tradition.

Thomas Aquinas teaches that all of our knowledge is rooted in our experience of the finite world. We are not endowed with a set of innate or inborn ideas. Aquinas also teaches that we can know what is beyond the finite, sensible world, that we can know the "metaphysical," what is beyond the physical. This is an obvious presupposition if any kind of religion or theology is to be possible, but it stands in conflict with the opposite presupposition of much of the philosophy and science of our own world, namely, that this physical world is probably all that we have, and certainly all that we know. To establish this possibility of knowing what is beyond the physical world, Rahner wrote his first major philosophical work, *Spirit in the World* (New York: Seabury, 1968): human existents as material do indeed exist in the finite, physical world of time and space and are very much part of it and it of them, but as spiritual existents they also reach beyond this world and transcend it.

To establish this, we must reflect upon those experiences of transcendence we have already considered. At the same time, we also draw upon the insights of those modern philosophies which have turned their attention to the human subject. This so-called "turn to the subject" in modern philosophy refers to the fact that in modern, transcendental philosophy it is the inquiring subject itself which has become the object of inquiry. In thus turning to the subject, modern philosophy has become "anthropocentric" as distinguished from "cosmocentric," not in the sense that it is interested only in humanity and not in the rest of the cosmos, but in the sense that it draws its basic paradigms for understanding reality from human existence. In following modern philosophy in this turn we acquire personal rather than impersonal categories in which to speak of human existence: self-presence, freedom, transcendence.

Moreover, we make this "turn to the subject" in order to establish, in the categories and logic of modern philosophy, our Thomistic thesis that personal existents do reach beyond the world in their experience of transcendence. Hence we ask: What are the limits of this transcendence, what is its term, what do we touch when we reach beyond ourselves in knowledge, freedom and love? This transcendence can be experienced as unlimited, as an openness which is unbounded and open in an absolute sense. We can use the image of a horizon to express this: our experience of the finite world opens us to a horizon which ever recedes as we move through the finite; there is always a "more" to be known and to be loved and to be lived. We are aware of it, but can never reach it; it is there, but it ever exceeds our grasp. By following our Thomistic starting point through modern philosophy's "turn to the subject" in what is therefore called "transcendental Thomism," we have arrived at an absolute openness of the human subject in its unlimited transcendence. This transcendence brings us not to a content of knowledge which we grasp, but to an absolute question. This experience of the unattainable and the incomprehensible we call the experience of mystery.

Can this mystery be more for us than an ever larger and deeper mystery, can we ever know more about it and thereby more about ourselves? If our experience of mystery is as Rahner has described it, not simply an as yet unsolved problem but something positively unknowable, then such knowledge cannot be of our own doing. It would have to be given to us to know, and in this sense revealed to us. If, moreover, it is of the very essence of human existence to be open and undetermined in its being and in its knowledge, then human beings experience themselves as those to whom ultimate meaning must come through history if it is to come at all. Human beings by their very nature are listeners for and possible hearers of the word of salvation and grace. This is the conclusion of Rahner's other major philosophical work, *Hearers of the Word* (New York: Seabury, 1969).

What has been acquired for theology through this philosophical analysis of the structures of human subjectivity? We have shown, through philosophical reflection on human experience, that human existence is transcendent existence, that it reaches beyond the finite world, that humanity can be known and loved by what is beyond that world, and can therefore know and love in return. We have thereby established a philosophical basis for doing Christian theology, we have made explicit and shown the legitimacy of those prior conditions or presuppositions which make what Christianity says both possible and intelligible. This provides us with a contemporary framework within which Christianity can make sense. But besides making sense, is it also true? Are we actually known and loved in this way? Is the ultimate and radical truth about us, and therefore the first truth in theological anthropology, a word of grace? It is Christian faith, and not philosophy, which says "yes."

The Theological Moment: Reflecting on Lived Faith

When people today encounter this "yes" of Christian faith and its tradition, it confronts them with two different but interrelated questions. First, can I make this "yes" my own, can I hear it as the final word of truth about my life, and thereby make Christianity's interpretation of human existence my own self-interpretation? Secondly, what is this word saying, what is it exactly that a Christian believes? The first question has to do with the grounds or the reasons why I believe; the attempt to establish the reasonable grounds of Christian faith is the work of fundamental theology. The second question has to do with the contents of Christian faith, the doctrines or beliefs in which Christianity expresses its interpretation of human existence. The two must be addressed together, for the question whether I can believe with intellectual honesty depends on an adequate understanding of what it is that I believe. The attempt to express this understanding is called dogmatic or systematic theology, but not in the sense of a rigid or closed system. Theological reflection on human existence cannot become a closed system, because human existence is not a closed system. It means, rather, that systematic theologians have certain key insights or basic principles around which they organize and in which they express the truths of Christian faith. We shall consider these basic methodological principles which give a particular shape to Rahner's theology before these truths are considered individually in later chapters.

Christianity, first of all, is a historical religion in the sense that it speaks not about eternal, necessary truths or an unchanging state of affairs, but about contingent, particular events, about events which happened in time. Its basic view of human existence, then, is not that of an ahistorical essence but that of a being in time, touched at the very core by what happens to it in time and by what it does in time. It sees in certain of these events a history of salvation, and it calls the expression of this salvific significance a history of revelation. Hence Christian faith is tied radically to history, and if it loses these roots it becomes a form of mythology or a form of rationalism.

The foundation of Christian faith, therefore, is the historical Jesus of Nazareth, the events of his life up to and including his death and resurrection, those events in and through which he became who he was and is. Christian faith is a response to this person, and this faith comes to expression in theologies about him, theologies which are called "Christologies" after one of the earliest of these theologies which expressed his significance by calling him the Christ. However little we can strip the historical Jesus of all of these Christologies and get back to him in test-tube purity, nevertheless Christians place their faith not in any one of these Christologies, but in the person about whom they speak. Christians believe in Jesus of Nazareth and express their faith by calling him the Christ or by using some other theological formula.

This situation confronts Christian theology with a twofold task. There is the need to know the historical Jesus by whatever means we have at our disposal, primarily the exegetical study of the biblical literature which constitutes our one source of historical knowledge about him. Without this there is simply no way of knowing whether the Jesus one comes to know by speculation about him or mystical experience of him has anything to do with the real, historical Jesus, or whether one has simply devised one's own mythology. Secondly, there is the need to express the theological significance of his person and life, that is, to formulate Christology in such a way that faith in him makes sense in ever new historical and cultural situations. Just as without the first task Christian faith can lose its roots in the history of the past, so too without this second task Christian faith can lose its roots in the history of the present. Karl Rahner raises the question whether we have not failed to take this second task seriously. Consequently, it is possible that there are many today who reject Christological formulas about Jesus, but perhaps are not really rejecting Jesus of Nazareth. Others, perhaps, are only too ready to repeat formulas from the past which no longer convey an adequate understanding of Jesus of Nazareth, but one that is distorted and tinged with mythology. Neither acceptance nor rejection of Christological formulas necessarily indicates whether one actually believes in Jesus of Nazareth.

This conviction leads Rahner to see that Christology must be done in two steps today. We must keep one eye on the past, on the history of Jesus and the history of what has been said about him in scripture and the subsequent tradition of the Church. The other eye must look to the present in order to develop a conceptual framework within which this past can speak to the present and actually be heard and understood in it. This framework is called "transcendental Christology"; it is not an addition to what we can know a posteriori from historical Christology, but the a priori horizon or framework within which the theological significance of those facts is expressed. It is called transcendental because it focuses on those necessary or universal structures within which all concrete human history takes place. Through discovering the common ground for the concrete history of Jesus and our own collective and individual histories today, transcendental Christology can express the universal significance of Jesus' particularity. Since, for example, in our philosophical reflection we have come to understand human existence as an openness which is simply unlimited and undetermined, and to which meaning must come through the actualities of history, the history of Jesus can be understood as the fullest actualization of that meaning and the fulfillment of the human potential for self-transcendence. Likewise, if we experience in ourselves human hopes which Christian faith says have been fully realized in the human Jesus, then his history touches ours at the deepest levels of our experience.

Transcendental Christology does not attempt to prove what happened, but to understand what happened in its universal significance. Just as the real potentialities of sound are not actual and known until a Beethoven creates his music, so too the real potentialities of human existence are not actual and known until they are actualized in a concrete, historical person. But once this truth is done and achieved and thereby known, in this event there is disclosed a new vision of all human existence, a new hope for everything human. For Christians this is what happened in the life of Jesus.

A Theology of Grace: The Supernatural Existential

This vision and this hope come to expression in a specifically Christian and theological anthropology, an interpretation of human existence rooted in the person and life of Jesus. To express the universal nature of the grace, salvation, and revelation Christians find in the life of Jesus, Rahner develops a transcendental theology of grace. The key concept in this theology is that of the "supernatural existential." This supernatural existential is not a "thing," but a concept used to explain how it belongs to concrete human existence to be called to what transcends our existence, to life with God. Hence grace is an "existential" as we used that term earlier in reference to self-presence, freedom and transcendence. If it is, then all people were created from the very beginning for grace; it belongs to the very essence of concrete human nature to be called to grace, to be able to find God in the particularities of all history. We can say, then, that the history of salvation and revelation are coextensive with the history of the human race, that there is a "transcendental" revelation, that is, that the God who came to be known through the history of the Jewish and Christian peoples can also be known through the history of all people, however different their way of conceptualizing and expressing this knowledge might be.

What Rahner has gained by interpreting the realities of Christian faith in his transcendental categories is clear when contrasted with other methods of interpretation. If, for example, human nature is understood as a closed or static structure given from the beginning of human history, and is not understood transcendentally as open to self-transcendence in history, then a history of salvation and revelation can only appear as something adventitious and extrinsic to human nature and its own history. It would appear as something added to it "from outside" and not as the realization of its own deepest potentialities. The history of grace, salvation, and revelation and human history as we otherwise know it would become two different histories, and the supernatural order of grace would exist side by side with "natural" or "secular" life as we otherwise know it. Then the particular history of salvation and revelation in the Judeo-Christian tradition would be understood in a highly particularistic and exclusivistic way, and the God it speaks of could only be known by a kind of biblical or ecclesiastical fundamentalism.

To counter these possibilities we can use our transcendental method to arrive at a renewed understanding of these realities. It is a renewed understanding, but not really a new one. For perhaps it is closer to the spirit of the New Testament's view that God "wants all people to be saved and to come to a knowledge of the truth" (1 Timothy 2:4), and to Paul's cosmic vision of the whole universe eagerly awaiting salvation:

"From the beginning until now the whole created universe groans in all its parts as if in the pangs of childbirth" (Romans 8:22). In enabling us to do justice to these scriptural statements, this renewed understanding perhaps also brings us closer to the contemporary evolutionary and historical view of the universe. For by making the offer of grace intrinsic to human existence, it makes it a universal offer. Because human existence is the conscious and free existence of a personal being, this offer is an experiential reality. Because, moreover, this offer comes not as one finite element in our experience among others, but as the ground and horizon of all our experience, it is integrated into the whole of existence in all its dimensions. Everything that is really human can be a "channel of grace," a finite mediation of our relationship to God.

Rahner's use of transcendental categories has given him a common framework within which to link the past with the present, and also to link the variety of religions and cultures in our own contemporary world, and, finally, to unify the "religious" and "secular" moments within our single human existence. Now there is one further step he must take to prevent the misuse of transcendental method and an idealistic misunderstanding of it. Because human beings are historical and social beings, transcendental structures of knowledge and freedom must be actualized in the world and in history. To go back to the example of Beethoven, there is no music in the potentialities of sound, but only when a Beethoven creates his music from them. So too, there is no actual knowledge of God and no free response to him except when actualized in the world and in history. Humanity's transcendental essence comes to be and achieves actuality in time and space; it has no existence of its own apart from the concrete world and concrete history. Hence Rahner emphasizes that humanity is indeed transcendence and spirit, but only in and through the particularities of our individual and social world and our individual and collective history.

To express this relationship of unity and difference, the polarity or the dialectic between these two equally necessary and equally primary poles in human existence, the transcendental and the historical, Rahner develops the category of symbol, or, more precisely, real symbol. It is of the very nature of human existence to express itself in order to be itself, and in this expression or symbol the symbolized becomes fully real. Hence the universal, transcendental possibility of salvation must become actual by coming to expression in concrete, particular histories of salvation, and the universal, transcendental possibility of revelation must become actual by coming to expression in concrete, particular revelations. The differences among the various concrete histories of salvation and revelation can be seen as the various symbolic expressions of the deeper unity underlying them.

We can speak of Jesus, then, as the concrete historical person in whom God's offer of grace and human response to this offer became flesh, became visible, audible, and tangible in the world; hence Jesus is a real symbol, a sign or a sacrament of this grace. Likewise we can speak of the Church as a sacrament or real symbol: by being the ongoing visible and tangible presence, that is, *real* presence, of this grace in the world, it is a visible sign of what is true of all the world. The Church as sacrament, therefore, proclaims a relationship not of God to itself, but of God to the world. Its sacramental activities are activities in which there is expressed and made explicitly religious a relationship to God which can be mediated by all finite reality. For implicitly and in its own secular language the world itself and its history are the primary sacraments of our relationship to God. Understanding church and sacraments as real symbols means that we do not encounter God for the first time in a church or in explicitly religious activities, but in human life. Consequently, the realm of personal freedom and ethical activity is not "applied religion," but the necessary condition for religion being a real and not an empty symbol. We can, indeed we must find God in all things.

In arriving at a symbolic understanding of the universe, Karl Rahner has arrived back at the point at which he began, his understanding of God as mystery. For if the world in all its facets and activities, the world of scientific inquiry, the world of artistic creation and the world of the most common and ordinary everyday life are all symbols of human transcendence, the ultimate reality symbolized lies ever beyond all the symbols, remains ever mystery. But in Rahner's vision this mystery which we can touch but never grasp, the mystery which we call "God," together with the mystery of the life and death of Jesus and the mystery of all human living and dying are one and the same mystery. For he has seen that being a Christian and responding to this mystery in faith and hope and love is also the fullest way of being human.

QUESTIONS FOR DISCUSSION AND
SUGGESTIONS FOR FURTHER READING

After reading about Rahner's effort to rewrite theology in a new key, one might naturally begin to reflect on one's own faith today. Stimulation for such a reflection may be found in "Thoughts on the Possibility of Belief Today," *Theological Investigations* 5, pp. 3–22. This is a rich and deeply felt introductory essay on the special situation of faith in the contemporary world. It asks: Is faith really human?

The experience of transcendence is fundamental to Rahner's thought. How would you illustrate what he means in terms of your own experience? It might be of help here to read "Being Open to God as Ever Greater," *Theological Investigations* 7, pp. 25–46. This is a moving example, from Rahner's more devotional writing, of what he means by our dynamism toward God as the horizon of all our activity. How do you understand Rahner's distinction between the first and second levels of reflection in theology? An earlier essay in which he argues for a first level of reflection in the education of both ordained and lay theologians is "Reflections on the Contemporary Intellectual Formation of Future Priests," *Theological Investigations* 6, pp. 113–38.

For a more extended treatment of Rahner's actual procedure in writing theology, one might consult "Reflections on Methodology in Theology," *Theological Investigations* 11, pp. 68–114, which contains his most comprehensive single consideration of his own method.

How would you yourself understand the distinction between the reflection on general human experience known as philosophy and the reflection on lived faith known as theology? In "The Current Relationship between Philosophy and Theology," *Theological Investigations* 13, pp. 61–79, Rahner shows philosophy's importance for theology but also argues that we should not, and need not, expect a complete, harmonious synthesis between philosophy and theology today. He also argues vigorously for theology's need to maintain a dialogue not only with contemporary philosophies but also with the natural and social sciences.

A first-level reflection on faith does not study the doctrinal history of Christianity in detail, but it is obviously dependent on that history. How do you understand this relationship? Discussion of the question would be helped by a reading of "The Faith of the Christian and the Doctrine of the Church," *Theological Investigations* 14, pp. 24–46.

2

Starting with the Human
ANNE E. CARR

Discussion of Rahner's thought should begin at his own starting point: human experience as a whole. This look at Rahner's anthropology, his understanding of the human, analyzes five basic dimensions of our experience: subjectivity or personhood, the horizon of knowledge, freedom and responsibility, salvation in history, and dependence.

ALL of us are mysteries to ourselves, our most familiar mystery. The question that each of us asks, the question that each of us is, endures as the mystery of our lives from childhood to old age and death. It is the human question, the question of the person. It is the question to which Karl Rahner's theology responds.

The texture and shape of any theology is most clearly suggested by its point of departure. Rahner's vision of the whole of theology opens with the human person, who is the "hearer" of the Christian message. Thus he begins, not with God, nor with Scripture, nor with the teachings of the Church, but with the person who is presupposed by Christianity as the hearer of its gospel. He addresses the person as a whole, both as human—in our everyday experience of ourselves, others, the world—and as Christian—familiar with and already influenced by the Christian message. Since he addresses us first as human beings, he describes an experience of existence that is accessible to everyone's self-understanding and to theoretical analysis, and thus he employs the reflections of philosophy. But since he works with the presuppositions of the revealed message of Christianity, he also clearly uses the discipline of theology. He asks, in short, what light can be shed on the question of the human person by an analysis of what the Christian message presumes as true about that person, each one of us. This focus on the meaning of the whole of human life, so distinctive in Rahner's thought, is signalled in the term "anthropology."

When theology at a first level of reflection addresses the *whole* of human experience, in its public and private, individual and social, obvious and mysterious aspects, it is not always possible to preserve precise distinctions between philosophy and theology. Since the strands of our experience, both human and Christian, are woven together in our lives, and our experience of ourselves is already modified by the historical experience of Christianity, we will not be able to distinguish the reflections of philosophy from theology with absolute rigor. The reality of Christian grace, whether it is recognized or not, has already touched our experience of ourselves and our world. And so we can begin our study of the person with the conjoined aid of both philosophy and theology.

This conjunction of philosophy and theology is crucial. In stressing the unity of our lives as both human and Christian, we are involved in a circle in which these two dimensions inescapably presuppose one another. Human life itself, understood through a philosophical anthropology, opens out towards the fulfillment of which the gospel speaks. And Christian life, on which a theological anthropology reflects, not only presupposes certain human structures, but is their ultimate source: the natural structures of human life as we know them are created by God as the prerequisite of the gospel. Thus there is an intrinsic point of contact between the human and the Christian dimensions in life, and between philosophy and theology, a unity within their abiding distinction. This pattern of unity in difference will be found throughout Rahner's theology, appearing, e.g., in discussions of nature and grace, secular and salvation history, the human and the divine in Christ. It is a fundamental characteristic of his thought which may be understood more clearly, perhaps, when studied in contrast to Barth's revelational approach or in comparison with Tillich's method of correlation. It means that human existence itself is created by and for the Christian message, that human life in its fundamental structures as intelligent and free is, at its core, a personal world intended for response to God's call.

Rahner addresses us as unique individuals, asking each of us as *his* hearers if the kind of analysis he proposes is not, in its general outline at least, the truth about our lives. Does it not correspond with what we already know to be the case about ourselves, even though we may never have put our entire experience into these words?

And everyone is then asked whether he can recognize himself as that person who is here trying to express his self-understanding, or whether in responsibility to himself and to his existence he can affirm as the conviction which is to be the truth for him that he is not such a person as Christianity tells him he is. (*Foundations*, p. 25)

What we hope to do, then, is to bring into clearer view what we have always known, but perhaps not reflectively recognized, as present in our ordinary and everyday experience of ourselves as persons. Five of these experiences form the outline for this discussion of Rahner's anthropology.

1. The Meaning of the Person

The first and most basic presupposition of Christianity is that the hearer of its message is a person, that is, one who can understand and respond. Thus Rahner's anthropology is not directed toward parts or aspects but toward the totality of the person. Unlike those limited or "regional" anthropologies which explain only humankind's biological, psychological or sociological condition, philosophy and theology deal with the whole. And the fundamental reality of the whole person is the experience of subjectivity, or personal experience. Rahner calls this "original experience," an experience so profound yet so constant that it can remain unnoticed in our lives. Although it is clear that our words will never be able to contain the reality they signify, it is this original experience that a theological anthropology attempts to express. It is important, then, in working through an anthropology like Rahner's, to be open to the experience he describes.

The experience in which we become conscious of ourselves as selves is one of radical questioning. We question various causes and explanations offered by the limited anthropologies of which we are aware. And we realize that no single cause, whether biological or cultural, entirely explains us to ourselves. We know ourselves as the product of numerous forces outside ourselves and yet as more than the sum total of ethnic origins, parental relationships, or social backgrounds. Our questioning of each single explanation we can find leads us to a place in which we stand outside ourselves. In opening ourselves to the unlimited horizons of such questioning, we have already transcended or gone beyond ourselves, and beyond the limits of any particular question or explanation. In a sense, this power of transcendence is infinite, never-ending in our experience. For every standpoint we reach, every answer we achieve, only leads to the new standpoint of a new question. The power of radical questioning, which is not so much something we have as it is that which we *are*, is the meaning of subjectivity. In the experience of confronting the self as a whole, we go beyond every partial knowledge, no matter how sophisticated that particular knowledge may be.

This experience of the whole makes possible all our partial, empirical and more obvious experiences of the self. Subjectivity is there, co-present in all individual experience as its prior ground, although it eludes the exact definitions which we can give to the particular parts of our experience. Subjectivity is present whenever one is being a self, prior to and present in all the analyses we give when reducing our experience and explaining ourselves by some casual explanation: "It's merely his Irish temper"; "It's caused by her father's attitude toward money"; "It's the result of a background of extreme poverty." The experience of subjectivity is more original than these origins and causes that we can so easily describe.

2. Transcendence and Knowledge

This is what Rahner means by transcendence as present in our ordinary experience: Everything can become a question for us. Each of our particular experiences occurs within a finite horizon of understanding. Inasmuch as we constantly move beyond every limited horizon of questioning, we are shown to be beings of unlimited horizon. This is the basic evidence for Rahner's argument that we are transcendent beings, or *spirit*. The more answers (and questions) we have, the more the infinite horizon seems to recede. An analogy from ordinary experience may help to clarify the meaning of horizon and the way in which it is only glimpsed, so to speak, out of the corner of the eye. We focus attention, say, on a particular goal in a particular context and concentrate our energies on its attainment. But even if we achieve our aim, we have already moved beyond it as we search for our next project, our next goal. Eventually we learn that every particular goal, even one that is very dear to us or pertains to some high human accomplishment, is ultimately limited, not fully satisfying, only finite. This kind of experience offers some comparison to the unlimited questioning of the human person as spirit, and indicates at the same time that we are not pure spirit. For we never reach the unquestioning and unquestioned resolution of all our questions.

The radical experience of this unlimited horizon of knowing can be

ignored, unnoticed, forgotten. We can give attention only to the concrete people and projects in front of us, not attending to the question
which is in the background. Or we can recognize the presence of the
question and implicitly decide that it is unanswerable or that it is finally
absurd. But if we allow ourselves to experience this fundamental question of our lives, it may emerge into clearer focus. Part of its mysterious
character, however, is that we are never entirely certain how we have
answered the question that is our own transcendence. Our words and
ideas about ourselves, the world, other people, may belie the fundamental answer we have really given with our lives.

One of the most basic and most controversial aspects of Rahner's
thought is his argument that this human transcendence is founded in the
pre-apprehension (*Vorgriff*) of infinite reality. The basis of all our everyday thinking and activity, he maintains, lies in this deeper consciousness of which we are seldom directly aware. It is a knowledge or
consciousness that is "pre-reflective," "preconceptual," "unthematic"
—adjectives which indicate a constantly present awareness that is not
directly grasped or conceptualized. It is "unobjectified" in that it is a
tacit awareness, a knowledge which is not made into an object for
mental reflection, but accompanies all our conceptual knowing. Such
knowledge is a dim but constant anticipation of the positive fullness
of infinite reality as the horizon of all our knowledge and freedom.

Could this pre-apprehension be simply the experience of nothingness?
No, for despite the fact that we do experience the absurd, the negative,
the powerless fragility of life, we also know the contrasting movements
of hope and positive choice. And we know, further, that our experience
is one, fundamentally unified in the person who is the subject of manifold experience—one's self. Thus we can argue that there cannot be two
primordial realities—a dualism in the ultimate ground of being. Rather,
the pre-apprehension or horizon of our lives, the ground of human transcendence, is that of a *positive* infinity. It is an infinite reality which
wills the limits and boundaries of the partial, fragile but positive beings
of our experience.

The pre-apprehension of being as positive, however, is not simply
self-evident and self-explanatory: the horizon of our experience as
human subjects remains mysterious and questionable. We do not know
ourselves as absolute subjects in perfect control of our lives and our
world, but as "disquieted by the appearance of being," "open to something ineffable" (*Foundations,* p. 34). We experience ourselves as subjects who do not create our selves and the space in which we live. We

seem rather to be those who receive being in limited, contingent fashion as a gift from the foundation of being beyond ourselves.

Only inasmuch as we are transcendent, tacitly aware of the infinity of being hidden and revealed in our experience, are we subjects, persons. We recognize ourselves as the product, not simply of some finite, particular series of causes and effects, but as grounded in the fullness of being itself and as the gift of that fullness. It is only in the horizon of transcendence that we are really able to know ourselves, and thus assume responsibility for ourselves as persons. Only in this horizon do we recognize what Pascal so vividly described: our greatness as transcendent spirit and our smallness as finite, limited, receptive beings. The paradoxical union of both elements is the meaning of human personhood.

This awareness of transcendence is not a particular experience which we have alongside others of sight and sound, persons, events, relationships. As the ground of these ordinary experiences, whether trivial or important, the experience of transcendence is more a constant way of being which is present in all other experience. Most important, it is not simply a concept of transcendence which we can try to think about as a topic to be studied. It is, rather, the openness to being which is always present and which we always are, within all the projects and plans, hopes and fears of our ordinary lives. It is that origin and background of our lives over which we have no control, a kind of question mark which is always present. For the experience of transcendence can never be pinned down adequately in conceptual language. Rahner believes it is glimpsed in mystical experience and in the ultimate and lonely finality of death. But the experience itself evades all our talk about it; it is quite different from the words we use to describe it. Yet there is no other way to bring such immediate experience to reflective awareness than through the mediation of words and concepts which can distort the very experience they are meant to signify. Thus such experience can be overlooked, ignored, avoided. But it remains as the "secret ingredient," the horizon of mystery which is always present to us and which constitutes us as persons.

3. Freedom and Responsibility

We noted earlier that when Rahner asks about the presuppositions of the Christian message, he addresses us as whole persons, both human and Christian, in our fundamental experience of ourselves. And Christianity, we said, presumes as the hearer of its message one who can listen and respond. Thus its anthropology implies not only knowledge but freedom and responsibility on the part of the hearer of its word.

Parallel to the transcendent character of knowledge, human freedom is not a particular piece of experience which can be isolated for analysis as in a laboratory experiment. This is what a radically empirical psychology attempts to do in fact, and so it fails to find evidence for genuine freedom. It finds only causes and effects, reasons and determinations, but never real freedom itself. For the realization of freedom in any particular instance is always accompanied by qualifications. Even in cases of law, where an individual is presumed to be responsible and called to account for particular actions, there is never absolute certainty about the extent of freedom. We can easily think of situations in which an individual acts in a certain way through a variety of determining causes: one may be unaware of all the implications of one's actions or mistaken about the facts; one may be moved by the pressure of fear, anger, terrible pain, misguided love; one may be under the influence of drugs or alcohol; in short one is not entirely free but at least partially compelled. And even when we are fairly sure we are acting out of authentic freedom, say in religious or interpersonal decisions, it is impossible to isolate the "pure specimen" from its surrounding biological, psychological, and sociological derivations and explanations.

Real freedom must be present in our experience, then, in a different way. We find our own freedom in the previous experience of being persons who are, as a whole, already given over to ourselves and ultimately responsible for ourselves. This experience of freedom is transcendental; it precedes, governs, and is present in the whole of our ordinary, particular experiences. It cannot be isolated in any individual part of our lives because it encompasses each of these in its overarching structure and scope. Nevertheless, like the transcendence of subjectivity and knowledge, transcendent freedom is not entirely hidden to us. For, as we have maintained from the beginning, our experience is one, unified, whole. Transcendent freedom is present precisely through the medium of everyday experience. We are aware of the "more" of transcendent freedom in our actions and choices, but in such a way that we never grasp it in its entirety. Thus Rahner distinguishes between originating and originated freedom, two moments always present in the single experience of freedom. This systematic polarity between transcendental and categorical experience is central in his understanding of human life; it refers to both knowledge and freedom.

Because of this, the experience of human freedom is ambiguous; it is subject to our own self-reflection and to the investigations of those sciences which study individual aspects of human existence. As we reflect on the unfolding of our own lives, it is impossible to know with perfect clarity the ultimate truth about ourselves and our freedom. We hope, we strive, but we are always uncertain about the final outcome of our judgments and choices. From a theological perspective, Christianity teaches that we seek our salvation "in fear and trembling" and that the final meaning of our lives is undecided until we die. If this is the case with self-reflection, our judgments about the freedom of other people are even more ambiguous. So it is with the judgments psychology, sociology, even biology, make about the presence or absence of freedom in the human situation. B. F. Skinner's behavioral psychology, e.g., may raise some powerful questions, but it need pose no ultimate threat to a Christian anthropology of freedom. Specific actions and choices indeed are the only bearers of human freedom, but as its partial, always ambiguous signs; they are incapable of complete analysis.

Freedom and responsibility, like self-awareness and personhood, are realities of *subjective* experience: we know them in our experience of ourselves as subjects. Thus they are precisely not accessible when the person is made into an object for scientific study. It is in this sense that freedom lies beyond, or transcends, the specific analyses of empirical or experimental investigation. Although freedom is constantly present in our experience of ourselves as selves, it eludes the microscope and the documentary camera. It may emerge in art, literature, film, but not so much in a specific object or action as in the suggestion, implication, or mood which evokes subjectivity and transcendence. Again the only test is to ask oneself whether something like this structure is not true to one's own experience of being a person, of being responsible and free.

For freedom is not something which one has, like a motor in a car, a tool which one can operate for good or evil according to circumstances. It is, rather, who one is as one creates oneself in time and relationships, the person one has already become, and the person one proposes to be in the future. It includes what one is in the worlds of family, community, business, politics, work of all kinds, and who one ultimately is in acceptance or refusal of the infinite and mysterious horizon of one's very existence. All human attitudes and concerns, styles of living and values are involved in what one does with one's life in freedom and responsibility.

This experience of transcendent freedom which is ingredient in the ordinary experiences of our lives can be ignored or rendered innocuous, just as our subjectivity can. We can blame our actions and choices on other people or events beyond our control. Responsibility can be shifted to our parents, our education (or lack of it), the "system," to what others have done to us or failed to do. But even if we thus categorically deny freedom and responsibility, our very denial is in fact an affirmation and movement of the transcendental freedom whereby we are responsible for our lives. We try to shift responsibility from ourselves in a choice or series of choices that is itself free and for which we are finally responsible. For our most original freedom has to do with the disposition of ourselves as whole persons. Our individual acts of freedom, from the most insignificant choices to important decisions about vocation, career, marriage, and family are truly free only inasmuch as they mediate and concretize our transcendental freedom. This freedom does not concern the objects of our experience but ourselves. As Rahner characteristically says, freedom is not the ability to do this or that, but the power to decide about and actualize *ourselves*.

Writing this way about freedom and knowledge as transcendental, Rahner is describing them in their formal or structural character. Indeed, the tangle of our lives as embedded in circumstances, events, and relationships may not appear to possess this lofty character of freedom at all. Precisely the opposite is often the case. We may feel ourselves to be almost entirely the product of forces beyond our control: we had no choice about our birth, our nationality, the color of our skin, our temperament, intelligence, talents. Our parents and the events of childhood shaped us long before we had the power to make conscious decisions. And our worlds have been shaped, without our consultation, by war, politics, technology, the media. For many of us, even our religious beliefs and moral orientations were planted long before we had the ability to make judgments and choose for ourselves. In distinguishing the formal structure or essence of freedom from its material content, however, Rahner's point is to demonstrate that transcendent freedom is the power which the person has, or rather is, with respect to these determining conditions of human life. Analogous to the general polarity between the transcendental and the categorical dimensions of experience, the polarity between the formal and the material elements of freedom illustrates how our freedom is implicated in what we choose to make of the very tangle of our lives. Our explicit or implicit decision to accept or reject what we have been given entails our responsible freedom whether we realize it or not. Cynicism or hope, despair or courage, indifference or love in the face of concrete circumstances shape our lives, indeed our very selves. We are in our own hands, and this kind of freedom cannot be escaped.

4. Salvation: Transcendental and Historical

With this analysis of the structures of human knowledge and freedom, Rahner has framed his systematic starting point for the more strictly theological question of salvation. If we understand transcendental freedom as the responsibility for creating ourselves in the given circumstances of life in this world, then we can see the intrinsic connection between personal existence and salvation. What Rahner has done thus far comprises a philosophical or metaphysical anthropology; none of the content of the Christian message has been invoked as proof in his argument. Yet it is a theological anthropology in that he proposes these observations concerning human experience as the formal and most fundamental presuppositions of Christianity about the human person. Thus the interlocking of philosophy and theology is apparent in his anthropological point of departure. But we notice also that it is a starting point in which the basic appeal is not to any philosophical or religious authority but to our own experience of radical questioning and of radical freedom.

Only if the foundation Rahner has laid is successful, can we follow him in his argument that salvation is not a future something that "happens" to us from the outside after this life is over, or a moral reckoning in which our sins and good deeds are weighed in the scale of God's justice. For salvation means precisely the ultimate validity of our real self-understanding and free self-realization before God. It is the confirmation of our way of understanding ourselves and what we have chosen to be, not simply in our words or ideas or actions but in our selves. Only in eternity can our freedom exist as final, complete, and fully actualized, for in time another moment and another possibility always follow what we have so far become. Before we begin to consider the particular events of the history of salvation, it is crucially important to understand that salvation always refers to this transcendental essence of the human person.

Having stressed the transcendental pole of salvation, Rahner turns with equal emphasis to the other moment within the single unity of human experience, our situation in the world, in time, in history. These categories do not signify elements which are secondary to the subjectivity and freedom of the person but are the very shape and medium in which transcendence is embodied. An analogy might be found in the inspiration of Bach; the inspiration transcends the individual notes as they are written or played, but is nevertheless absolutely dependent on those notes for its expression. In stressing the intrinsic and reciprocal relationship between transcendence and history, Rahner notes that any aspect of human history may be the carrier of transcendence; the particular experiences, actions, and aspects of our various histories together form the prism through which our transcendent natures are realized.

Historicity is the metaphysical term which denotes those determinations of our very selves (time, world, society, history) which are the given context in which we are situated. It signifies the world of other persons and things which are inescapably part of us, so primordially intrinsic to our existence that historicity is a permanent structure of human being. It is an "existential," that is, a dimension of our very being as persons. Historicity is both that which we must accept—whether we enjoy our lot or simply bear it—and also the context in which we exercise our creativity and freedom, the very fabric from which we design our lives. It imposes limitations, to be sure, but possibilities as well. It is the material, the only material possible, in which we come to the realization for which, as spirit, we continually strive.

Thus, too, historicity constitutes the context of salvation. Since the question of salvation is put to us fundamentally in our freedom, and our freedom is historically situated, we understand the original meaning of the idea "the history of salvation." Rahner argues that human history as a whole is coextensive with the history of salvation even though the two aspects of history are differentiated. The history of salvation is hidden, only vaguely discerned in ongoing secular history. One cannot be very certain what final significance for the history of salvation there was in the Russian Revolution, for example, or John F. Kennedy's presidency, or the student movements of the 1960s. This ambiguity of historical events is deepened by the fact that because history continues, the impact of particular events is never finished and ready for final appraisal—not, that is, until history itself comes to an end. That the history of important events and figures is rewritten in every epoch testifies to this continual reassessment on the human level. Moreover, since each of our lives, and the lives of groups and societies are bound up together in an intrinsically social existence, there is a fundamental unity in both the history of humankind and in the history of salvation. And both impinge, in their differentiated unity, on the personal history of every individual.

5. Dependent Personhood

Rahner completes his anthropology with a reaffirmation of the mysterious character of human personhood as we experience it. Having stressed the transcendence and freedom of the human spirit, he concludes with an emphasis on our radical dependence as persons. For we experience ourselves, he suggests, as not entirely in control but rather at the disposal of the other: other people, other things, and finally an other which is the presence of mystery. He calls this ultimate other the being of mystery. How else can we name it? It is both revealed and concealed to us and constitutes the incomprehensible ground of our existence.

True, as we become aware of the elements of our own historical conditioning, our very awareness in some sense brings us beyond those conditions. We do transcend our origins, especially as we become more conscious of them, but we never leave them behind entirely. Suspended as it were, a midpoint between the finite of our situation and the infinite of our transcendent powers, we never become completely self-sufficient, never fully realize the potentials of our selves, our worlds, our personal or social histories. Nor is it possible simply to withdraw from the interpersonal world of time and space into a kind of interior isolation. And no matter how fully we exercise our transcendence in creative lives, we are constantly receiving our very existence from an unknown source beyond our control. What we make of our lives is always a kind of compromise or synthesis between available possibilities on the one hand and our own consciousness and freedom on the other. And what we make of our lives is never fully comprehended or completely open to our introspective assessment. We remain unknown even to ourselves, not in this or that part of our lives, but in their ultimate totality, in what the subject of all our experience finally is. To the extent that we do approach the truth of ourselves, it is with the awareness that we are not entirely in our own hands.

With this affirmation of the human person as dependent, we have prepared the way for introducing the question of God in relation to human experience. We repeat, however, our proviso about the work attempted thus far. All of the words and concepts, the ideas and structures we have proposed have been on the level of reflection, a mediate level which is secondary to the experience they describe. The whole purpose of these words and ideas is to evoke the experience they reflect, to lead us to see that, beyond the words, the self-understanding so described is our inescapable experience whether we explicitly accept it or try to refuse it. In the end, it is clear that no words can adequately capture that experience of transcendence and dependence, of who we are as free subjects living in time and history.

Questions for Discussion

Before moving to the question of God in the next essay, it is important to absorb the significance of Rahner's point of departure as a theologian. Several issues can serve to illuminate some implications of his anthropological starting point. First, there is the significance of Rahner's primary assertion about the unity of the human person. Does he prove this unity, or does he assume it as self-evident when he differentiates the aspects of subjectivity and personhood, transcendental knowledge and freedom, historicity and dependence? How important is this idea of unity for his discussion of the pre-apprehension of infinite reality? Do we experience this unity in our lives in such a way that we can understand it as the basis for knowledge of the positive infinity of being?

Second, there is the question of the theological significance of Rahner's fundamental appeal to experience. Does it comprise a stronger or weaker argument than an appeal to the authority of scripture, or to Church doctrine? It would probably be helpful to relate it to various appeals to reason, to philosophical arguments, for example, like Aquinas' proofs for the existence of God. Reasons may fairly easily be suggested why Rahner's starting point is more necessary today than, say, in the thirteenth century.

And third, there is Rahner's own presupposition about the conjunction of philosophy and theology. Not everyone agrees that both disciplines must be involved in reflecting on the foundations of Christian faith. How would he respond to a critic who finds his anthropology "too Christian" to be authentic philosophy and "too philosophical" to be genuinely Christian? In discussing these issues, it might be helpful to analyze Rahner's statement that ". . . the Christian message itself creates those presuppositions by its call" (*Foundations*, p. 24). Then each of us is left with the final question whether this anthropology ultimately succeeds or fails to persuade us of its validity. If it is convincing, then the initial step of Rahner's argument for the intellectual integrity of Christianity has been achieved.

SUGGESTIONS FOR FURTHER READING

"Theology and Anthropology," *Theological Investigations* 9, pp. 28–45, is a key essay in which Rahner briefly demonstrates his transcendental method and the intrinsic relationship of anthropology to every theological theme.

"The Dignity and Freedom of Man," *Theological Investigations* 2, pp. 235–63, is an early essay in which Rahner explores the notion of human dignity, the freedom of the person, and human freedom in relation to the state and to the church.

You might read "Theology of Freedom," *Theological Investigations* 6, pp. 178–96; in this concise and especially clear piece, Rahner discusses human freedom in a theological perspective as freedom from and toward God, as the realization of subjectivity in love, and the mystery of freedom in its context of guilt and liberation.

Advanced students of Rahner's thought will want to study his early philosophical writings: *Spirit in the World* and the extensive portion of Joseph Donceel's translation of *Hearers of the Word* available in *A Rahner Reader,* pp. 1–65. These provide the more detailed foundations for Rahner's anthropology.

3

Within the Holy Mystery

MICHAEL J. BUCKLEY

The constant questioning in human experience leads us to talk of God—for God is the context of all reality and experience. The language we use to talk about God, and the knowledge we claim to have, are the subject of this essay.

INESCAPABLE and incomprehensible. The context in which I live. The atmosphere around and within everything I grasp or love. The mystery which human beings call God—and even as a word, God is inescapable.

The Word "God"

We do not make our language. We are born into it. Much more does language make us what we are. It gives us the concepts with which we think. We contact things within language. It shapes the way in which we touch reality and allow it to touch us. It supplies the possibilities for communication, for reaching beyond ourselves into the lives of others. We exist with others through language. We possess our language together. Language constitutes a human openness. It frames the questions we consider and the answers we give. Deep in language, part of its initial and primitive tradition, is the word "God."

Strange that we have such a word. Most things that we name, we encounter, come up against. Trees, chairs, rocks, human beings—these things we find about us, here and now. But God . . . ? Yet the word ranges through all our speech. Strange that it should be there. To name what we experience as mysterious beyond all naming. The word emerges in a thousand different moments. It can be trivialized in invective or invoked in prayer or produced for ceremonial rhetoric or come

out of the deep silence of overwhelming crisis and death. The word
exists and continues to mingle in language no matter how it is treasured
or eroded. It is ineluctably there even for those who refuse it any reality
beyond language. Even the atheist, the "godless," keeps the word
alive—present and provocative.

Does the word mean, or merely point out? You don't run up against
God, but the word does function like a proper noun. It does not simply
signal another individual within our experience, but somehow it does
point out. And it does more. When you say "Yahweh is God," what
are you saying? You are not saying nothing. Human beings have died
for statements like this. We translate the word "God" from one language to another. It must, then, mean something. It both serves as a
proper noun, and also carries meaning.

What do you mean when you use "God"? The name only initially
seems to say nothing about itself. If you pause over the word, weigh it,
examine it for the experience which it contains and echoes, the word
which seems faceless and without contour serves well to speak of the
One who is not another thing, who is the nameless, silent context for
everything we name. Think of it for a minute. "God" brings a new situation into serious speech. Everything else comes into a whole before
it—everything else as a whole faces this word, whether persons, the-
aters, friendships, life or death. Each of these are "what is brought
forth" or "what is created" or "what looks beyond itself." No matter
how radically things differ among themselves, they stand over and
against "God" as having this in common: They look to Him as origin
or as goal or as the ocean out of which they came. The meaning of
"God" is here: Everything regards Him or depends upon Him or comes
out of Him. Everything faces Him. This is His meaning: "God" must
make sense of everything else, must draw it into a unity. In this pervasive dependence upon Him, however differently explained, all things
come into a community among themselves and the meaning of "God"
is experienced. Thus the word names the One who mysteriously unifies
everything and so is always present. "God" can summon up all of reality as its correlative. Everything becomes His "creation"; it stands over
against and dependent upon Him; it only is because He is. The word
names that which alone calls reality into a whole. Of course the word
can remain overlooked and unheard, its depths wasted or unrealized,
because "God" integrates the totality which is always present.

If the word were to disappear, what else would bring us before the whole of existence? What else would lie within the questions about the meaning of everything or about a lasting value of our own life? What else would confront us so strongly and demand continual transcendence and an abiding sense of responsibility? What else in the manifold preoccupations of our lives would challenge us to think of life as a coherence, even if our thoughts give way to bitterness or stoic rejection of the possibilities which this word suggests?

To forget this name, if only as a haunting question, would be to forget what human beings now are: men and women whom issues about meaning and totality have drawn into wonder and poetry. Without this word, human beings would settle down to an ideology whose limits would be taken as absolute—rather than continually questioned—or to a routine of the everyday taken as definitive. "Only a flicker / over the strained time-ridden faces / Distracted from distraction by distraction / Filled with fancies and empty of meaning / Tumid apathy with no concentration / Men and bits of paper, whirled by the cold wind / That blows before and after time." So Eliot described the twilight of such a world. Each moment would become a unit in its own right. Everything would finally add up to . . . nothing. If the word dies, in all of its transpositions, the human dies with it. As long as there are human beings, men and women before whom the question of their own existence and the meaning of "the world" tells with poignant force and who feel a final responsibility for the quality of their lives, the word "God" will figure in their questioning and in their longings. Even if it exists only in question, the word is inescapable in a life that is human. It is the word in which language and the human situation which it embodies bring to consciousness the question or the answers, the disavowals or the affirmations, about ultimate meaning and ground. It is this word which evokes and confirms our humanity.

It is within the human that the word "God" gets its meaning. Not that God is simply the human writ large, as Feuerbach would have it; this would mean that men and women extrapolate the human, but do not transcend it. The real meaning of this word, one that moves beyond its erosion in casual use or in easy colloquialism, is admittedly found in prayer and the quiet self-possession, fidelity, and love in which men and women deepen their lives. We let the word tell on our lives in those moments when transcendence moves beyond any single individual within experience, beyond anything functioning as a limited object of experience and consciousness, to rise towards that "in which we live

and move and have our being.'' It is within the transcendence of knowledge and love that the word God is allowed to tell its real meaning.

The Knowledge of God

1. A Prenote: Experience and God. In the history of Western thought,
there have been two general ways of affirming the existence of God.
One argues from the *notion* of God, that He must be; the other argues
from the analysis of *experience,* that He must be. The first of these is *a
priori;* the second is *a posteriori.* Catholic tradition has favored the second. But the experiences which lead to God are hopelessly dwarfed if
they are limited to the experience of the external—as if we learned
about God the way that Californians know about Australia or that astronomers initially argued to Neptune.

Boats leave for Australia from San Francisco; people arrive who
report it; its name and its history appear in books and newspapers. It
would be madness to deny that Australia exists, but many of us have no
direct experience of it. In the nineteenth century, astronomers noted
variations in the orbit of Uranus, deflections in its movement which
could only be explained by the presence of another planet as yet unob-
served by any telescope. From these "perturbations," Adams and La-
Verrier deduced the existence of Neptune, its size and position, before it
was sighted on September 23, 1846. Too often Catholic tradition has
reduced the affirmation of God to similar deductions of the non-ex-
perienced. Frequently the movement of inquiry towards God has been
treated as if the inquiring mind were a neutral investigative ability uncovering the warrant for its assertions within what is simply external.
But this is radically false: the mind is not neutral and God is not unex-
perienced. Nor is this procedure required by the *a posteriori* tradition. *A
posteriori* experience can be both of ourselves and of our world. In the
intersection of these two, in the fullness of experience, God is found.

The world intimates God, and it does so because human beings find it
finally insufficient to answer their questions. The world raises questions
for human beings which it does not answer, but to evoke a question is to
suggest and to anticipate an answer. On the other hand, the drive of the
mind is the anticipatory experience of God, because the drive of the
mind is for a coherence that "makes sense" out of everything. And the
drive towards coherence is embodied in every question we ask.

This conjunction, then, of the questioning subject with the questionable world brings a person to what is beyond either. We know something by "transcending" it, by going beyond it as we describe it in general terms and discover the general influences which have brought it about. Because we are not locked in, fixated on, a single or particular thing, we can transcend it; because we can transcend it, we can know it.

It is not the case that God is simply given by nature; nor is God simply given by the orientation of the mind. Rather, God is given as the orientation of the mind when it moves through nature in its drive for truth—the truth that is the coherence of nature and the satisfaction of the mind. Nor is it the case that the mind moves toward mystery and infers that it is real. Rather, the mind moves toward reality and finds that it is finally and radically mystery.

Note how the drive of the mind for meaning intersects with the world which confronts it: God is the orientation of the mind when it is geared to ultimate reality and to the final truth about the world. God is mediated by the world because the world points beyond itself; it requires transcendence even to be understood. The spontaneous movement of the human person towards God is inevitable as mind and nature meet in the question.

2. Meaning and Context. What is given when I am aware of something? A number of things. First, the object I encounter and am conscious of—the thing itself—is obviously given. It is not that I am conscious of something and infer that it exists. Rather it is given. It is the focus, the "theme" which I am conscious of. Secondly, at the same time, in a vastly different way, I am conscious of myself. I know the other as the *object* of my awareness; I know myself as the *subject* who is aware, as the one who is knowing. This is quite different, but quite as real as the object of knowledge. Thirdly, I know my own *act* of knowing; I know that I am knowing. The thing of which I am conscious is known as object; I myself and my concomitant act of knowing are known as subject and its action. These three are irreducibly given—I do not infer one from the other. They are irreducibly distinct—I do not identify one from the other. They are irreducibly related—all three are causally influential within my experience of any thing.

These three are given together in the activity and passivity of experience—but is that all that is given? Obviously not. These three factors are given within a *context* of reality. To know the object and to know myself and to know my own act of knowledge—all of these imply a context or a situation within which they are known. And this context is given, not inferred, just as the subject and the act of knowing and the object are given. The context is given "non-thematically," i.e., like the subject and its acts, it is not the "theme" or the focus of my consciousness.

The context is the background, or the atmosphere, or the "horizon" of both the subject and the object. It identifies with neither; it encompasses both. What is more, this context is the radical direction for any act of inquiry or questioning, because the context gives coherence—"makes sense out of"—both the subject and the object. For example, if I am asked why there is life on this planet and not on Venus or Mars, my explanation will refer to air pressures, humidity, the laws of gravitation, the sustaining atmosphere, etc. If I look for the explanation of the Brownian movement of tiny particles, I go beyond the particles to water molecules involved in thermal motion. In the awareness of myself as subject, I am conscious of myself existing dependently within a world of things and a texture of the interpersonal. In all of these cases, I look to the context for explanation. Each datum, given in a question, is "transcended" in the movement towards its understanding. And the point is that I transcend each spontaneously. The orientation of the mind moves beyond each of them in an effort to explain. The human mind goes spontaneously to the *context* to answer questions about any object. It does so because the human experience is that this object can be understood, that it makes sense—but *not* finally in terms of itself. Its intelligibility is ultimately derived from its context. In other words, both the subject and its object depend for their explanation, for their intellectual coherence, upon their context. The mind's movement towards understanding is a steady, transcending movement towards context.

3. Human Subjectivity as Movement Towards Infinite Context. Why is it that we look spontaneously and continually to further contexts to explain our human experience? Why this constant dynamic drive towards new discoveries? The instinctive thirst of the mind, its openness and its demands, is for a completeness of meaning. We experience that each of these things which we encounter demands an explanation and yet does not offer that explanation with any completeness. This is their limitation: They provoke a question which they alone cannot answer. They raise but cannot answer the question of their own coherence. This is to experience that they are finite, limited and dependent. The longing of the mind goes beyond them—beyond anything so limited, so finite.

This is what Rahner means by asserting that the drive of the mind is toward the infinite.

For at the same time we experience in anticipation that explanation can be forthcoming. We ask questions continually and expect that they will be answered or at least that the answer lies somewhere. This prior experience both of the opaque givenness of an answer within a question and of an orientation towards full understanding lies within our readiness even to begin to question and inquire. We look to the context because we have the prior, unthematic awareness that the context can explain; it is from the context that we expect explanations to be forthcoming. This means that we experience both that reality is finally intelligible even before its coherence has been disclosed, and that this final coherence does not lie with the limited object of immediate consciousness, but with its context.

The context of reality and of explanation—the horizon given with every limited object—is ultimately something radically different from limited objects or the set of limited objects. It does what they cannot do; it finally integrates and gives coherence. In this, it is limitless or infinite. (Infinitude here is not endless extension. It is completeness without limitations. Here it is described functionally. It is the ability of the context of reality to account both for itself and for all the things which depend upon it.) Whenever we ask a question, we begin a series of questions which can take us to this horizon of all reality and to an infinitude which is utterly different from the finite things we directly and immediately experience. Ultimately the coherence or explanation of the finite is not finite. The movement of the mind towards fullness or completeness of meaning and truth is a movement towards the infinite context of reality.

The drive of the mind is towards this transcendent context, one that is always other than what is grasped, one that always lies on the other side of "why?" Conversely, this transcendent horizon evokes human transcendence—it is the situation, the direction, and the source of human transcendence. We think whatever object we think within this context; we encounter and are aware of whatever we meet, within this context. This context is always given in the unity of mind and nature.

Granted that we spontaneously move towards such a final coherence or complete explanation. Is there such an explanation? Whence this persuasion that things must make sense and that the mind must be satisfied?

Why must one assert the final intelligibility or the infinite context of reality?

It is impossible to argue to the presupposition that things finally make sense. Any "proof" would presuppose it. But two things can be underscored in the conversation about infinite intelligibility.

First, we do experience that the mind moves towards the real, that it is geared to reality, and that a sign of serious mental disintegration is what we call "removal from reality." We do experience that things deliver "sense" or "meaning" or "intelligibility" to the inquiring mind. Reality and mind seem made for each other. The drive towards reality and towards a final coherence to reality are the same. The mind is impatient with appearance—as opposed to reality—and it moves in dread away from nothingness or chaos. Why is it that there is joy in the experience of living, or horror before the blotting out of death, or a sense of fulfillment when after tortuous investigation the meaning of an event begins to dawn? The radical drive of human subjectivity is for the real.

To assert that there is no final coherence, no meaning in terms of which the universe makes sense, is to assert that the drive of the mind is radically deceptive or pathological, and that the individual units within the world may be understood, but that the whole itself is meaningless. But it does not take a great deal of thought to realize that if the whole is meaningless, the parts are ultimately meaningless. As Michael Polanyi has pointed out, meaning is always a matter of total context. This is why any experience of intelligibility, no matter how small or seemingly insignificant, is so crucial; for to experience that any particular thing delivers meaning and intelligibility, is to experience that the whole is intelligible. The daily moments in life present this in a thousand ways: the dawning curiosity of a child, the dynamic dedication of a scientist, the games people play, and the pervasive sense that the meaning of the human situation is not finally absurdity. One cannot "prove" a final coherence, for to demonstrate it would be to presuppose it; what is critical before all else is to see that this final coherence is a given in the coherence of particular things.

Secondly, to deny final intelligibility—that is, that "things make sense"—is to assert it. To say that the world is absurd or that the mind moves towards final ambiguity, is to affirm meaning and a definite intelligibility: Its meaning is that it has no coherence. This statement confers a definite structure on reality, an intelligibility analogous to things within our own life that are an unintelligible chaos. Absurdity or ambiguity is the absence of that meaning or order which we have found elsewhere. The contrast is noted and called absurd or ambivalent. Now, however, this absence is taken as a definitive structure and imposed upon the whole of reality. But this won't work. Chaos or absurdity is like the hole in the doughnut—an absence within the experience of the real. It is only the real which allows this absence to have its "presence." To take the absence, then, and make it the context of reality, is to assign it a reality which it denies. To erect ambiguity as a final intelligible structure, rather than a present state of consciousness, is to assert what you deny: Unintelligibility is made final intelligibility; the void is made the real context of the real.

To summarize, then: When one experiences anything, one experiences also the actuality of its context. These reflections have suggested that the context of reality is experienced in three ways. It is that *within which* I experience anything directly, as the given situation of the real. Since it is non-thematically experienced as conferring integrity and coherence, it is that *towards which* I move spontaneously in all my questions and decisions. It is that which leads me continually to transcend each and every object in search of the explanation of the object. The context is, finally, the *source* which evokes and opens up the possibility of all human transcendence. This infinite context, direction and source of human transcendence is what we call God.

4. Holy Mystery as the Context of Reality. God is, then, both a given of reality and an experience of the knowing subject: a given of reality insofar as He constitutes the situation of anything we encounter; an experience insofar as He is non-thematically present as the orientation of human transcendence towards coherence.

To say that our knowledge of God is *a posteriori* does not mean that we look into the universe with a neutral ability to know and discover God along with a thousand other things. It does not mean that human beings have discovered God as they have discovered planets. The whole drive of human knowing is towards God, towards final coherence. He is the context within which any thinking and knowing takes place. It is within our human transcendence—a transcendence which takes us beyond anything finite—that we know something of God as the One who always lures us on beyond whatever we grasp and as the context within which we know.

This is to say, paradoxically, that God Himself is incomprehensible.

You cannot transcend the infinite. There is no further context by which the infinite context is made coherent. God is His own coherence, complete ("infinite") in Himself and giving integrity to all else. This is the riddle of human knowledge. We transcend the finite towards the infinite; we comprehend what we know in terms of what is incomprehensible. Incomprehensible reality—this is what we call Absolute Mystery.

Thus, for human subjectivity to come into its own fullness is to come before Absolute Mystery. To find myself, to rescue myself from distractions and superficiality by allowing what is deeply true about myself to emerge into presence, is to find myself within this context—one that I cannot finally get my hands upon, one that every deep drive for meaning and love indicates, and one which every thing speaks of but nothing finally delivers. Each thing which I directly experience points to this last and ultimate context by which it is finally to be understood and by which the world is finally to be integrated.

Mystery is thus inescapable. Everything indicates it. Mystery is not what I do not know. I do know it. I know it as Mystery, as the final context of my life. I find it like a permeating atmosphere within and among the things I touch. But none of these is the Mystery. Each of them only speaks of it.

Mystery is not that which I cannot know. Mystery is that which I cannot exhaust, which I cannot go beyond, which I cannot transcend. In this sense, Mystery is incomprehensibility—I can never enclose it in definition. For Mystery is the endlessly intelligible. It is its own explanation and the explanation of everything whose reality raises a question.

This is what it means to be aware of and to live within Mystery. It is the initial experience of the infinite context of reality, given in both the orientation of the mind and the relativity of things. Mystery is the term towards which the mind moves in its orientation towards knowledge and explanation and in this transcendence grasps what is comprehensible. Can one say that he or she experiences God? Yes—but so differently from any other experience. God is experienced within my direct experience of other things. God is experienced as the context within which I know what I know. Like the experience of the self, God is experienced within the experience of knowledge—not from it or by it. God is experienced as the horizon and the "lure of transcendence." All subsequent metaphysical and theological reflection needs to return again and again to this experience—the fundamental experience of the human grasped by Absolute Mystery.

In this sketchy phenomenology of knowledge, the transcendent emerges as given. A similar descriptive process could be done in an examination of human freedom and human love. Both of these demand that persons be present to themselves, that they be responsible for themselves so that they can give themselves to others in friendship and affection. To possess oneself, to be responsible for oneself, is possible only to the degree that one is not determined and controlled by something outside of oneself. In other words, freedom is possible only to the degree that one can transcend other forces and other objects. It is because we love the infinite that it is possible for us not to be coerced by anything finite. It is this orientation, this kind of love, that makes human beings free. And it is this freedom that allows us to love others, to give ourselves freely.

The Mystery towards which we move in knowledge is also the one towards whom we move in love. It is this Mystery which opens our transcendence, and it is in love that we desire it. For the experience of God can deepen into the experience of God as personal. As infinite Mystery, God is not less but more than we are. For this reason the Mystery within which we live is holy; the knowledge of Mystery and the love of the infinitely good becomes the ground of prayer and worship. It is this Holy Mystery which gives us to ourselves. It is this Holy Mystery which allows us that transcendence of knowledge and freedom in unity which alone makes us human. But how is it really that we are moved to speak personally of this fathomless Mystery which contextualizes all reality?

A Personal God

The word "God" is inescapable, and the most daily, routine aspects of our existence give meaning to the word as we are drawn in the transcendence of knowledge and freedom to what is utterly beyond ourselves. But what can we know of this Mystery? How can we speak of it?

The problem is a profound one. Language tells upon the way we think. Words fasten upon the things we know and either reveal them or distort them beyond recognition. If we use words hewn from the things around us for God, we reduce Him to a thing around us. We will not come to God but to idols. Yet, the only source of words is our immediate experience with sensible things. We have words for water and vision and happiness—because they enter into our immediate experience with the world around us. How then talk about one who is not given directly by experience, but as the context of experience?

But if you notice, the problem is not just about God. It is also about ourselves. When we speak of our mental life, for example, how do we do it? We talk in terms of ancient metaphors: We say that we have "concepts" or "understanding," possess "insights," form "ideas," and make "judgments." All of these words are originally metaphors, whose richness constant usage has suppressed. We know that understanding is not the same thing as actual sight, but we call a moment of understanding "insight," because it is something like "seeing into" what was previously opaque. Something like, but quite different. We stretch the language to handle subjective, spiritual experiences which are not immediately tangible.

Ordinary language stretches this way all the time. We say that a man defending his country with arms is a "patriot"; we say the same thing about a nurse working in the wards of an army hospital; we say the same about a worker in a factory or a teacher who attempts to instill a balanced love for one's country. Each of them is called a patriot. But if you looked at their actions, hardly one would resemble the other. Each of them is a patriot, but each in his or her own way.

Now how about God? Does language function the same way? Many people have thought so. But it won't work. God is not another thing who does something in "His own way." We know how a GI or a nurse is a patriot, because we can see what they are and what they are doing. But God? What God is, is incomprehensible. What God is doing, we know not because we see God but because we see God's effects. Our language has to reflect the way that we know. We know God as that upon whom all things depend. We know God as the transcendent ground of all things. So our language must stretch to fit what we know. All of our statements about God are meant in this sense: God can be named as the cause of what we see; but as the transcendent ground, God can never be incorporated into a common system with them—the way that metaphors about insight and analogies about patriots do.

What is, comes out of God and bespeaks God—as any effect is symptomatic of its cause. Not only language, but things themselves thus become symbolic of God: Everything bespeaks the richness of its transcendent cause.

Something like this is true in any interpersonal relationship. When you are kind to me, when any number of gentle, thoughtful gestures come from you into my life, gradually I come to have some idea of how deeply kind you are. Each of these moments in which you author a letter of congratulations, a word of consolation, a helpful suggestion for pressing work—each of these moments embodies your kindness because they come out of your kindness. Your kindness cannot be simply identified or described by any of its effects within my life, but it is in these moments that I get some glimpse of the whole disposition of your life which lies behind them and which is embodied in them. Somewhat similarly, we know and speak of God through and in His effects within our life—we name Him as the transcendent source out of which all things come and through and in which they continue to be. All things are symbolic of God.

Analogous language about God indicates this: that any reality we know exists in God as in its source. When we use "good" of God, we do not use it in the same way that we speak of the "good play" in football or the "good doctor" or the "good afternoon"—each in its own way. We mean that what we find good here, in all of its variants, we assert of God transcendently as its source. There is always a tension, then, in what we say about God—a tension which is only removed at the cost of projection and idolatry. We take the word "good" from our immediate experience and predicate it of God. Yet at the same time, we deny that God is good like a play or like a doctor or like an afternoon; we deny that God is good in any way that we know. And finally, we assert that He is good as the transcendent ground of all goodness which we know, as the one in whom goodness is realized preeminently as in its source.

The statements about God, then, are analogical statements, but in quite a different way from those of "patriot." They assert something of God not by an analogy like "patriot," but by an analogy of language which indicates ultimate dependence or transcendence. For it is the transcendent movement towards final coherence and love which gives us God as "subject." Any predicate which we assign to God from the world around us must be caught up in this prior and radically purifying movement of transcendence.

For, oddly enough, these statements of the analogy of transcendence are much closer to what is original in our experience. What is most radical about human knowing is its transcendence, its moving beyond this or that individualized object to the transcendent context of them all. In fact, it is this movement which makes possible our knowledge of individual and particular things, since all knowledge is obtained through contexts. When we "stretch" to talk about God, we touch the radical experience which makes us what we are. We realize what we are.

Only in this context can we talk about God as person. Philosophers such as Fichte have attempted to remove this predicate from God—not because they disbelieved in God but because they denied that God was another individual alongside others, with the limitations that human subjectivity and freedom embody, one who defines himself over and against another. To name God as this kind of "person" is simply to project another human being, writ large. The history of religion has indicated that projection is a normal failure of religious consciousness, and this history gives weight to their hesitation.

Only the analogy of dependence or transcendence can prevent the charge of projection. It simply asserts that the source of reality must possess what it is the source of, and possess it in a preeminent purity and fullness which we have never directly experienced. When we predicate subjectivity and personhood of God, we are not saying that God is a person like a human person. We are saying that God is the ground of all personal reality and that this reality is realized in God as its transcendent source. We are saying that God is more than person as we know it. That personal reality which in us is limited and defined by another, is found in God without limitation and in its radical originality. God knows and loves as is only possible for the source of knowledge and love. How is this realized in God? That we do not know. To answer this question would be to grasp the nature of God. Statements about the personal reality of God, like any other statements about God, move into mystery as words which are taken from individualized experiences are allowed to merge back into primordial origins.

But such reflections simply allow us to assert that God is personal. It is another thing to *find* God personal. In the first, we are talking about philosophic argument; in the second, about religious experience. It is God who must fill the empty, formal assertion with historical experience: through prayer, through moments in our lives in which we sense God's challenge and nearness, through the supremely graced presence which God has taken in Christ Jesus and in the pervasive integrity of the Spirit. It is here that piety and very original religious practice take their cosmic importance, in a holiness of life in which one accepts and experiences the personal reality of God.

The Dependence and Autonomy of Creation

The word "God" continually summons human beings to consider their lives as a totality. The experience of transcendence carries every act of knowledge and love beyond itself to the presence of Mystery. The dialectic of analogy allows us to think and to speak haltingly and truly of Mystery. This total experience of language, transcendence, and analogy spells out what we are: creatures. Language confronts us with God, at least as a question. Transcendence reveals God's reality as a haunting presence which is the ground and horizon of all reality and truth, as the direction towards which we are borne in consciousness and freedom. Analogy allows us to find meaning in this relation, taking words originally coined to deal with the immediate or the direct and referring them back to the incomprehensible source of the realities they name. Language, transcendence and analogy compose an interdependent world, *each* of whose elements feeds into the others and is, in its turn, supported by them. *Each* of them indicates the fundamental human experience, a radical orientation towards Holy Mystery: Language is given its meaning by transcendence and is justified in its use by the dialectic of analogy. The total experience is that of a creature.

The full meaning of creatureliness is only available through revelation; the more profound our awareness of God, the more thorough our knowledge of ourselves. Yet even with the most general human experience, our experience of being creatures is given. In the experience of transcendence, we are radically and inescapably oriented towards Holy Mystery as the context of reality. To be a creature does not refer immediately to an episode at some distance from the present. It refers fundamentally to a relationship that is always present. To be a creature does not refer to one relationship among others, as if it were another instance of the general relationship of dependence. It refers to an absolute and unique relationship of utter dependence, unlike any other in my experience: The total dependence upon Mystery as upon the context of reality which gives direction to the movement of inquiry and establishes the freedom of choice and personal responsibility. The first instance of creatureliness is not an event in or out of time in which the world came to be or in which I came to be—an event I have heard of, but not experienced. The first instance of creatureliness is this experience of total dependence and radical orientation towards Holy Mystery.

To be a creature is to experience God as ground and, because of this, to experience Him as radically different. God is not another thing in my experience. He is the context, the ground of "every other thing." He is not a direct object of my awareness and my choice; He is the situation which makes this awareness and this choice possible and which explains every object. In subsequent reflection I can thematize this Holy Mystery. Yet the reflection is not the experience. The thematization always has a note of artificiality because I am treating what is essentially unthematic as if it were possible to focus directly upon it.

God is ground and radically different; it is not God who needs the world, but the world which needs God. It is not that God and the world compose a larger unit, make up a system greater than either of its parts. This would not be to have God as absolutely different, but as another— albeit larger—element within the world. What we experience, however, is radical dependence, not interdependence. To include God within a system with the world, as Whitehead does, is to reduce Mystery to a functional interconnection with other parts, one of which determines and sustains the other. It is only when the opposite is seen, when one is faithful to the experience of transcendence, that God as the absolutely different emerges. Only when one grasps something of the independence of God's Mystery, can one grasp how freely God establishes what is other than God's own life. Only in His Freedom can human beings sense something of how gratuitously and unconditionally they have been loved. Because God does not depend upon the world, He does not have to create; He does not need the world to fill out some internal lack. Yet God does create, does originate that which is not God, so that, as will be developed later in this book, there would be a world to which God's own life could be communicated. It is the independence of God which allows Him to love us into existence. The choice by which the world is given to itself, brought into being, is creation. Absolute dependence is simply another expression for creation out of nothing.

Oddly enough, the more complete our dependence upon God is, the more radical is our human autonomy and personal freedom—a point which neither Nietzsche nor Sartre ever grasped. Dependence upon God is not like dependence upon another thing in the universe. God is not another being in the universe; God is source. One could argue that dependence upon another being, something with which we exist, can sometimes take away human autonomy. Whatever be the truth of this, whatever be the judgment of its validity after any number of critical distinctions, it is radically false when applied to human dependence upon God. For genuine reality is not threatened by the ground of all reality; on the contrary, reality is established in its freedom and autonomy by its ground. The dependence upon God is that which establishes my reality, not what denies it. We are infinitely different from God—with the absolute difference that creation has brought about—and we never merge amorphously with God. The created does not merge with the uncreated. Creation is the guarantee of our autonomy. Our autonomy is precisely the effect of the action of God.

While creation establishes the validity of the world, it also demythologizes it. There is only one God and nature is not a part of Him. He is absolutely different from nature. Nature is not worshipped, for it is not God. It is finally the material for the creative power of human beings. What is more, nature is not the privileged locus for finding God; it is neither His most profound effect nor His most poignant symbol. The human is. Human beings are finally what bespeak God, not only in the depth of their endowments but in the radical direction of their lives. For to be human is to be radically directed towards God through knowledge and love. It is within this transcendence of knowledge and love, within the experience of the personal, that even wordless nature is caught up and borne back to God. This transcendent orientation constitutes the uniqueness of the human person, and in this orientation the human gathers all of nature into a knowledge and love which returns all things to their source in Absolute Mystery.

Questions for Discussion

The preceding pages have advanced an argument whose lines have been drawn by Karl Rahner in the third chapter of *Foundations of Christian Faith*. Rahner's reflections have suggested that "God" is a word which summons all reality into a totality and human beings into a profound sense of self-responsibility; that the human dynamics of knowledge and love reach out to God as the Holy Mystery which contextualizes all other knowing and love; that the symbolic nature of the world allows us to know something about this Mystery as source; and that the total orientation of our humanity which is discovered in this world, in this dynamic, and in this dialectic of analogy becomes radically present to our consciousness as the experience of being created.

What are some of the questions that are suggested by these reflections?

First, what is the weight that the word "God" finds in human usage? What kind of a world emerges when you use it seriously? Is it possible to use it in such a way that it cannot be heard? Heidegger speaks of a "forgetfulness of being" as lying at the root of the disorientations of Western philosophic thought. Is there an equally pervasive, possibly far more subtle "forgetfulness of God" which lies at the heart of much contemporary religious and theological reflection and speech? Has "God" become too easy?

Secondly, Rahner asserts that human transcendence, in the experience of knowledge and love, discloses God as Absolute Mystery. How would you rephrase or correct or criticize this assertion in terms of your own experience? How would you describe the way this Holy Mystery is present in every love, as well as in all knowledge—so that in loving anything "one is implicitly loving God"? Or, taking another tack, how does God emerge in your own religious history and in the expectations of your life?

Thirdly, how is it possible to speak of God without the projections which Freud makes the essence of such religious language? Can there be a knowledge of God which does not reduce the Mystery to the human but deepens it as the absolutely different? How is the Mystery that is God related to the revelation that is Jesus Christ, and why is it that this revelation is salvific?

To allow yourself and your reflections to stand within this kind of questioning is to come before God with an openness that waits upon Him. To question with reverence and steady perseverance is to move towards God, the Absolute Mystery, in a deepening knowledge and love which can become the contemplative fullness of human life.

SUGGESTIONS FOR FURTHER READING

In "The Man of Today and Religion," *Theological Investigations* 6, pp. 3–20, Rahner discusses how the contemporary world poses a particularly urgent question for any religious affirmation of God's reality and presence.

"The Experience of God Today," *Theological Investigations* 11, pp. 149–65, explores the extent to which the experience of God is affected by the special situation in which the human person exists today.

In "The Experience of Self and the Experience of God," *Theological*

Investigations 13, pp. 122–32, Rahner argues again that the experience of God constitutes the enabling condition of the experience of the self, and that the experience of the self is the condition making it possible to experience God. This unity allows for an inner integrity between the love of God and the love of neighbor.

"The Concept of Mystery in Catholic Theology," *Theological Investigations* 4, pp. 36–73, is one of Rahner's most famous essays; it shows that mystery constitutes the fundamental reality of the incomprehensible God, present to every human person in the experience and lure of transcendence and offered to all human beings through grace as their ultimate destiny. All of the "mysteries" proposed by Catholic dogma are aspects of this one mystery with which Christian revelation confronts humanity.

"Thomas Aquinas on the Incomprehensibility of God," *Journal of Religion* 58, Supplement (1978): S107–S125, locates Rahner's theology of mystery within the teaching of Thomas Aquinas and holds that this illumines the contemporary understanding of the human person as the question for which there is no final answer.

4

The Bonds of Freedom

BRIAN O. McDERMOTT

The search for meaning is carried on in freedom—the scope and goal of this freedom are characterized here as nothing less than the totality of our lives in union with God. In the process of trying to arrive at this goal, we are confronted with a fundamental option: a "yes" in openness to our shared humanity or a denial of ourselves. In this option, the power of original sin in us is dominated by God's own loving self-gift.

WHEN converts to Christianity recount the story of their passage from the old life to the new, the language they use can often be black and white. Whether it is Paul of Tarsus describing his slavery under the Law and freedom in Christ, or Thomas Merton in our own time narrating the days of sin at Columbia before his conversion and life of grace as a Trappist monk, the impression conveyed is unmistakable: *then,* sin and guilt and unfreedom, *now,* grace and light and freedom.

Converts can be forgiven this language, for their conversion marks a watershed in their lives which is experienced as a total passage from death to life. But from the point of view of the gospel, which inspires Rahner's reflections on freedom and guilt, it is much more likely that there is no period of a person's life and no sector of human history which has been, or will be, simply graceless, untouched by the redemptive influence of Jesus Christ. Yet just as truly we can and must say that there has been no period of history which does not need redemption. Following Rahner's lead, our own reflections will trace the contours of human freedom in a world redeemed yet threatened by radical guilt, where that freedom, oriented to final fulfillment, hides within itself a dark possibility called original sin.

History: Redeemed or Unredeemed?

I remember once having a conversation with a Jewish acquaintance and coming finally to that most disturbing of topics: the Holocaust. My Jewish friend thought that the Holocaust was the greatest challenge to the truth claims of Christianity. He asked point-blank: "What good has the cross and resurrection of Jesus done for history and human life, when such a thing as the Holocaust, and countless other atrocities, have occurred in human history?" The question is a profound one, and in a sense has no "answer" in the ordinary meaning of the word. I did not try to respond, but was stopped short by his anguish. Later, upon reflecting on our conversation, it occurred to me that no one is able to step out of human history and observe what history without redemption would look like compared with a redeemed history. We cannot presume—unless we simply choose to—that our history is unredeemed, just as we cannot suppose that our history would be empirically the same if not redeemed. The genuine humanity that has been achieved, the values nourished and fidelities lived out, all deeds of love and justice and generosity call for explanation, especially if one believes our world in no real sense redeemed.

The large question which my friend raised is also the more personal question of the meaning of my own life. Talk about salvation and redemption is not foreign to most citizens of technological America. We are the most religious and secular people around! Cults from East and West promise their American initiates salvation from the meaninglessness of technopolis, while the human and natural sciences proceed apace in university and corporate research and development, uncovering the mechanisms which make us tick and giving us, so it appears, salvation in the form of control. If our parents are not responsible for our behavior, then our genes are, and with clever adjustment our destiny can be assured.

But the very quest for meaning, whether through cults or through assuming the reins of technological control, signals an inalienable feature of being human. We are responsible for our lives, we are given over to ourselves, we yearn to understand as keenly as possible and to control as thoroughly as possible all the empirical aspects of our lives. We are summoned to know the conditions which affect our behavior and to uncover the causes of good and evil in society and personal life. This search for meaning about the objective, circumscribable features of our human life together on planet Earth is a quest which goes deeper and wider than any particular examination of any particular segment of our experience. Physics cannot explain why physicists seek the light, and neither can psychology, for it too is a search for light. Physicists and psychologists offer interpretations of particular regions of human life. But the interpreters themselves are, finally, doing their interpreting as a way of assuming responsibility for their lives, as a way, in other words, of being faithful to themselves as human beings drawn to the light.

Responsible Freedom

There is not any activity in which we engage, there is no personality trait which marks us as who we are, which does not find an explanation in biology, psychology, sociology or some other empirical science. There is no region of our human lives which is not explainable. But the existence of sciences which explain my behavior, the objective answers to scientific questions about the human phenomenon, bear witness to the central and pervasive truth that as a human person I am under an imperative to understand, explain, give an account of myself. As the explanations mount up and grow in complexity I can choose to hide behind these explanations by saying to myself: "This is what I am without remainder, except of course for what tomorrow's science will have to add to the account." Or I can choose to recognize these explanations as the stuff of my freedom, as the account of *what* I am empirically but not of *who* I am called to be. For in the light of this latter perspective, all the empirical explanations of what I am point to pathways of my life as I inalienably live it myself in a way which is open to the light or closed to it, selfish or self-giving, attentive to the mystery of my life or denying or evading it. In other words, all the motivational and quantitative explanations of what I am can become the field in which I live out my life in gratitude, or the hiding place where I avoid my responsibility.

No particular science can disclose or decide that I am nothing but a finite chunk of reality, or field of energy, rounded off and totally enclosed in a grid of equally finite quantities. A decision to view my life in that way transcends quite literally the data on which it is based. How I am related to the whole of reality is a matter of intelligent decision and understanding freedom, not a scientific conclusion. So too, holding oneself open for more, for possibilities that cannot be measured by science or ordinary common sense, is equally a choice. In each of these choices I am thrown back on myself: Which kind of person do I choose to be and become in all my particular choices and actions—open to a possible "more" or closed in a finite circle of meaning and value?

This is what the best of Christian tradition has meant when it talked about freedom. Here freedom referred most profoundly not to choosing this value or that, but choosing in an ultimate way—as the deed of my entire life, through all the pathways of particular choices—*who* I wished to be, a person either open or closed to the mystery of my life.

Each of us has one life to live. Each of us is who we are through the living of that one human life, with all the particular circumstances which mark that life. Born into this particular family, maturing, choosing a livelihood, marrying or remaining single, suffering and rejoicing, I become myself, and no other. When that one life comes to its end in death, I have become who I am. Not someone who *is* only at the instant of dying, but the one person who has come to be through all the life experience I have undergone and chosen. A human life is an inextricable pattern of doing and being done to, of activity and passivity. Yet the passivity on one level can become the material of a more profound activity—the doing of my one life. Viktor Frankl speaks of this when he writes about his experiences in a concentration camp. He was physically, and, in many ways, psychologically, imprisoned. Great violence was done to him. Yet he was able to transcend his imprisonment through love of his wife and his desire to write and create. Even the cramping and destructive circumstances of prison life became in a mysterious way the context and material of his desire to be and remain human, to be more than a mere object. This happened not in some romantic flight of fancy but in a quiet, secret yet persistent effort to choose who he wished to be even in those horribly straitened circumstances. He did not allow himself to merge without remainder into his circumstance. He remained a person, broken in body and psyche to a great degree, but living his one life even in that brokenness, putting a personal stamp on the ash-grey moments of life in prison. Even what we did not choose for ourselves in our lives can become the expression of who we desire to be.

Freedom Has a Goal

Because we are called to become persons, our freedom is something final, that is, it is goal-oriented, but in a real sense the goal is nothing other than ourselves, as we come to be in authentic solidarity with all other persons.

Christian faith says something very significant about the nature of this freedom we have been exploring. The choices which we make are not only the way in which we choose who we shall be and become, but the choices are responses as well to an invitation, or rejections of an invitation, which makes itself felt in all the many goals, values, dreams, attractions which lure us on in life. When I choose to marry, or to begin a certain business career, or make a decisive change in my life, I am not only choosing myself, who I want to be, but I am choosing myself in relation to the Mystery of my life, who is God. Christian faith does not view choosing self and choosing a certain relationship to God as two separate actions or decisions. Rather, my choosing to be a certain kind of person, say, an accountant or teacher, involves a whole set of directions and actions which express a response to the invitation of the Holy Mystery, an invitation to allow the Mystery to love me and to draw myself to itself as I try to become myself. In choosing in a way which is open rather than closed I am allowing myself to be "defined" not only by my desires or my self-chosen actions, but also by the Mystery of God who desires to be the atmosphere, horizon, and final goal of all my life experiences.

The Dark Possibility of Freedom

The possibility exists, however, that my life can take a very different turn. One of the mysteries of my human freedom is that in a whole series of decisions which on the surface may appear innocuous enough, I may be choosing to become a thing, rather than a person, a closed system of behavior, energy and outlook which at heart is—heartless. Now choosing to be a thing is vastly different from being a thing. Let stones and trees and seashore and automobiles be what they are—but human beings can choose to be persons or to become beings who are closed to all loves and all authentic creativity. The prospect is devastating, but tragically possible. The outcome of such misused freedom is not the rigidity of body or waywardness of psyche which mark old age, but a rigidity and paralysis of spirit at the heart of all that human being is and does. This utter impersonality is the final condition of those who choose to be wholly alone, for and by themselves alone. This is to choose to be a thing, to choose total excommunication as the shape of one's life in violation of and indeed contradiction to one's deepest, most authentic call. This call is inscribed ineluctably in one's being and it is a call to be in communion, to be in relation with one's true self, all the human community and through that, in relation to the Holy Mystery of one's life, whom Christian faith calls God. A painful accident of life such as the loneliness of our large cities is one thing, but profoundly chosen loneliness, real spiritual aloneness is something else again; then one has chosen the hell of the false self, the hell which consists in being without the other.

Such a final choice is dark and unintelligible; it literally does not make sense. No psychological or spiritual theory can explain it; it has no explanatory cause other than the person who so chooses to be: "I am this way because *I* choose to be this way." The responsibility, and here the word becomes an accusation, is nowhere to be located but in the person.

In closing myself I say, in a single spiritual movement, "no" to self, God and the human community. On this level I have not simply misunderstood; the final disposing of myself before God and others is not liable to mistake. Mistakes are possible on all levels of my being except the level of my single freedom which is my one human life lived unto finality. On this level, understanding and freedom are inextricably intertwined and we choose to understand ourselves in a way which knowingly contradicts an authentic self-understanding. At this level I am my own person, one with myself and responsible for my understanding and freedom. No one and no thing stand "behind" me to absorb or deflect that responsibility out of me into itself.

This final condition of self-chosen slavery, thingness, frozen impersonality, is almost unthinkable for us. Its preparation is hidden and most often gradual. Jean-Paul Sartre, in his monumental *Being and Nothingness,* has detailed the dimensions of such "bad faith," how I choose what is contrary to authentic life and love and at the same time choose to view the choice as life-giving and good. The negation is made, on a certain level, to appear as an affirmation, and only later on, if at all, will I recognize explicitly what all along on a deeper level I knew already, that the choice was for death rather than life, because it chipped away at a trust, or hurt a covenant in my life, or perhaps allowed egotism to deaden a love or eviscerate my sense of justice.

The tragic irony involved in all this is that the pattern of choosing to be thing, to be a non-person, lives and draws its energies from a dynamism at the heart of the person toward personhood. The denial of the Holy Mystery of God and the rejection of the self is a mockery of true self-achievement, a miscarriage of one's life. Self-assertion, when it is actually egotism unto death, is a final self-denial. A promise and power of personhood are denied by a choice, or more probably by a series of choices, which are signs of a self-chosen impotence, self-chosen non-being, annihilation as far as one can choose it. Thus a negation of this order and range is not simply the counterpart to a possible "yes" to life and its mystery, for the former stands in inalienable reference to the "yes" of life: the "yes" God speaks to life and the unchosen and eternal orientation to God which makes me the person I am in my deepest nature. Even my "no's" in life bear witness, in their own way, to a yearning for life and expansion. A "yes" has been inscribed in my being from the time of my entrance into the human community, a "yes" I can live out or deny, but it asserts its presence in all affirmations of the good or surrender to the evil.

A False Dilemma

The modern atheist challenges these assertions in many forms. One basic rejoinder to a conception of life as oriented to Mystery is to assert that authentic human freedom and a divine sovereignty cannot exist together, because they necessarily enter into competition. Either I am a self-creating person or the object of an infinite, controlling subject. Either God *or* human freedom! The challenge is not an easy one to answer, because it does not bear simply on some historical clash between, say, an emergent humanism and ecclesiastical authority (such as in the Enlightenment), but calls into question one's understanding of both freedom and God.

Two considerations offer a Christian approach to this challenge. First of all, there is a growing awareness in our world that human persons learn to love and live well only if they first receive love and care from others. There is something about the special character of freedom such that love is its cause. But the notion of freedom and the notion of "being caused" do not seem to square easily. After all, freedom is sometimes spoken of as *causa sui,* self-causing, quite the opposite of being caused by another. But love "causes" in a way specifically different from all mechanical or impersonal modes of causality. Love offers nourishment to other persons to be and become themselves, their own most authentic selves. Love achieves that kind of thing. All other forms of causality determine something else, they affect something else as object. But when I love someone, and try to be faithful to that love, I am engaged in a twofold desire: to offer my true self to the other person and to encourage the true self of the other. Freedom and receiving influence from the other on this plane are not competitive or displacing, but rather imply each other.

The second consideration is that the displacement that takes place between two human persons, whether physical or psychical space is involved, is due to their finitude. For example, the rhythm of give and take which goes on in a friendship, the backing up and stepping forward, is a characteristic which is the consequence of two finite persons being individuals, no matter how intimately they are in each other's life. At its best, Christianity has tried to think consistently about God's relation to human beings as the relation of the infinite with the finite, where God's presence in the life of the person is what makes possible and sustains the freedom of the creature, precisely because the creating and self-communicating activity of God is a twofold activity of *infinite love*. Christianity claims that God's creative and self-communicating love is at the heart of God's "sovereignty" vis-à-vis the world; it is not in competition with human freedom. This claim is compelling to anyone who recognizes that this love, which is infinite, creates the difference of the creature and the union of the creature with the reality of God.

Sometimes people who are good Christians unwittingly nourish the atheist challenge when they protest: "All that is good in my choices and actions comes from God, while all that is evil and mediocre is due to me, and not to God." There is a certain plane on which such a statement can be truthful—when in prayer and praise we confess God's goodness and our own frailty. But, from a more theological point of view, we need to view this statement with great caution. Because love "causes" the other person to live his or her own life, the good choice and good deed in my life is more my own precisely because God, in a way proper to his infinity, is cause of my own good deed or choice. A good choice is more my own than an evil choice, because the former is more dependent on God than the latter is. Love causes healthy independence in relations. The beloved depends on the lover for encouragement toward healthy autonomy which is fruit of the union between them. We are returning to an earlier reflection here, because it can protect us from falsely letting God "devour" our good deeds, so that we are left in his sight, naked and garbed, as it were, only in our transparently evil deeds.

The Horizon of Freedom

Christianity offers a serious response to the person who asks whether our freedom, the freedom of our lives, is situated exclusively in the sum of finite loves with which we may be blessed. For it holds out the hope that there is a sustaining love which is *the* situation of my life and freedom and which can be absolutely relied upon. In all our loves there is the mark of the absolute, at least in the form of desire. We say "forever" when we are loving well. Even a second and third marriage these days is often enough the expression of this search for "forever"! We are too critical in our age to believe that desire indicates possibility of fulfillment, but the Christian conviction is worthy of a serious hearing, namely that there is an unbreakable love sustaining us in our loves and failures, not as competition but as the secret power at work wherever we experience the autonomy and freedom that are love's power and mystery.

Talk of "freedom's situation" raises another question which introduces us to a further conviction shared by Christians. What sense does it make to speak of God's love for us as the situation or atmosphere of our freedom, when the distinct impression one gains from hearing Christians speak is that at the beginning of each human life original sin weakens that person? "In sin we are born" seems to be the Christian view. Adam and Eve, paradise, Fall, inheritance of guilt, concupiscence and the need for baptism all are part of this picture. It sounds as though God's love comes on the scene at a later, subsequent moment, or at least shows up in an effective way only later, when a *contingent* action, baptism, which occurs for only a few, undoes original sin, which *necessarily* affects everyone. Precisely because relatively few people are baptized, it would appear that most of the children of this world are under the power of original sin. What does this say about the power and sovereignty of God's love in a broken world? Is the doctrine of original sin simply the translation into common sense of the ordinary person's conviction that evil is all about us but the deeds of goodness are fragile and rare? After all, people sometimes hold that the doctrine of original sin is the one doctrine which they know to be true from experience. Whatever they may mean by original sin, it at least refers to the power and visibility of evil in our world, and American Protestant theologians such as Reinhold Niebuhr have written eloquently of the power of this symbol to express the intrinsic tragic character of our human condition.

At the beginning of these reflections I said that redemption should not be narrowly conceived by Christians as affecting only a portion or region of human history, as though there were on the one hand a graced side of life and on the other a simply graceless dimension. But a serious challenge to this perspective seems to be Christianity's own view that the condition called original sin precedes temporally the graced state which only baptism makes possible. It cannot be denied that this is the position adopted by many Christians in the history of the Church. The theology of St. Paul acknowledges an experience of "before" and "now" which is undeniable. But the same apostle is the preacher of a salvation which is universal, touching all of human existence. If we are saved, all of us is saved and redemption is at work in the lives of all. In the light of the death and resurrection of Jesus, Paul would never allow sin to be more powerful than redemptive grace. The power of sin has in principle been broken, and redemptive grace affects human existence prior to any free choice made by human beings, including the choice to baptize or to allow oneself to be baptized.

St. Paul is no stranger to the power of sin at work in the world. Indeed, in the letter to the Romans he offers what stands with the early chapters of Genesis as the classic portrayal of the mushrooming growth of sin when people become accomplices to its power. But the same Paul is convinced that we live, thanks to Jesus Christ, in an already redeemed world. Is it going too far to suggest that the redemption which Christ has brought about affects each person who enters the world at least as profoundly as the sin and evil which still stalk the human stage?

If the Christian takes seriously the grace of Christ which abounds all the more where sin once abounded, to paraphrase Paul, then the whole of a human life and the whole of social life must participate in a real and fundamental way in Christ's redemption. But if this is so, what becomes of the Christian doctrine of original sin?

The Power of Sin

A theologian like Rahner is deeply persuaded that there is a profound realism in Christianity, a realism which goes beyond today's optimism and tomorrow's pessimism. There is a double character, theologically speaking, to our human existence from the start of our lives. First, we are marked as loved, loved by God the Father, through the redemptive life, death and resurrection of Jesus and in the sending of the Spirit. One could call this the original redeeming grace. It is original redeeming grace because it is the deepest horizon of concrete life—the saving love of God, as distinct from particular situations such as loving parents, various friends, the encouraging experiences of community, and so on. It is God's love as it affects us before we make any choices in life. This original or fundamental redeeming grace is God's choice for us, as loving and forgiving Lord, God's choice to be, in a redemptive way, our goal, beginning, savior. If it could have its way, this love would become the all-encompassing and exclusive horizon of my life and the life of the human race, inviting and empowering the full, authentic freedom of each person and each community.

On the other hand, as we have noted, each person and each social group in human history is marked by the power of sin at work in the world. Before you or I make any choices about our lives we are touched interiorly by this power. The logic of this power is equally total; if it could have its way, it would become the all-encompassing and exclusive horizon of my life and the life of the human community. Its thrust is totalistic, indeed totalitarian. "The power of sin" is an expression which can sound mythological. It certainly is mythic, in the sense that it is a way of talking about "something" which cannot be spoken about in simply rational, logical terms. Scripture sees particular sins and specific forms of moral evil as manifestations of the power of sin ("sin" in the singular). The mythic way of speaking is not accidental or extrinsic to what is being talked about here; it is worth noting that, in Christian tradition, Satan was conceived of as a fallen creature, not as the substantially Evil One.

The doctrine of original sin is an effort to express on the level of discursive reason the role sin plays in human life prior to a person's exercise of freedom. Traditionally, for Roman Catholics, that role has been one of depriving the person of sanctifying grace, that is, depriving the person of the share in God's life which God desires for his creature. Rahner does not deny this doctrine, but he does maintain that everyone born into the world is influenced on the deepest level of personal being by two unequal forces: the power of God's redeeming love in Christ and the power of sin opposed to Christ. Being redeemed and being subject to sin are two fundamental dimensions, or existentials, of our life from its inception. These existentials are not simply juxtaposed or parallel, for the negative dimension is encompassed, as it were, by the redemption wrought by Christ. The negative existential can be interpreted in the light of the saving existential in a twofold way. First, it is a fundamental dimension of our existence in the world, and of such a kind that, if redemption in Christ had not occurred, it would be the all-encompassing horizon of my life, and of all human life. Second, it is the dimension which is oriented even in a redeemed world to becoming the final posture of every individual person in that person's history of freedom. It is total in orientation, but not total as actuality at the beginning of the person's life. Only the complete and final "free" complicity of the person can permit that dimension to become the totally deformed shape of the individual's life.

There is a dynamism in us which we have not brought about through our own choosing, and this dynamism invites us to go it alone in life, to choose separation, radical selfishness, "thing-ness," which is eternal death and the tragic mockery of authentic selfhood. But another dynamism, more powerful because it is God's doing in us and for the same reason more authentically who we are, is present too. If we cooperate with this dynamism (in a cooperation which itself is gift in us), it will allow us to belong in authentic solidarity with our brothers and sisters, with ourselves, with God in Christ and the Spirit. Total loneliness and complete belonging are the radical choices. But they are not choices which face us as external goods or values. Rather, they are dynamisms within us, and we can align ourselves with one or both of them in differing degrees as we grow as members of the human family.

This theological way of talking about existentials, dimensions, dynamisms within our lives is an attempt to express the *most* fundamental aspects of our life in relation to God and other people. They must be distinguished, but not separated from the empirical, contingent factors which make up the concrete particular situation of every human person born into the world. The family I was born into may have been blessing or curse in my life. The genes I inherited may be healthy or deficient. The empirical circumstances of my life are profoundly important in my salvation history, but not exclusively so. Christian faith maintains that God's *redeeming* love and the freedom of the person blessed by that redemption are the most powerful circumstances in human life.

Redemption through the Community

Does this suggest that Christians should view salvation merely as an I-Thou relation with God, ultimately apart from the social character of human life? If so, the belonging which saves seems to be simply a belonging to God!

Rahner sees things differently. On the one hand, salvation is the gift to the individual, and no one can take another's place in freedom. Each person is an absolute in history. And yet redemptive grace is given to the individual through the community. The good news in all this is that

God's own life in the Holy Spirit has created the community which mediates this redemptive grace to all, a community called Church. Redemption is present and at work in all people because the Church exists, not because all people are called to be members of the Church. God's effective desire to save all (1 Timothy 2:4) is not restricted by the temporal and spatial limits of the sign he has raised in the midst of human history. The presence of the Church in human history is the presence of the infallible sign created by God to manifest saving grace among all people. Rahner's conviction regarding the role of the Church as sign for a universal reality is born of his view that the Incarnation and the pouring out of the Spirit affect all of human history. In a real but mysterious way all peoples are linked to Christ's community of salvation in the Spirit. Even a simple gesture of acceptance into the radically redeemed human community can mediate redemptive grace to the infant, according to Rahner. The adult involved in this event need not be explicitly aware that this is what is going on, but the effective presence of the church in history creates bonds which place that person in a situation of salvation which they are invited to ratify as they mature. It is an unsoundable mystery of human life that some people are born into circumstances that are materially, psychologically and spiritually favorable, while others are born to a world which is deprived in many ways—abusive parents, destitution, mental retardation. No theory can make this mystery transparent. But Rahner's recognition of "original redemptive grace" and "original sin" is his translation of the scriptural conviction that our broken world belongs to Christ in the Spirit, and that this powerful truth is stronger and more fundamental than the concrete circumstances of my life compared with someone else's.

Questions for Discussion

Rahner defines human freedom in terms of our capacity to determine who finally we shall be before God. Does this way of speaking allow us to appreciate how particular attitudes or actions are free or unfree? Does it give too much weight to the fundamental choice involved in all choices, and not sufficient weight to the concrete particulars of our lives and the material of our choices?

The phrase used above, "original redemptive grace," is not Rahner's but this author's. Do you think this is an appropriate way to express Rahner's insight that each person born into the world participates in the redemptive and justifying grace of Christ, since the human race has in principle been redeemed already by Christ?

If one agrees with Rahner's insight, then a further question arises. What is the importance of baptism in such a view? Does it not appear that this sacrament of initiation is as important for Rahner as membership in the visible Church, neither more nor less?

Finally, an area of Rahner's reflections which calls for closer examination is his position that original sin is an existential of human life, and not simply a condition that affects us prior to baptism. In what ways is this existential a different force in our lives after sacramental entrance into the Church? Indeed, what does "original sin" mean as a reality in itself in a redeemed world? Rahner has tried to re-think the doctrine of original sin in a creative and faithful way. The continuity and difference with the doctrine we grew up with as children can be a most fruitful way of learning in a deeper way what it is the Church invites us to acknowledge and confess when we speak as Christians of original sin, the bond of freedom.

SUGGESTIONS FOR FURTHER READING

"Original Sin," in *Sacramentum Mundi* 4, pp. 328–34, is a helpful brief overview of Rahner's understanding of original sin in relation to the official teaching of the Church.

In "The Sin of Adam," *Theological Investigations* 11, pp. 247–62, Rahner offers a contemporary reflection on the meaning of the "Fall" of "Adam" and on the universality of the grace of Christ.

"Guilt—Responsibility—Punishment within the View of Catholic Theology," *Theological Investigations* 6, pp. 197–217, develops Rahner's understanding of freedom and responsibility in relation to the question of guilt and punishment.

"The Theological Concept of Concupiscentia," *Theological Investigations* 1, pp. 347–82, is an important early article dealing with the finite and composite character of human freedom in a broken world. The article develops a basic distinction between human nature and human person in terms of which the traditional concept of concupiscence can be understood today.

5

The Invitation of Grace

JOHN P. GALVIN

Rahner's vision of the relationship between God and the world is centered in his theology of grace. He sees grace primarily as the offer of God's own life to humanity, an offer which promises fulfillment to what is most fundamental in our experience. This conception is developed in ways that are important for our understanding of God as Trinity and for the relation between nature and grace.

THE Christian message is in principle quite simple: It is the gospel of salvation in Jesus Christ by a God of infinite mercy and love. "For God so loved the world that he gave his only Son, that whoever believes in him should not perish, but have eternal life" (John 3:16). Yet, as Dietrich Bonhoeffer observed in a letter written from his cell in Berlin, fundamental Christian ideas like salvation and grace "are so difficult and so remote that we hardly venture any more to speak of them." While traditional explanations of these ideas seem strange and in many respects unsatisfactory, the hollow rhetoric of many attempts at modernization betrays the presence of trivialities devoid of substantial meaning and unworthy of serious attention.

Discouraged by this state of affairs, we may understandably be inclined to resign ourselves to the conclusion that words such as grace should be consigned to the scrapheap of language as no longer serviceable in the contemporary world. It may seem that here, if anywhere, we would do well to heed Wittgenstein's advice and keep silent about that of which we cannot speak. Still, like Bonhoeffer, we continue to suspect that something new and even revolutionary may lie hidden under the standard words, something otherwise unavailable and desperately needed by a fragile and threatened humanity if we are not, as Michel Foucault put it, to "be erased, like a face drawn in sand at the edge of the sea." And as long as this is so, we can hardly justify abandoning the search for a more adequate understanding of their meaning, however arduous a task this may promise to be.

One possible source of assistance is Karl Rahner's vision of the relationship between God and the world: his theology of grace. I would not venture to suggest that the total answer to our perplexity can be found here. But Rahner's conception of grace, which constitutes the unifying thread pervading all his work and providing its distinctive character, is extraordinarily appealing. It invites the reader to join in examining Christianity anew, from a perspective which affords a comprehensive view in which the disparate elements of the Christian faith coalesce into an organically integrated whole. If we are to pursue this invitation, it will be necessary for us to study Rahner's theology of grace in some detail. Many who have not been deterred by the inevitable effort have found the investigation quite rewarding.

God's Offer of Self as Human Salvation

"God himself as the abiding and holy mystery, as the incomprehensible ground of man's transcendent existence is not only the God of infinite distance, but also wants to be the God of absolute closeness in a true self-communication, and he is present in this way in the spiritual depths of our existence as well as in the concreteness of our corporeal history" (*Foundations*, p. 137).

With these words Rahner expresses in his own terminology the central conviction of Christianity. Human life and human history are not doomed to meaninglessness. They do not develop and end in ultimate absurdity or Sisyphus-like frustration. Our longing for salvation, our search for wholeness, is destined to achieve fulfillment.

In what, however, does this salvation consist? For Rahner, it is nothing other than God himself, present to us in unsurpassable nearness. Hans Küng has recently asked, in his *On Being a Christian,* if any reasonable man today wants to become God, and commented that "our problem today is not the deification but the *humanization of man.*" Küng's precise meaning is difficult to determine, for his remarks may simply be intended as valid criticisms of certain types of theology and spirituality. His implied question about the relationship of grace and humanization is certainly legitimate and important. Nonetheless, this formulation of the issue seems to insinuate a false dichotomy between humanization and the enjoyment of unsurpassable closeness to God. As will be argued in more detail toward the end of this chapter, "humanization" and "divinization" are not alternatives, and the offer of grace is neither distraction from nor addition to genuinely human concerns. Far from destroying our humanity, God's self-gift is the offered fulfillment of the openness that is most fundamentally and most typically human, an openness which no created reality can satisfy. Nothing less than God's offer of himself can ultimately advance our full humanization.

By self-gift or self-communication of God, we mean simply that God offers himself to us in unsurpassable proximity: the giver is himself the gift. God does not merely give us finite gifts, nor merely communicate to us truths about himself. He offers us a presence which surpasses his relationship to us as the infinite but distant horizon of all our acts. In keeping with its nature, this divine self-gift takes place on a personal level, not in the objectified manner in which sub-personal reality might be conferred on the beneficiary of a bequest. A full personal relationship with God is established only in one who responds positively to the divine offer, with at least implicit faith, hope and love. (Theologians frequently reserve the term "divine indwelling," as alluded to in John 14:23, for this intensified relationship in which God's presence within us has elicited a positive response on our part.) Nonetheless, it is legitimate to speak of God's self-communication to designate the presence of the divine offer as such, apart from our response. For the offer as such has initial effects, and helps constitute the situation in which our response takes place.

It is clear from the nature of God's self-offer that the initiative must lie with God. But we are not thereby condemned to passivity. A "salvation" which did that would hardly be salvific. Still, the fulfillment of our openness is something which we receive as a gift, not a product of our own making. "We love, because he first loved us" (1 John 4:19).

Though the primary gift is nothing other than God himself, the divine presence is inevitably accompanied by effects in the one to whom God is present. These effects are not identical with God himself, but rather created and finite. For this reason, the Scholastic theological tradition has distinguished between uncreated grace and created grace. Uncreated grace is God himself as present in the recipient; created grace is a divine gift, other than God but above our natural powers, freely given to us by God. The precise characteristics of created grace vary according to the circumstances of the recipient, particularly with respect to the individual's fundamental response to God's offer of self.

For an accurate grasp of Rahner's theology of grace, it is essential to keep in mind that he attributes priority to uncreated grace. Many Catholic theologians see divine indwelling as a consequence of the presence of created (sanctifying) grace. One prominent author, Charles Journet, has even gone so far as to write that "grace is like a net we throw over the Trinity to hold it in captivity." Such theologians refer to "actual graces" to account for the operation of grace in instances in which sanctifying grace is not (yet) present. Rahner, on the contrary, is prepared to speak of God's self-communication even in situations in which the divine offer has not been accepted. This enables him to consider created grace in all its forms as effect of God's self-communication, at least as offer. He thus explains both "actual graces" and "sanctifying grace" as diverse effects of the one divine self-gift. The result is a more personal and more unified conception of our relationship to God, one in which "grace" refers primarily to God's presence within us, at least as offer.

Although God's self-communication is present throughout our lives, it does not reach its definitive stage until our death, since only then is our acceptance or rejection final. The difference between our present state and the state of final perfection which we hope to enjoy after death is expressed well by Paul: "When the perfect comes, the imperfect will pass away . . . Now we see in a mirror dimly, but then face to face" (1 Corinthians 13:10,12). Drawing on this imagery, theology has traditionally used the term "beatific vision" for the definitive state of salvation. For an understanding of God's self-communication, it is important to realize that the differences between grace during our lives and the beatific vision at their conclusion do not derive from arbitrary divine decrees, as if God were holding back on something we could enjoy now. The differences are rather a consequence of the temporality which is a constitutive dimension of human existence and human freedom. The fulfillment hoped for at the end of life is the unfolding of a gift already present and operative now; conversely, the grace effective now is but the bud destined to blossom fully at the appropriate time in the future. (There remains of course the fearsome possibility that an individual will culpably block this development and thus fail to arrive at the goal.)

Even in the beatific vision, the result of God's self-communication is not a synthesis of God and ourselves. If the statement we quoted from

Küng is meant merely to exclude this, then Küng's intention is beyond objection. God always remains God, the holy mystery, the ultimately nameless One beyond human comprehension. We for our part remain genuinely finite, genuinely human, though transformed by the gift of God's love. Even if absorption into God were possible, it would represent destruction of human nature, not its fulfillment. It is precisely because God communicates himself to us as God that he is able to be the infinite fulfillment of our unlimited openness.

Our relationship with God in grace provides a starting point for an understanding of the doctrine of the Trinity. While it is impossible to examine this doctrine in detail without extended consideration of the person and work of Jesus Christ, some initial observations may be made here, if only to indicate the relationship of faith in the Trinity to other aspects of the Christian message.

The basic principle is that the way God reveals himself corresponds to the way he is in reality. In more technical theological vocabulary, the "economic Trinity" (God as he reveals himself in the history, or economy, of salvation) is the same as the "immanent Trinity" (God as he is eternally in himself). Were this not so, God's self-communication would not be genuine self-gift and self-revelation. Thus our threefold experience of God, the holy mystery—as incomprehensible ground of his own self-gift, as present for us in our concrete history in Jesus Christ, and as transforming us in the innermost core of our existence— rightly leads us to speak of Father, Son, and Spirit, not only in our experience of God, but in the one God himself. In traditional language, we speak therefore of three "persons" in the one God. In order to avoid spontaneous misunderstanding of what "person" means in this context, Rahner has suggested that the term "ways of subsistence" might be used as well. (The English translation of *Foundations* speaks of "modes of presence.") Obviously, any terminology has certain liabilities. The important point here is not the terminology as such, but the realization that the doctrine of the Trinity is an essential presupposition and implication of fundamental Christian convictions. Far from being a superfluous addition to the Christian faith, it represents a compact summary of major themes of Christology and of the theology of grace.

Human Response

In keeping with the freedom and personal character of both the offer of grace and its human recipient, God's self-communication is directed toward our knowledge and freedom. Since its purpose is to enable us to enter into immediate knowledge and love of God and thus find salvation, it does not achieve its final goal until freely accepted by its recipient. Such acceptance is itself a gift of God's grace, though not to the exclusion of our activity and responsibility. The divine offer makes its own acceptance possible through its initial effects on the recipient.

Thus the divine offer may be present in us in three different ways. First, it may be present simply as offer and appeal to human freedom, but as yet without personal response on our part. Even in this initial stage it has certain effects which transform the situation in which we exist. The two remaining forms presuppose our response. The offer may be present and accepted in an act which is both an event of grace and a deed of human freedom. The purpose of the divine offer is to achieve this result, which is often called the "state of grace" in traditional terminology. But, finally, the offer may be present in rejection by our freedom. Yet even in this instance, the offer does not vanish without a trace but remains, providing the possibility of forgiveness and involving the unrepentant sinner in a fundamental self-contradiction, since the God whom the sinner rejects is the One who offers fulfillment of the sinner's basic human longing.

To guard against a possible misunderstanding, it must be stressed that neither acceptance nor rejection of the divine offer should be imagined as necessarily taking place in an explicit manner, nor as occurring in a single, clearly defined event which could be isolated from the rest of life and recognized as decisive upon subsequent reflection. The offer of grace is present, modifying our consciousness, throughout the whole of our lives. As previous chapters have suggested, all deeds which engage the depths of our freedom affect our relationship with God. Acceptance and rejection of grace are thus not limited to acts with visibly religious content. They take place in any true exercise of our freedom, even if the specific act seems to have nothing to do with God. The fundamental way in which the offer of grace is accepted is genuine love of neighbor (see Matthew 25:31–46; 1 John 4:7–21).

A few words on the currently popular topic of the experience of grace (experience of the Holy Spirit) may help to clarify this point. Since divine self-communication has a transforming effect on human consciousness, it is possible and legitimate to speak in a certain sense of experiencing grace. Neither the realities which we experience nor we who do the experiencing exist in a purely natural state, untouched by grace, and our experience is inevitably affected by this fact. Great caution, however, is in order here. Experience of grace is not exactly like other experiences. It differs significantly from the experience of other objects of our knowledge, like the experience of a chair or table, or even that of another person. The closest suitable comparison is to our experience of ourselves as subjects of our own actions, as distinguished from our objective knowledge about ourselves. Nor is experience of grace restricted to special moments or unusual circumstances. It cannot be isolated from our other experiences and does not necessarily entail explicit recognition of grace for what it is. For these reasons, it is at least normally impossible for us to distinguish concretely between grace and the other factors which are always joined to it in our consciousness and knowledge.

In addition, it is important to remember that we cannot determine through introspection, with an absolute certainty which could not be false, whether grace is present in us in the modality of acceptance or of rejection, or simply as offer awaiting response. In the words of the Apostle: "With me it is a very small thing that I should be judged by you or by any human court. I do not even judge myself. I am not aware of anything against myself, but I am not thereby acquitted. It is the Lord who judges me. Therefore do not pronounce judgment before the time, before the Lord comes, who will bring to light the things now hidden in darkness and will disclose the purposes of the heart" (1 Corinthians 4:4–5). While serious self-assessment is not impossible, definitive self-judgment is beyond human ability.

The Universality and Freedom of Grace

God's salvific offer of himself is made universally—at all times and in all places where human freedom exists. It is not restricted to certain individuals or groups (for example, to Christians) or to those who live during or after the time of Christ. Rather, as 1 Timothy 2:4 states, God wills the salvation of all, and so offers himself to all. This, of course, provides no guarantee that the divine offer is actually accepted by everyone, though the Christian is not forbidden to hope that this will prove to be the case. The universality of the divine offer has far-reaching implications for understanding the history of salvation and the significance and role of Jesus Christ as universal mediator of salvation; these will be major concerns of the following three chapters.

In keeping with its character as a personal relationship, God's self-communication is a free act of divine love. To grasp this fully, it is necessary to abstract temporarily from the problem of sin. That the sinner has no claim on God's mercy is readily intelligible. But God's self-communication is not free only with respect to the sinner. Even a sinless humanity could raise no binding claim on this manifestation of divine love.

The issue we are addressing here has been discussed since the Middle Ages under the rubric "nature and grace." In this context, the common word "nature" is used in a particular technical sense, in which it does not refer to all that actually exists, nor to what may be distinguished from "artificial" or "cultural" products of our own making, but rather to whatever in our existence can be distinguished from grace, sin, and their respective effects. Using the term "nature" in this legitimate though abstract sense, we can pose our problem in this way: How can our nature be such that we are both conceivable without grace and yet capable of being fulfilled in the most complete way possible precisely through grace?

To account for the freedom of God's self-communication, it is insufficient to appeal solely to God's freedom in creation (freedom to create or not), for the issue is precisely the freedom of the offer of grace to a particular creature. Our intelligence and will, for example, owe their existence to God's creative goodness, and would not exist without his free act. Yet they are not strictly speaking gifts *to* humanity, for they are constitutive elements of our human nature. If God's self-communication were part of the nature of a given creature, or if a creature had by nature a right to grace, then God's offer of himself to that creature would not be free gift to a freely chosen partner.

This stress on divine freedom brings several questions. Is this divine freedom compatible with the conviction that God's self-gift is constitutive of human salvation? Is it not self-contradictory to say that our salvation consists in a gift which God, our creator, could freely have withheld? Is there an explanation which both preserves the freedom of God in offering grace and yet avoids envisioning grace as so extrinsic to our lives that it could no longer realistically be considered constitutive of human salvation? At the very least, any theology which asserts that God's free self-gift constitutes human salvation is compelled to explain how its position is coherent.

In order to resolve this dilemma, Rahner introduced the notion of the "supernatural existential" into the vocabulary of theology. This technical term has since been associated with his thought. An existential is a basic structure which permeates the whole of human existence; it is not a localized part or region of our being, but a dimension pertaining to the whole. Our being in the world, or our being with others, could serve as examples. The adjective "supernatural" is added in order to indicate that this existential, unlike others, is not given automatically with human nature, but is rather the result of a gratuitous gift of God. The divine offer of self-communication forms a constant dimension of human existence, always present, yet not part of human nature as such, affecting the whole of our being and directing us toward unsurpassable nearness to the triune God of grace and eternal life. The supernatural existential is the initial effect of the offer of grace, even prior to human response. It is present and operative universally, and constitutes one of the factors in the situation within which our response takes place.

While the notion of the supernatural existential enables us to avoid thinking of grace as extrinsic to our lives without compromising its freedom, it does not in itself solve the problem of the relationship of grace to our nature. To address this aspect of the question, Rahner draws on the traditional Scholastic concept of "obediential potency." An obediential potency is a capacity which is open to fulfillment yet not frustrated or meaningless if the fulfillment is not granted. Rahner considers our openness to being, our existence as spirit in world, as obediential potency for the self-communication of God. This potency is not a separate faculty or regional section within us, like our ability to breathe, but rather our human nature as such. If the divine self-communication did not occur, our openness toward being would still be meaningful as the condition for the possibility of human knowledge and human self-disposal in freedom. We would still have to do with God, though only as the distant horizon of our existence. But because of this same openness we are by nature possible recipients of God's self-communication, listeners for a possible divine word. While the actual offer of grace transforms our concrete existence, it does not destroy that which characterizes us specifically as human—our finite openness as spirit in world. And, since the obediential potency for grace is precisely human nature as such, God's free fulfillment of this capacity through his self-gift automatically becomes the most central factor in human existence. "Divinization" and "humanization" are not alternatives between which we could choose; in the actual world in which we live, they are one and the same goal of our existence.

With the aid of these two categories, we can express the freedom of grace without making grace extrinsic to our lives. Because of the super-natural existential, grace is always a part of our actual existence. Far from being confined to a particular portion of our lives, or being present only when we deliberately advert to its existence, grace is operative in all we do. Our nature, as unrestricted openness toward being, is obe-diential potency for the offer of grace: open and even directed toward it, yet not strictly requiring this highest fulfillment of its potentiality. Grace thus remains free gift of God and yet, when freely given, takes its place at the very core of human existence.

Because of our concentration on the relationship between grace and human nature as such, the relationship between grace and sin has not been in the forefront of our discussion. This emphasis is also typical of Rahner's writing on the subject. Nonetheless, while it is important to avoid reducing grace to a means for overcoming sin and the damage it has wrought, it is also essential that the problems discussed in the previous chapter not be overlooked. In the actual order in which we live, grace includes the healing dimension of overcoming sin, as well as the dimension of elevating our nature, for God's self-communication is able to override any obstacles it may encounter.

Perhaps at this point we can return to the passage with which we began our discussion, and now grasp Rahner's meaning with deepened understanding: "God himself as the abiding and holy mystery, as the in-comprehensible ground of man's transcendent existence is not only the God of infinite distance, but also wants to be the God of absolute close-ness in a true self-communication, and he is present in this way in the spiritual depths of our existence as well as in the concreteness of our corporeal history" (*Foundations,* p. 137).

Questions for Discussion

This is not the place for scholarly discussion or criticism of Rahner's conception of grace. Our purpose has simply been to introduce its more important themes. To do anything beyond this would require more ex-haustive presentation of his views and his arguments on their behalf, as well as a more extensive and nuanced critique than is possible or desir-able here. But a few questions may be raised by way of conclusion, in the hope of promoting deeper understanding of Rahner's thought and further discussion of its implications.

First, one of the most striking elements of Rahner's thought is his in-sistence on the universality of the offer of grace and on the presence of grace, at least as offered, in every aspect of our lives. How does this affect our conception of the church, and of the importance of being a baptized Christian? What is the value of specifically religious acts such as prayer, if they are not the only place in which we encounter or respond to God? Does Rahner's conception of grace lead to either secularism or sacralization of the whole of life, or does it provide an authentically Christian vision of the presence of God in the world?

Second, what are the consequences of the distinctive characteristics of the experience, or consciousness, of grace? To what extent, if at all, is it possible to identify a particular experience as a result of grace? Is it possible to have a religious experience which is purely the result of God's gift of himself—one untouched by our religious and cultural environment and by our own personal characteristics?

Third, how would you evaluate Rahner's relative neglect of an explicitly biblical theology of grace? While the fundamental notion of the self-communication of God unmistakably incorporates certain Pauline and Johannine themes, other major elements of Rahner's thought are less directly related to biblical foundations. Is this a deficiency or is it necessary to address pressing issues not explicitly raised within the New Testament? Are there elements in the New Testament views of the relationship of God and humanity which are not adequately presented in Rahner's conception?

Finally, Rahner's theology of grace, like any other, has its own particular characteristics. Two of these are the stress on divine self-communication as gratuitous fulfillment of human nature rather than as overcoming of sin and evil, and the concentration on the individual (rather than the Church) as recipient of grace. While other perspectives are not denied, they are not in the foreground. What is to be said for and against these options? What is their validity in the current situation of Church and theology? Do they constitute a tendency to blur the gravity of sin and evil, or promote an individualistic conception of our relationship with God? Or do they effectively illuminate particular dimensions of the divine self-communication?

As important as these questions may be, they do not detract from the significance of Rahner's achievement. His theology of grace has enriched Christian reflection on a topic of paramount importance, and it provides us with a promising point of departure for further meditation on the inexhaustible mystery of God's love for us and for all in Jesus Christ.

SUGGESTIONS FOR FURTHER READING

"Reflections on the Experience of Grace," *Theological Investigations* 3, pp. 86–90, is a useful, meditative introduction to Rahner's thought on grace and also shows its relationship to his many writings on spirituality.

"Concerning the Relationship of Nature and Grace," *Theological Investigations* 1, pp. 297–317, and "Nature and Grace," *Theological Investigations* 4, pp. 165–88, are famous essays on an issue of major importance for understanding Rahner's conception.

The entries "Existential, supernatural," "Grace," and "Potentia oboedientialis" in the *Theological Dictionary* of Rahner and Herbert Vorgrimler, pp. 161, 192–96, 367, are valuable compact summaries.

"Some Implications of the Scholastic Concept of Uncreated Grace," *Theological Investigations* 1, pp. 319–46, is rather technical, but will be instructive to those familiar with Scholastic theology.

Finally, *The Trinity* contains not only Rahner's chief work on that subject but also a brief presentation of his theology of grace.

6

A History of Grace

THOMAS F. O'MEARA

Now we turn to consider how the self-gift of God is revealed in history. Grace and salvation are seen to be operative throughout—from the dawn of human time, through a multitude of religious movements, towards a climax in Christ. Revelation is the realization of how God's grace acts in history, and this essay also outlines the main features of this concept.

KARL Rahner enjoys questions. His writings and his lectures often begin with the posing and the savoring of questions.

From 1965 I remember the first day of one of his courses in Munich. The semester's series of lectures bore quite a general title, and so we wondered just precisely what topics Rahner would treat during those autumn months. That first day Rahner spent three hours not by lecturing but by asking questions, all sorts of questions about interesting areas of theology we might discuss, problems left unanswered from the Church's past, new issues raised by an uncertain if technically advanced world.

Rahner always begins his theology with our personality and with our own life, with our times and with our future. Currents at a deep level fashion our questions; in the sea of our existence the waves are the questions of life. He begins to think about faith not with biblical texts or past philosophies but with our existence at this particular point of geography and history, with our questions.

What are my questions about words such as "religion," "faith," "church"? I can employ a church like a country club or I can drop out of it. The churches, once stable beacons in American society, are now questioning, changing, renewing, adapting. Has my faith been weakened by an ecumenism which not only reaches out to all Christians and Jews but to the religions of Asia and Africa? One step into these questions is like that afternoon when Rahner asked only questions; a first question introduces many more.

Questions about the presence and identity of the Christian faith flow from the new unity of the world. Transistor and Telstar have brought the world even closer together than jet travel did. The world has one future. But how, then, is Christianity important? Looking at the millions in China, at celebrations in Moscow's Red Square, looking at New Delhi's Indians moving towards a sacred river, or at the followers of Islam flying to Mecca on sacred pilgrimage, we ask: Is Jesus Christ, unique Son of God and future Lord of the World, to fade or to shine?

Karl Rahner is one of the best Christian thinkers with whom to search for some answers to these problems about the relationship of God's action in Christ to the totality of the world's religious history. For his world of grace is a history of grace. God's love and plan are revealed not all at once but in time over the course of centuries. Salvation history is not simply a few biblical stories about Abraham and Moses and Jesus; it is the very history of the world rooted in and completed by God's Word made flesh in Jesus of Nazareth. God, because God is love and wills to save all, has graciously embraced the whole of human history. God's grace and justification have been concretely and historically realized in human history. For the believer the history of the world is a history of grace. What seems to be an endless stream of blood and sweat has a meaning because beneath and within it is the expanding power of God's presence. The history of the world seems to dominate, to have the last word and to dictate the terms for all of our lives. But in fact the history of the world does not have the final word for us. The history of grace is the ultimate history, the final and most valuable story. Jesus' preaching was not about many dogmas but about a view of reality, reality from God's point of view. One profound truth Jesus preached in parable and word is that the goal and completion of history will not be death and despair, suicide and self-hate, but that it will be life: fulfillment and meaning born of cross leading to resurrection. But this view is hard to believe, and this vision is difficult to glimpse. Faith allows us, if not to see, at least to hold to a conviction about the transitoriness and incompleteness of history, so that deep within us the conviction grows that our own lives are part of a history of grace.

A History of Grace within a History of Earth

In parts of Asia, in the Philippines, in the interior of Brazil, there are tribes on the move, hunting and harvesting. With few belongings, they survive in a humid jungle of fruitfulness and violence. Their loves and children, their fears and accomplishments are like ours. Yet they watch a cycle of killing—of animals and enemies—without emotion. Tender, almost permissive within the family and tribe, they might kill their foes. Sickness is warded off by magic; if illness spreads, the witch doctor is clubbed to death. In a park of the past they live in the stone age, that period ten thousand years ago from which we all came.

Usually Christians would ignore these people or precipitously race to convert them. An American fundamentalist missionary would convert the paleolithic tribes at any price to save their souls from the evil he sees everywhere. But ancient ruins or surviving tribes make the past tangible for us today. They challenge us to reflect upon God among us. In our instant world, a tribe can be both past millennia alive and the subject of a television special winning prizes in Venice and San Francisco. How is tenderness in their psyche able to be combined with the daily cycle of life and death? Are those hunters the norm in our vast history? Are we the exceptions?

In an introduction to Teilhard de Chardin's *The Appearance of Man*, Robert Francoeur relates our long past to our brief present. Let us propose a comparison of mankind's history with a calendar year in which one "day" equals four thousand years of human history. In this scheme, January first would witness the appearance of our *Homo habilis* ancestors one and a half million years ago. They could walk erect and use the most primitive tools. Speech, as we know it today, evolved very gradually during the first three months of our "year." Man's evolutionary progress was at best tedious and halting: fire, first for protection from the cold and wild animals and only much later for cooking; tools chipped from stone; the skills of hunting; the slow concentration and involutions of the cerebral cortex. Summer came and went without much change in our ancestors, and autumn was two-thirds through its course when Neanderthal man finally appeared around November first. The first indications of a religious belief can be seen in the burial sites of the later Neanderthaloids, around December 17 in our scheme.

By December 24 of our hypothetical year, all the non-*sapiens*, or

primitive forms of man, had died out or been absorbed by the more pro-
gressive and modern Cro-Magnon man. Agriculture began around December 28 and the whole of our historical era, the brief six to ten
thousand years for which we have records, is nestled in the last two
days of our "Year." Socrates, Plato and Aristotle were born about 9
A.M. on December 31; Christ at noon, and Columbus about 9:30 P.M.
The final hour of December 31, from 11 P.M. to midnight New Year's
Eve, embraces all of the nineteenth and twentieth centuries.

Not only does the Christian faith profess that God enters history, but
it suggests we might find "history" in God. Within the Godhead there
is plurality, interaction, and relationship between Father, Son, and
Spirit. Christianity speaks of birth and generation in the Trinity; Son and
Spirit are on missions to us, are sent into our history and our psyches.
And so it is not surprising that our human life and God's presence in it
is a *history*. Because God's very nature is a giving-birth and a reaching-
out, his stance towards us is one of self-communication, of love-born
communication. And we too are obviously historical—we have parents
and we have children; we live in a period of history and in a landscape
of this part of the planet Earth. It is not simply that we are objects in
history but rather that, as Martin Heidegger pointed out for us, history
pervades our being: we are historical, we have historicity. Historicity
means *I* am living at this moment in this place. Science fiction likes to
spin stories about time machines enabling someone to travel backwards
to Arthur's England or to Plato's Athens. Perhaps such a move out of
our own historicity is no more possible than a move out of our own personality. The alienation, the confusion of leaving my history would be
intense, and it might end—as do schizoid attempts to leave one's own
personality—in madness. God's patient actions and words in the midst
of our history are necessary so that we might be reached in the concreteness and sensuousness of our lives. And so if God is to reach us as
we are, it will be in history.

Do not most Christians have the impression that God's revelation,
God's own history of loving contact with us, began somewhere in the
Middle East with Abraham? Christianity has become a religion of the
past, whereas Jesus intended it to be a movement for the future. Instead
of adoring and creating the sacrament of God in history, Emmanuel,
Christians have spent their time recreating "Bible Land." We gain the
impression that the history of salvation existed only for a few decades in

a remote place. If so, how is it a saving history for the world, how is it my history of salvation, how is Christ the center for which the entire religious history of the world longs?

Beginning with humankind does not only mean listening to stories about Abraham and Moses. They lived rather recently among sophisticated cultures and developed religions. They are not the first opening of the history of God's presence, even for the bible. We should let God's activity extend itself into the story of the entire human race past and present.

There is only one world. Our planet is united by that collective, social disaster we call the Fall, and by its special invitation to God's future. There is only one God touching us. For us living in the twentieth century, time and geography expand the range of the dialogue between God and our race. We experience God's own life through the story of humanity and through our own story. This one story is the history of the presence of God—a saving history within secular history—through at least a million years. The history of humanity's quest for meaning and peace meets the history of God's active presence, and the two histories disclose a deeper dimension, a dimension which can truly be called a "saving history" or a "history of grace."

Moving back thousands of years, we can see grace and sin operative in social, tribal conditions. Culture modifies freedom, conditioning God's action, altering ideas about right and wrong. We find cave paintings, objects of burial ritual, bones, skulls. When our recent ancestors, the dead Neanderthaloid or Cro-Magnon man, were interred in the caves which we would stumble upon later, the triumphs of civilization, the wealth of cities from Thebes to Houston, lay tens of thousands of years in the future. Over the cold plains of upper Europe, winds moaned, and tribes moved south. Yet these men and women, whose features seem simian, puzzled as we do over faith's enduring questions before the future and before the great absence.

These men whom scientists had contended to possess no thoughts beyond those of the brute, had laid down their dead in grief. Massive flint-hardened hands had shaped a sepulcher and placed flat stones to guard the dead man's head. A haunch of meat had been left to aid the dead man's journey. Worked flints, a little treasure of the human dawn, had been poured lovingly into the grave. And down the untold centuries the message had come without words: "We were human, we too suffered, we too believed that the grave is not the end. We too, whose faces affright you now, knew human agony and human love." (Loren Eisley, *The Firmament of Time* [New York: Atheneum, 1971], p. 113)

Humankind evolved culturally just as surely (and as slowly) as it evolved biologically. The span of freedom, the reach of self-transcendence, conditions God's presence and our acceptance of God's presence.

Our history includes not only my personal history and God's trinitarian activity within and around me. It also includes my freedom and my fallenness. They are the place where God meets me; they, like electric charges, influence and direct my own history.

The believer knows there is one thing faith and hope depend upon: God's history of love and promise among us. There is *no neutral world*. All men and women at all times live in a fallen world in which violence is common, life uncertain, guilt and sin present. Yet, at the same time, no tribe is so primitive, no mother in the Ice Age so immersed in magic, that their calling to future fulfillment goes unanswered. The trace of God is as present to the personality of all as light is to eyes. Religion and faith struggle to see the history within our history. A divine atmosphere pervades. The history of the human race and religions and cultures are visible expressions of humanity's story: the history of God.

The Spirit's constant presence does not withhold from a free person the possibility of rejecting God, rejecting everything. There is, also, a history of reflecting God's grace. The violence accumulated through the history of rejecting God—we call that the Fall. Human life is a dialectic in freedom between grace and sin. What is rejected in sin is not a law of moral goodness but something deeper. We say "no" to God, to ourself, to God's invitation for a future perceived in faith. The history of God is ignored; the history of humanity is maimed. The real life of a man and a woman is a dialectic between presence and sin.

The History of Religion

There is no gray world.

Most Christians imagine the world in this way: a large circle has an inner circle placed within it. The inner circle is white and represents the Christians (mainly western, mainly white); around the core of believers and church members is a thin rind colored black (sinners guilty of sexual or homicidal crimes); the large remainder of the sphere is gray. The gray sphere includes the masses of China, the slightly religious businessman in Singapore, the villagers of central Africa or the tribes of the interior of Brazil. Modern Christians are too kind and too enlightened to condemn them to hell. Yet, how are these people contacted by grace— for these villagers or businessmen do not belong to Christian churches? Whether in Shanghai or São Paulo, they populate an intermediate world, the real world of much of the human race.

There is no gray world. For the New and Old Testaments, for Augustine and Thomas Aquinas and Luther, there is no gray world. Fundamentalists who black out all of the large circle, painting in a universal perdition unless one is saved by scriptural words, have a theologically possible, if dubious, position. But it is incorrect because it fails to appreciate the universality of God's love and because its understanding of Jesus Christ's role is superficial. The Judeo-Christian tradition intends by the stories of Adam, Eve, and the Fall to state that there is one human race, that every woman and man live in the same existential situation. There is no world of just living—life apart from mystery and presence. Every human person is a high peak around which swirl the blasts of grace and sin.

There is an innate tendency in religion and in religious people to be narrow. The theology of a wider history of salvation tries to do justice to God's love for *all*, and to the length and variety of the history of the human race. Teilhard de Chardin constructs a cosmic view of grace beneath every drive of sex and war and art, reaching for Omega. Karl Rahner begins with the universal presence of a hidden grace in all women and men. Vatican II stated that all peoples comprise a single family with one origin and one final goal, God. God's providence, God's light and God's saving goodness extend to all in various forms. Any form of exclusivistic fundamentalism which ties God to an external word or form, even those held dear by the churches, reduces the gospel to the ludicrous, and when a faith makes the gospel incredible, the vision is at fault. The number of members of the Asian world religions increase, and will continue to increase geometrically.

The history of all religion is also the history of salvation, for the history of the world is the history of God's presence to our world. Salvation is humanity's desperate awareness that it is radically loved, created to live on. The history of salvation did not begin with Abraham; what begins there is a particular, public, recorded religious history. In the history of religions, grace struggles to become mature and human, to become powerful and visible. Presence permeates slowly. Before Christ, in all of history, God is present humanizing and socializing humanity, preparing our race for civilizations where the Spirit can be well received.

The history of religion is also the history of the abuses of religion. Religion and violence are mixed in sacrifices and wars, begetting genocide and slavery. The history of religion is the history of humanity's corruption of the presence of God whispering to it. Humanity corrupts even its adoration of the holy. Religion parades magic, idolatry, false views of God—God as playfully evil, God as appeasable judge. One of the mysteries of God's presence is God's reluctance to step in and correct humanity's evil. God never dominates our freedom, despite an ageless desire to accelerate our movement toward higher life.

Having plunged unreservedly into the colorful picture of human history and the history of religions, and having seen there a more complex presence of God at work, we are ready to draw some distinctions. The varied history of the world is not the same as God's activity we call grace and revelation, but it is the place of God's work among us. God's activity we call grace; God's word we call revelation; the place where God acts and speaks is our consciousness, life and history. The history of salvation is not a history of miracles from Bible Land. The history of salvation is the history of grace present in all of history, as God's special action towards us over and beyond our creation as men and women. The history of salvation includes all of the world's religions. They do not exist apart from salvation history; they are the products neither of demons nor of abstract philosophies. We believe God's special word will ultimately be found in the full event of Christ and Christ's Spirit. Yet, the history of religion is part of the history of salvation as it leads to the total Christ. It is that Christ, crucified and risen, who leads the human race deeper into the Kingdom of God; that Christ is fully present to all of the human race only at the end, when history finds its fulfillment and God is all in all.

We are accustomed to hear that the Old Testament leads to Christ. Judaism has recorded the history of salvation moving close to its center in Christ. What of the other great religions of the world—Islam, Buddhism, Hinduism? Are they part of salvation history that leads to Christ? Are they, too, each in their own indecipherable way, "special salvation histories" looking to find a fulfillment which will in fact be Christ? This is one of the deepest problems for the Christian faith today—the relationship not only of the length of past history but the breadth of religious history to a belief that Christ is *the* definitive religious figure. Rahner's coherent approach to salvation history isolates no religion, but includes all in God's history of self-communication to peoples. But how they are all fulfilled in the history of salvation we consider "special," in the evolution of God's grace towards the event of Christ—that remains a mystery and a promise.

God in History

Religions struggle for light. The Judeo-Christian revelation has only one message: We are not alone. What every religion tries to express about God, Israel heard clearly: that God was not remote but intensely active in our history. To believe is to confess the entrance of God. Three thousand years before Christ, people had reached the social capabilities of mature religion. Had there been earlier special interventions, prehistoric heightenings of God's invitation barely heard in the plains which are now the suburbs of Peking? We do not know.

The history of religion had been mainly a history of implicit, indeterminate presences of God. But we are flesh and blood. We live through colors and sounds. Our emotions and our sexuality, the tricks of memory and neurosis must be constantly supported by the concrete. What is less concrete than presence! Events, missions, martyrdoms, the explosion of religion in politics are dramatic moves by God to make God's presence visible. From this point of view, the Judeo-Christian tradition is correct in emphasizing the history of Israel, for its tradition puts on display the concrete presence of God with people:

> God's self-revelation in the depths of the spiritual person is a certain "state of mind." (We mean this in the psychological not the emotional sense.) It is produced by grace, it is inarticulate, in a sense taken for granted, not formulated into objective propositions. It is not informational knowledge about religion but a consciousness, a pervasion of our psyche. But this gratuitous, unobjective, self-revelation of God (not yet formulated into special statements of a particular religious belief) has to be translated into something objective. For only if it is objective can it become the principle of man's concrete behavior. (*Theological Dictionary*, p. 411)

Karl Rahner is here describing the divine milieu surrounding our personality. Grace is present to us, and our freedom responds to its probes.

But these impulses are subtle, while we live in a world of speed and danger.

The history of God's revelation grace moves from the implicit to the explicit, from the mysterious to the concrete. The prophets of Israel show an increasing depth in understanding God and humanity, whose relationship slowly becomes that of lovers. The political and tribal aspects of religion decline; mercy and inner authenticity master superstition. The future comes through pain as well as through glory. As God's history expands, a person's vision of self deepens. Our future includes personal redemption as well as national survival. In every religion the attempt is made to reflect at the borderline of the conscious and unconscious upon God's presence and to make that sensed reality concrete in the form of creeds and rituals. In the religions of the human race we find success in this enterprise and we find failure. Revelation and grace are mingled with ignorance and error just as the two mix in our own psyches. Yet God is guiding this process, making revelation concrete for the sake of the human community. We have applied the term "history of salvation" to all of human history. Therefore, it is helpful to distinguish between the general history of salvation, where religion and God's presence are universally present, and the special history of salvation, a segment of religious history in which we discern a more powerful, a clearer activity and direction by God. That evolving brightness and distinctness in Word and Spirit come to sharpest expression in the special saving history of Israel, culminating in Jesus of Nazareth, the Christ.

History in Christ

Saving history and my story are somewhat the same. They have the same basic components: the complexity of life and the presence of God. When this history of religious evolution and Spirit becomes concrete, it appears simply as an enlarged version of the story of each of us. My life is always concrete, lived out in cities and battlefields and conference tables. The dialogue between myself and presence takes place in my choices. It is grace present everywhere—in Brazil, in Assyria three thousand years ago, in Jerusalem destroyed or rebuilt. The history of salvation is not a chronology of unusual heroes and saints, but the history of people responding in a variety of ways to an increasingly intense presence of God.

The time of Jesus was, like our own, an age of turmoil, of many as-

cending movements and collapsing institutions. Crowding at the edge of
Jesus' life were revolutionary Zealots with their extremist branch, the
Sicarii; observant stubborn Pharisees; establishment Sadducees; monastic Qumran. The surrounding Mediterranean world was a seething caul-
dron of religious quest. Mystery religions of Greek or Syrian or Egyp-
tian background competed with apocalyptic sects. Sophistication and
communication encouraged massive preoccupation and discontent with
religion. Into this world Jesus, son of Joseph, carpenter and prophet,
was born. God's special gift of life to us which we call ''salvation'' or
''redemption'' (for now and for the future) has a history because we
human beings have a history. The history of grace reaches its climax in
our world in a human being, because we are human beings.

Jesus of Nazareth can truly be called, according to the meaning of the
New Testament, God and man. Nevertheless, he is not utterly different
from us: in him those two elements of salvation history—the human and
visible dimension and the divine and subtle dimension—are present. In
the Christ they are present in a particular intensity which our lives lack;
in Jesus of Nazareth the divine and the human are calmly and irrevocably *one,* while in us they are dimensions which struggle for unity and
which can be repressed or lost. Rahner writes: ''It is only in Christ that
we Christians have the possibility of making a radical distinction between the categorical history of revelation in its full sense, and the formation of human substitutes for it, human misinterpretations of it''
(*Foundations,* p. 157).

The history of salvation reaches its climax, its leader, its sign and
promise in Christ Jesus. After the coming of his Spirit, that saving history continues. The Kingdom of God—which is a biblical name for the
history of salvation—comes in Jesus with greater intensity, but the
Kingdom is not yet here in its triumphant fullness.

Jesus Christ, true God and true man, is our climax in religious history
not only as an individual savior. He is a sign, a pattern of God's plan
for our situation, for just as the Word of God immerses itself in the historical individual, Jesus, so this union is a contact with and affirmation
of every man and woman. Jesus' incarnation speaks to the entire evolutionary history of our race, drawing it forward to the future which Jesus
has anticipated: resurrection.

Who is Jesus Christ? The history of grace shows Jesus Christ is one
of us. However different he may be, he is the climax of the human con-

dition we have been describing. Our situation—a backdrop of freedom, vocation and sin—is a history in which the self-communicating presence of the mystery we name "God" and our own personal quest meet. In Jesus of Nazareth both reach the highest level of intensity; they meet never to be separate; they meet as one. The self-disclosure of God driven by love pushes outward until God becomes the object of his love—a human person. Standing in that history on both sides of the line of spirit, Jesus is the personal intensification of God's presence and the crucial prophetic figure of public religion. Jesus Christ is the place where God's presence struggles to make itself most tangible, visible, attractive. Jesus is the key example of the human religious situation; the successful union of the passionate love of God and the religious quest of all of us.

The Word of Grace

We have been speaking about history and story, about a widely saving history and about a particular life history of Jesus the Christ.

What Christians call "revelation" means the *word* about the world of grace in which we live out our lives. Revelation is the proclamation of what is happening for us as God's gift of God's daily presence; it is the interpretation of the meaning and future of our own lives from God's point of view. Revelation is the history of grace made verbal.

The last lines of the Gospel of John indicate that no human words, Greek, Chinese, or English, can adequately convey *who* Jesus, the Word of God made flesh, truly is. All of salvation history has an atmosphere of mystery. Our own stories, because of their openness to God, and God's saving history within and beneath world history, are always more than we can grasp. Only at the end of history will we humans understand history, and only when we are indissolubly one with God will we fully understand our lives. What academics research the mystics strain to experience in quiet solitude . . . but revelation and grace are always more than our faith and hope caught up in their silence.

Rahner draws upon modern philosophy for the expression "transcendental," a name for the richness of our personality. "Transcendental revelation" is not the nature of our psyche but the general presence of God which permeates often in an unobjected way through our consciousness. Transcendental revelation is not revelation about a transcendent God but the meeting in our own personalities of the richness of our selves and the action of God. "Categorical revelation" is revelation articulated, expressed in words, drawn from events and peoples. Categorical revelation is the biblical record of special saving history.

"At various times in the past and in various different ways, God spoke to our ancestors through the prophets; but in our own time, the last days, he has spoken to us through his son" (Hebrews 1:1–2). Revelation comes to us in the midst of peoples' histories; it emerges out of lives lived in world history, but it comes to us with particular intensity through men and women conscious of being set apart as bearers of revelation. Some would call them "prophets"; others might prefer "mystics," "gurus," "holy ones." Looked at theologically and correctly, the prophet is none other than the believer who can express the transcendental experience of God correctly.

Because we naturally interpret our experience and ponder inwardly over our individuality and our destiny, reflection upon salvation in history has been going on as long as history itself. With the Hebrews this interpretation, this revelation, is intensified, collected, retained, and written down. With the Jewish experience we have not only an intensification of the history of salvation leading to its climax in the Christ, but a richer receptivity and record of that history—revelation.

Revelation, then, should not mean for the believer a series of startling pieces of information, a kind of heavenly television program on the religious world in review. Rather, revelation is our psychological interpretation of the history of salvation. Since, however, we see into God's plan in history only darkly, through faith, both God's light to understand it (revelation) and our grace-born acceptance of God's presence (faith) are God's gifts, facets of grace loose in the world. In Jesus Christ, the Word of God and God's story were one. So in our own lives, we should struggle to let our faith be our eyes into the real world of God's grace. We should move away from any attraction to spectacular revelations about the next year or the next life. Rather we should open our life to the fundamental truths of our Christian faith not as memories but as a future-looking hope. The history of salvation must express itself in the words of revelation, but those words should lead us to history and to our life's story amid grace.

The Future of History and Grace

We are mistaken if we believe that the only time of salvation history was the years the bible records, that the high point of history was those few years of Jesus' public life. The apostle Paul has a different view. He sees the history of salvation, God's plan for the world, as entering upon an extraordinary and final intensity with the passion and resurrection of Jesus. After Jesus, God's grace,the Kingdom, is triumphant. Although all of us must learn by and pass through the cross, a victory is assured.

What we call the Holy Spirit is the Spirit of Jesus, the Risen Christ. That Spirit contains the dynamic of a stronger, more vigorous history of grace. The history of salvation does not freeze with Jesus' own triumph, nor does it reach its only climax then. It continues: all of our lives are sustained by and pour into this history, which is not only the history of politics and economics but the history of God's activity within history. "Kingdom of God," "Grace," "Spirit"—all of these are names for what we have been calling the "history of grace" or the "history of salvation."

The Kingdom of God is a phrase for the new and final era in God's history. Now God's spirit becomes more accessible to us, burns more intensely within us. The Kingdom of God is not a heaven of souls above us, but a dynamism that sweeps all of history towards God. And yet the Kingdom is not fully present, and so Christianity is critical of all utopias on earth, of easy political transformations of this history or this politics into paradise. The Kingdom is neither within nor without us; it is the atmosphere of all our decisions. The Kingdom grows, slowly, never localized in one nation or one church. The Kingdom of God is intensified presence in the world. Wherever men and women respond, there is the Kingdom.

We began with questions. Questions should be exercises in learning, or, as Heidegger put it, the piety of thinking.

The future is always a question. The gospel announces we are in the final age, the new era. This, however, along with the lengthening span backwards of the human race, raises questions for a history of grace. To say God's Kingdom comes and the Holy Spirit is sent is to raise not doubts but questions about the presence of God in politics and economics, in personality and culture.

Through our individual histories we live in that larger history of salvation whose center is the risen Christ. This world now remains one of grace and sin, of success and neglect, of joy and suffering. Eventually, the history of salvation will merge with resurrection. And the resurrection of Jesus Christ is a strange event. It is a moment belonging to the end of history, projected backwards into the midst of history. As a promise for every man and woman, it is "normal." For faith, Christ's personality was so enlivened by God's Spirit that it survives death. That love which we now grasp through dark faith and rare flashes of experience will at the end of time be so strong that its power will pour through our own entire personality. Our belief looks forward to the victory of grace in our stories, to a time when salvation will rush through history to explode in resurrection.

QUESTIONS FOR DISCUSSION AND SUGGESTIONS FOR FURTHER READING

Rahner argues that human history as a whole has a unity of purpose and direction, but that secular history and salvation history must be distinguished within it. How would you explain the difference between world history, the history of nations and cultures, and the history of salvation? Two important essays on this topic are: "History of the World and Salvation-History," *Theological Investigations* 5, pp. 97–114, and "The Order of Redemption within the Order of Creation," in *The Christian Commitment,* pp. 38–74. In both these essays Rahner holds that the history of grace is coextensive with the history of the world.

Is it really possible to affirm both the universality of the history of salvation and Jesus Christ as God's final Word, the center of human history? How does Rahner's approach influence our understanding of religions such as those of the American Indians or Africans, Buddhism or Islam? Two basic essays on these questions are: "Christianity and the Non-Christian Religions," *Theological Investigations* 5, pp. 115–34, and "Church, Churches, and Religions," *Theological Investigations* 10, pp. 30–49. Here Rahner holds both for the absolute claim of Christianity and the undeniable presence of grace in other churches and religions.

The concept of revelation is at once a very simple and a very complex one. How do you understand it, especially in terms of biblical revelation? In particular, from Rahner's perspective, how does the categorical revelation found in the Old and New Testaments flow from the transcendental revelation in the consciousness of people touched by God? It would be useful to consult Rahner's essay on "Revelation" in *Sacramentum Mundi* 5, pp. 348–55. Also, for a condensed but important treatment, see ''Observations on the Concept of Revelation,'' in Rahner and Joseph Ratzinger, *Revelation and Tradition,* pp. 9–25.

One might also consider now the relation between revelation and Church doctrine. Among various essays on the subject, see ''Considerations on the Development of Dogma,'' *Theological Investigations* 4, pp. 3–35.

7

Discovering Jesus Christ: A History We Share

J. PETER SCHINELLER

In the first of two essays on Christology, the distinction between historical and essential (or transcendental) Christology is explained, and the first of these is discussed. Starting with living faith, we follow the path of the first disciples and learn to confess Jesus of Nazareth as the Christ of God. This entails an understanding of the life of Jesus, his death and resurrection, and the way we may approach historical knowledge of his existence.

For almost two thousand years Christians have made an extraordinary claim. From the millions of persons who have lived and died on this earth, one, they maintain, Jesus of Nazareth, is the key and center of all human history. They claim that the life, the teaching, and the person of Jesus sheds light on every dimension of human experience. He is the final and full revelation of God to human history; more than any other person who walked this earth, he has the words of eternal life (John 6:68).

How can one begin to make this faith claim intelligible? And since it is a faith claim, how can one make it credible for others? These are the questions addressed in the area of theology known as Christology. Christology treats of the person, message, and significance of Jesus Christ for Christians and, indeed, for all persons.

Before examining the basis and intelligibility of the Christian claim, we should analyze further what is present in that claim itself. The Christian is one who believes in Jesus as Lord and Savior, as the Christ or anointed one sent by God. While individual views concerning Jesus will vary, the belief common to all Christians is that in and through a faith relationship to Jesus Christ, they are finding God, and hence salvation. This faith relationship to Jesus Christ differs from a relationship to any other human person, insofar as Christians affirm that Jesus lives on as risen Lord, present with the Father in glory. Christians affirm that by encountering the life, death, and resurrection of Jesus, they are encountering the mystery of God's own self, and are being offered divine forgiveness and life. Christians who wish to deepen their understanding of Jesus Christ should begin by taking seriously their vital faith relationship to Jesus:

> . . . In the first place a Christian may and must accept without hesitation and courageously the "Christology" which he is living out in his life: in the faith of the church, in the cult of its risen Lord, in prayer in his name, and by participating in his destiny up to and including dying with him. (*Foundations*, p. 294)

We do not begin reflection on Jesus Christ by attempting to step aside from our faith relationship to Jesus, or by denying it; rather we attempt to bring together the resources of scripture, tradition, human reason, and reflection in order to deepen and build the faith we already live. In this way, one will "always have your answer ready for people who ask you the reason for the hope that you all have" (1 Peter 3:15). After such an initial expression of the faith in Jesus Christ from which the Christian lives, a move to theological reflection can be more fruitful. This reflection must turn to the history of Jesus and the history of belief in him. In addition to this particular history, it must also reflect upon the more universal or essential aspects of Christian faith. In this way, just as there are two moments or aspects in all Christian theology, namely the historical and the essential, so too these must be included in reflection on Jesus Christ.

Historical and Essential Christology

The historical approach explores the historical testimony about the life, death, and resurrection of Jesus, as found especially in scripture and in Church tradition. An essential approach examines the necessary conditions in the human person which make possible a genuine capacity to hear and respond to the historical message of Jesus Christ; it is developed as part of a religious anthropology, and is also known as a transcendental Christology. These two approaches are mutually dependent, for in the final analysis, the essential approach presupposes familiarity with the data of the historical approach, and it can never be developed without such historical experience as its presupposition. So too, the historical approach cannot remain merely an examination of discrete, unrelated historical data; it must be unified and grounded in a more general philosophical anthropology.

We may note here that, corresponding to these two approaches to Christology, we have divided our discussion of Rahner's Christology in *Foundations* into two chapters. This one will focus on the history of Jesus (examining *Foundations,* chapter 6, subsections 2, 5, 6, 8, and 9). The next chapter will explore the philosophical, traditional, and doctrinal aspects of Rahner's Christology (related to *Foundations,* chapter 6, subsections 1, 3, 4, and 7).

The historical approach to Christology is also referred to as a Christology from below, or an ascending Christology. The expression "from below" indicates that this reflection begins with Jesus as a man in history; by considering his teaching, activities, death, and resurrection, it gradually ascends to acknowledge him as the Christ of God. This approach contrasts with a Christology "from above" or a descending Christology, which begins from the doctrine of God as triune and then shows how the second person of the Trinity became man in the course of human history. The prologue of the Gospel of John exemplifies this latter view: "The Word was made flesh, he lived among us" (John 1:14).

The historical approach, therefore, means following and even reenacting the path and process by which the first disciples came to believe in Jesus as the Christ. A beautiful example of this approach can be found in Luke's account of the two disciples on the road to Emmaus (Luke 24:13–35). The two disciples had been friends and followers of Jesus of Nazareth, a great prophet by the things he said and did. But his death seemed to dash their hopes, and so they were leaving Jerusalem, the holy city. Not even reports of the empty tomb stirred their faith. It was only when Jesus met them on the way and explained that he had to suffer and die, only when he broke bread in table fellowship with them that their eyes were opened. Then they recognized that the Jesus they had known really was the Christ and was now risen Lord.

In this manner, the historical approach invites each person to follow the process that led the first disciples and apostles to the confession of

Jesus of Nazareth as the Christ of God. For the most significant data on who Jesus was, on the shape of his life and message and how this led to belief in him as risen Lord, one must turn to the New Testament. Here one must rely upon the research of biblical scholars. In accord with the findings of these scholars, employing the best methods and resources for understanding the scriptures, we find that the synoptic gospels disclose the basic elements and characteristics of the ministry of Jesus. They also disclose how the first disciples came to faith in Jesus as the Christ.

Basic Structure of the Life of Jesus

In dialogue with modern biblical studies, the following elements can be considered a faithful report on the life of Jesus (*Foundations,* pp. 246–64). Jesus, born a Jew, took part in the religious life and culture of Palestine. This involved worship at the temple and synagogue, familiarity with Jewish laws and customs, celebration of feasts and praying the scriptures. Within this tradition, Jesus intended to be a religious reformer rather than a radical religious revolutionary.

He was, however, a radical reformer insofar as this involved breaking the lordship of the law, which had often put itself in God's place. He continually fought against legalism, asserting for example that "the sabbath was made for man, not man for the sabbath" (Mark 2:27), and recalling that it was not against the law to do good or to save life on the sabbath (Mark 3:4).

He seems to have known that he was radically close to God. Precisely for this reason, he saw himself in solidarity with social and religious outcasts because his Father loved them. The full extent of this compassionate and forgiving attitude is seen in his constant association and even table fellowship with tax collectors and public sinners.

As a reformer, his preaching centered on the Kingdom of God. "This is the time of fulfilment. The reign of God is at hand. Reform your lives and believe in the gospel!" (Mark 1:15). Jesus realized that in his personal call for repentance and conversion the nearness of God's Kingdom was becoming present in a new, unique, and unsurpassable way. Even though he preached not so much about himself as about the Kingdom of God, this preaching necessarily involved a claim concerning his own person. Those who heard his words were forced to a decision not only about the Kingdom message, but about the very person of Jesus.

The message of the Kingdom was set forth in parables and stories such as the good Samaritan, the prodigal son, the sower and the seed, and the widow's mite. Here Jesus disclosed a world where the love of God was ever present and the invitation to a response of faith, hope, and love was offered.

While the full unity between his person and message would be seen clearly by the disciples only after the resurrection, the basis for this unity was present in the ministry of Jesus through claims which went beyond those of the Old Testament prophets. Jesus seemed to experience and live out of a special relationship to the Father, one of unique sonship, and he saw himself as exemplary for us in our relationship to the Father and in the Father's relationship to us.

An essential part of his prophetic mission was to gather disciples who would follow him and his teaching and share personally in his proclamation of the nearness of God's Kingdom. Jesus also performed signs and wonders that affirmed that the new closeness of the Kingdom had come through him. "If it is through the finger of God that I cast out devils, then know that the Kingdom of God has overtaken you" (Luke 11:20). These works or miracles were personal calls and manifestations of God's saving activity, directed to a particular situation or person in need. In addition to confirming the authority of his teaching, the miracles also serve to prepare the disciples for the highest manifestation of God's power in the resurrection of Jesus as risen Lord.

It seems likely that Jesus hoped his preaching and teaching would result in the conversion of those who heard him. But in light of the resistance which he faced, he probably began to see that his mission and preaching was leading him into mortal conflict with both religious and political leaders. He began to see his mission in the pattern of the prophets, knowing well how often prophets are rejected. Growing opposition and rejection, however, did not deter him from his mission, and "he resolutely took the road to Jerusalem" (Luke 10:51). He was willing to face the fate of the prophet. Even death he would face freely and resolutely, accepting it as the inevitable consequence of fidelity to his mission, the mission given him by the Father. "Father, if you are willing, take this cup away from me. Nevertheless, let your will be done, not mine" (Luke 22:42).

The movement of Jesus towards death on the cross was also an obstacle to his own disciples. Their incipient and weak faith was not yet strong enough for the message of the cross. Whether and to what extent Jesus saw his own death in any explicit way as a sacrifice for the world can remain an open and unanswered question. In tracing the path to faith in Jesus as the Savior, it is sufficient to show that he accepted his fate in willing surrender to the mystery of God, and that he maintained his claim to an identity between his person and message, in the hope that this claim would be vindicated by God even in his death.

The Resurrection—From Death to Life

The ministry and teaching of Jesus had sparked the beginnings of faith in the disciples. But his death on the cross seemed to shatter that faith. Nevertheless, the resurrection faith of the early Christian community is a historical fact, in spite of the cruel and tragic death of Jesus. Even the most sceptical or secular of historians cannot deny that the Christian phenomenon begins to make its impact upon the ancient world between the years 30 A.D. and 90 A.D. The disciples did gather together and proclaim Jesus as their risen Lord, even if we must admit that there is no direct claim that anyone saw Jesus rise from death to new life. In this sense, therefore, the resurrection of Jesus is not witnessed to as a historical event that can be established as having occurred in a definite time and place. None of the gospel accounts, varied as they are, tries to present witnesses to the actual event of the resurrection of Jesus. What the scriptural witness does offer in different settings are powerful encounters in which the disciples come to experience the spirit of the risen Lord Jesus in their midst. The more precise nature of these resurrection appearances is difficult to determine.

> So far as the nature of this experience is accessible to us, it is to be explained after the manner of our experience of the powerful Spirit of the living Lord rather than in a way which either likens this experience too closely to mystical visions of an imaginative kind in later times, or understands it as an almost physical sense experience. (*Foundations,* p. 276)

For Jesus himself, the resurrection does not mean a return to life in the temporal sphere, nor a return to biological existence as in the story of the raising of Lazarus; rather it signifies the ultimate saving of his life, the seal of God the Father upon all that he stood for and preached in his pre-Easter life. Jesus, who had made claims to be the final prophet and word of God, who claimed that the nearness of God's Kingdom was present in his teaching and ministry, is the one accepted and vindicated by God the Father. His claim to be the final prophet, his life of filial obedience to the Father, is divinely accepted and validated. All that he had taught and stood for is now shown to be truly God's own word. And so Jesus, in his person and not merely in his teaching, can be acknowledged as the final word of God. The graced and saving word of God's love to the world is fully expressed, and indeed even identified with the person of Jesus of Nazareth. His death which seemed at first to be the frustration and collapse of his career and goals, the final passivity, is now viewed as the culmination of his life of faithful surrender to the Father.

For the disciples the fuller realization of who Jesus was and is gradually unfolds in the early community. The development of Christology towards the finished writings of the New Testament gospels and letters evolves from two sources. These would be first, the growing experience of the Christian community of Jesus as risen Lord, and second, the continued reflection, from the viewpoint of Easter, back upon the public ministry of Jesus. The early Christians now see more clearly that "God was in Christ reconciling the world to himself" (2 Corinthians 5:19). The claims Jesus made in his pre-Easter ministry had their basis in the one true God. The first Christians begin to express the significance of Jesus and his continuity with the God of the Old Testament by seeing him as the fulfillment of the prophecies. They begin to apply to Jesus, even in his pre-Easter life, titles of honor such as Son of God, Lord, Christ, and Word of God. This creative and inspired interpretation of the person and life of Jesus forms the model and basis of Church tradition. Eventually these interpretations are reformulated and expressed in conciliar statements such as those of Nicaea and Chalcedon. The fuller meaning of the saving significance of Jesus for all persons is thus preserved and handed on for later generations of Christians.

In the same moment in which the disciples acknowledge Jesus as risen Lord, he is confessed to be their Savior. For it is their conviction that the reconciling and forgiving love of God has broken into their lives in and through their encounter with Jesus. While this breakthrough of divine love was seen in partial ways during the public ministry of Jesus, it was most fully revealed in Jesus' faithful and loving acceptance of the Father's will on the cross, and through the Father's raising him then to glory.

In and through Jesus of Nazareth, therefore, God's loving and saving grace is revealed and fully established in human history. This saving will is seen to be God's deepest and most constant attitude to the world, offering the possibility of life with God to all persons. Rahner succinctly summarizes the new saving reality in the world because of the death and resurrection of Jesus:

> We are saved because this man who is one of us has been saved by God, and God has thereby made his salvific will present in the world historically, really and irrevocably. (*Foundations,* p. 284)

The life, death, and resurrection of Jesus are the real and effective sign of God's saving will in and for the world. God who spoke in many and varied ways in the history of Israel has offered the final and full Word of saving love in his Son, now acknowledged as risen Lord (Hebrews 1:1–4).

The Path of History—Our Path Today

In this brief outline of a historical approach to Christology, we have reconstructed the process by which the first disciples came to acknowledge Jesus of Nazareth as risen Lord and Savior. The emergence of Christological faith came slowly and painfully for the first Christians. It must be noted that this process is not all that different from our own, and it can be highly instructive for us.

Even though most Christians were probably taught from their earliest years that Jesus is the Christ, that he is the divine Son of God and Savior of the world, it is also clear that at some point in the Christian's life, whether as adolescent or adult, that person made the faith he or she was taught into their own. Like the disciples on the road to Emmaus, the Christian today at some point affirms that Jesus indeed is more than a prophet and is the very Word and Son of God. Through prayerful reflection on the scripture, in the social and liturgical gatherings of the Christian community, we too come to experience the power and presence of the risen Lord. He is no longer a truth that was simply taught us, or a person we read about in scripture, but is acknowledged as Lord over our lives. Our own ingrained longing for the fullness of life is now seen as linked inseparably with the pattern and example of Jesus, who passed from death to the fullness of life, as risen Lord. In and through his human nature, now glorified with the Father, Jesus is the one who mediates and manifests most fully the gracious love, life, and truth of God into our lives. We continue to experience Jesus and his cause as living and victorious, and we dare to affirm that he among all the figures of human history "has the words of eternal life" (John 6:68).

One lasting value of this historical approach is its strong affirmation that Christianity is a historical religion and speaks about particular events in time. It is not mythological nor based solely upon human reason. It is of the very nature of Christian faith, a faith that wishes to understand Jesus as the absolute savior, to be interested in the history of Jesus. By situating the foundations of Christianity in the history of Jesus, this approach always keeps before our eyes the full humanity of Jesus. This contrasts somewhat with much of Christian tradition which has tended to emphasize the divinity of Jesus Christ. In its more extreme forms, such an emphasis upon divinity results in a mythological view of Jesus where he only *seems* to be human.

Since a historical approach relies heavily upon the New Testament, it calls for collaboration with biblical scholars who have particular expertise with the New Testament. The methods and results of such scholarship must be respected and even allowed to challenge the formulations of Christology. At the same time it must be admitted that there is no unanimity among biblical scholars in interpreting every point of the New Testament. We can and must reasonably accept the best available consensus of biblical scholars on the point at issue.

The historical approach results in what may seem to be minimal details concerning the life of Jesus. While the nature of the biblical materials does not allow us to draw up a full biography of Jesus of Nazareth, this does not mean that research into his public life and ministry is of no significance. The New Testament evidence can show that Jesus saw himself not merely as one among many prophets, in an unfinished line to the future, but that he understood himself as what might be termed the final or eschatological prophet, and as eschatological savior. That is to say, in Jesus was found a new and unsurpassable closeness of the saving love of God, to such an extent that those who encountered Jesus had to decide whether or not to accept the God who in him had come so close to earth.

As a general principle in understanding the New Testament texts about Jesus, it must be admitted that there is or can be a significant difference between who a person is and the extent to which that person can verbalize or express his or her identity. The point of this difference is that Jesus' self-understanding during his public ministry need not necessarily and unambiguously coincide with the contents of developed Christological faith. We need not demand that all or indeed any of the titles later ascribed to Jesus (such as Son of God, Christ, Son of Man,

Lord) fully correspond to his own self-understanding, nor indeed that Jesus employed any or all of these titles in his public ministry. It is quite possible in fact that he may actually have refused or denied some of the titles that subsequently were ascribed to him in the writings of the New Testament. The precise way in which Jesus expressed and verbalized a messianic consciousness remains unknown.

In accord with the emphasis upon the humanity of Jesus, the historical approach affirms that Jesus, in his human consciousness, stood at a created distance from God, in freedom, obedience, and worship. His verbalized and expressed self-consciousness had a history which necessarily involved growth and learning. On this level, he may well have been threatened by crises of self-identity as he moved through new and surprising experiences. All this need in no way contradict the traditional teaching of the Catholic church that Jesus' soul possessed the direct or immediate vision of God from the first moment of his existence. This teaching need not entail that Jesus must have always been explicitly aware of this vision, or that he could conceptually express or objectify what was involved in the vision. His vision of God could remain unthematic, and hence the teaching is clearly reconcilable with genuine human experience and a genuine historical consciousness in his religious life before God and human persons.

Further Implications of Christology

Christology should not be viewed only in the limited sense of studying the person and work of Christ in relation to Christians. It should also have implications for the Christian's way of life and interpretation of the world. Two specific areas where this becomes significant may be mentioned here: the relation of Christian and non-Christian religions and the Christological shape of common human experience.

First of all, Christians today necessarily interact with people who are deeply religious but are not Christian. How does Christian faith regard and relate to the religious traditions of these people? From the insight gained into the boundless love of God revealed in and through the life, death and resurrection of Jesus, we dare to speak of the universal saving will of God. With the New Testament, we say that God "wills everyone to be saved and reach the full knowledge of the truth" (1 Timothy 2:4); this universal offer and possibility of salvation is echoed in the documents of the Second Vatican Council—for example, in the Decree on the Missions, art. 7; the Dogmatic Constitution on the Church, art.

9–17; and the Pastoral Constitution on the Church in the Modern World, art. 19–21. Christians believe that Jesus Christ is the savior of all people, that God and his mercy do not work the salvation of non-Christians independently of Jesus Christ. Thus Protestant theologians also account for the possibility of salvation through Christ but without explicit membership in the Church by speaking of the "latent church" (Paul Tillich) or of the "hidden Christ" operative in history (Reinhold Niebuhr).

If a non-Christian is saved, it is only through Jesus Christ. A person affected and eventually saved by the grace of God in Jesus Christ might rightly be called an "anonymous Christian." Instead of regarding non-Christian religions, and even atheistic humanism, in a totally negative fashion, the Christian can truly learn from them, since the grace of God in Christ is or can be operative in these traditions, as it is in the hearts of all men and women. Note that there is no question of making such religious traditions equal to Christian faith in its salvific significance; Christology as elaborated in its historical and essential moments shows Jesus Christ to be the definitive or decisive revelation of God. There is ultimately one movement of God to the world of persons, and this plan from its eternal origins was to be realized and actualized in and through the incarnation, cross, and resurrection of Jesus Christ. But we can speak of the presence of Christ in other religions as the presence of Christ in and through his Spirit (*Foundations,* pp. 311–21).

Moving from these general considerations on the relation of Christianity to non-Christian religions, we must also ask how and where human beings beyond Christianity actually respond to the grace of Christ in their own life situations. Here, based on the universal offer of God's grace in Jesus Christ, we can speak of a searching or inquiring Christology present in the hearts of all persons. Examining the actual shape and form of grace in the life, death, and resurrection of Jesus, we can speak of three attitudes or actions which are manifestations of an anonymous or implicit Christianity. There is first, the everyday call we experience and respond to in loving our neighbor; second, an attitude of bold hope for the future in spite of circumstances that suggest fear or despair; and third, an attitude of readiness for and acceptance of death not as the sheer victory of emptiness but as an openness to life (*Foundations,* pp. 293–98). These three basic experiences refer to central areas of human existence; if a person is actually practicing them, it is only because that person is acting from and responding to the grace of God that was fully manifest in the life of Jesus. Each of the three areas involves an attitude of self-transcendence, a self-transcendence possible only through the grace of God. These attitudes, therefore, witness to the hidden or anonymous, but operative grace of God which Christians name as the grace of Christ, since it is mediated through and perfectly exemplified in him.

The deepest and simplest summary formulation of the essence of belief in Jesus as the Christ can be seen if we truly believe and act in accord with the conviction expressed in the parable of the last judgment in the Gospel of Matthew: "What you do to the least of the brethren, you do to me" (Matthew 25:40). Jesus Christ allows himself to be found anonymously in the brothers and sisters, especially in the poor, the hungry, the imprisoned, and the stranger. In living this parable, a person is practicing an absolute love which gives itself radically to another person. In so doing one affirms implicitly in faith and in love that Jesus is the Christ. This is so because such self-transcending hope and love is searching for a God-man, for someone who as man can be loved with the absoluteness of love for God. In his life, death, and resurrection as the God-man, Jesus Christ makes possible the absoluteness of this love for a concrete fellow human person.

Even those who call themselves Christians must take as their own the words of the distressed father in the gospel story who exclaims, "Lord, I believe, help my unbelief!" (Mark 9:24). Thus Rahner writes wisely and soberly:

> A person is always a Christian in order to become one, and this is also true of what we are calling a personal relationship to Jesus Christ in faith, hope and love. (*Foundations,* p. 306)

These words are particularly fitting as we conclude this essay on the historical approach to Jesus Christ. This mysterious, yet life-giving relationship to Jesus Christ must deepen and take on new meanings for us today, as it did for the first followers of Jesus in their own time and history.

Questions for Discussion

The path to faith in Jesus Christ is a path through history: the history of Jesus, the history of those who first followed him, and the history of Christian believers through the centuries. Such a historical approach, gaining favor in theology today, is not to be accepted uncritically. Areas for continued discussion arise, for example, regarding the biblical foundations to this approach. There seems to be a pluralism of views about Jesus Christ in the New Testament. How unified and how divergent are the four gospels in witnessing to God's love in Jesus Christ? In addition, scholars differ in their interpretation of the biblical material. Which scholar or which trend does one follow? And if, in accord with the historical approach, one attempts to move back to the earliest traditions concerning Jesus, how do the later traditions, such as the gospel of John, function in the formulation of a Christological position?

More generally, can one rest easily with a Christology that necessarily seems always to be open to new data, interpretations, and evaluation from New Testament scholars? And can one, using the historical approach, speak of Jesus in any absolute way as eschatological prophet? Does not the historical approach prevent us from taking one person or event and making that person into the center and key of all history? How does the message of Jesus, the man from Nazareth almost two thousand years ago, retain its truth and power across the oceans and across the centuries?

These challenging questions serve to remind us that the historical moment of Christology must continue beyond the New Testament, for the history of Jesus as risen Lord only begins when he is no longer present in the flesh. Christology must take into account the development of Christian faith and doctrine beyond the New Testament, through the Church councils, and on into the present. The Word of God did not cease penetrating human lives with the apostolic age, and so the experiences of Christians throughout the centuries must also contribute to Christological reflection. In addition, as Rahner has constantly demonstrated, there is the transcendental or essential moment of all theology and hence of Christology. The following essay will continue reflection upon Jesus Christ in the light of the continuing history of Jesus, and in the light of the transcendental moment of Christian faith.

There are further questions. One must ask whether the theory of the anonymous Christian and the universal offer of God's grace in Christ does not undercut the significance of the specific historical mediation of God's grace in Jesus Christ; does it not weaken the need to be explicitly Christian, as well as the urgency of the Christian mission to nonbelievers? How does one keep a balance between the concrete, historical figure of Jesus that is emphasized in the historical approach to Christology and the universal effect and implications of that life for all times and places? There seems to be a perennial challenge to hold the proclamation of the boundless and infinite love of God in creative tension with the belief that this love was totally enfleshed in one who walked this earth like us, Jesus of Nazareth.

We can look at non-Christians with the confident belief that the boundless love of God in Jesus Christ is offered to them and affects their everyday lives. In fact, if they are loving their neighbor and living in trust and courage towards the future, they may be more alive with the grace of God than Christians are. This leads us to conclude with a reminder to those who call themselves Christian. The other side of a positive attitude to non-Christians is a self-critical attitude to one's own Christian faith. That is to say, not the person who cries out "Lord, Lord," but the person who does the will of the Father will enter the kingdom of heaven (Matthew 7:21). Is it not our continual challenge to *be* and *act* Christian not in name only, but in deed and in truth? The Christian is one whose life, attitudes, conduct, and eventually even death are shaped and formed by the power and example of Jesus the Christ.

SUGGESTIONS FOR FURTHER READING

"The Two Basic Types of Christology," *Theological Investigations* 13, pp. 213–23 is a clear presentation of the two contrasting approaches to Christology based upon the transcendental and historical aspects of human experience.

In "Remarks on the Importance of the History of Jesus for Catholic Dogmatics," *Theological Investigations* 13, pp. 201–12, Rahner argues that in spite of the difficulties of interpreting the New Testament, the historical nature of Christianity demands that we interest ourselves in the history of Jesus. Another helpful essay on this topic is "The Position of Christology in the Church between Exegesis and Dogmatics," *Theological Investigations* 11, pp. 185–214.

With "Anonymous Christianity and the Missionary Task of the Church," *Theological Investigations* 12, pp. 161–78, Rahner expands his views on the anonymous Christian and responds to criticism that it undermines the missionary thrust of the Church.

You might also consult: "Incarnation" and "Jesus Christ," in *Sacra-*

mentum Mundi 3, pp. 110–18 and 192–209; ''Resurrection'' and ''Salvation,'' in *Sacramentum Mundi* 5, pp. 323 f., 329–33, and 405–9, 419–33, 435–38. These encyclopedia articles develop particular aspects on questions of Christology.

8

Anticipating Jesus Christ: An Account of Our Hope

OTTO H. HENTZ

"Essential" or transcendental Christology relates our historical faith in Jesus to the transcendence ingredient in our concrete human experience. In Jesus, God has united human experience and God's self-giving love, for in Jesus the two are made one.

WHAT startling claims we Christians make about Jesus Christ! Christ is the one mediator between God and humanity. He is the savior whose teaching and life, whose very person has redeemed everything human. Moreover, because of Christ we make startling claims about ourselves, our world, and our history. The measure of authentic human life is the very life of God. The transcendent mystery of Love gives itself to us in personal intimacy, summons us to personal union, so that God might be "all in all" (1 Corinthians 15:28).

The basis for such startling claims is our confession that Christ is God incarnate, the God-man. Jesus Christ is not one more figure in a series of religious geniuses, like Buddha and Confucius, or one more divinely inspired prophet, like Jeremiah and Isaiah. In his person and destiny Christ is the decisive revelation of the mystery of God and the mystery of human existence. The event of Christ is a unique act of God in history, an act which is in fact God with us: "God was in Christ reconciling the world to himself" (2 Corinthians 5:19).

Christians are concerned with the person of Christ not merely because of his authority and the decisive power of his saving mission. At stake is the very meaning of salvation, the meaning of human existence. In the person of Jesus Christ the transcendent God becomes present with us in our history in an unsurpassable way. In his person, Christ reveals fully and finally the infinite dignity and eternal significance which belongs to all human beings. Because of what Christ is, the God-man, we know that always and everywhere the weight and worth of human existence can be adequately measured only by the self-giving love of God.

The real challenge in accepting the God-man is not simply to accept that God exists, that God is creator, that God speaks through prophets, that God acts in some way to save us. The real challenge is to accept that we human beings are the very ones with whom God shares divine life and love. But if Christ is true man and true God, then we, called to be co-heirs with Christ, are the ones in whom God means to become "all in all." Unless we acknowledge that we too are shaped at heart for eternal union with God, the God-man must seem to us an unreal, fantastic individual. That destiny, personal union with God, is the good news revealed in the person of Christ; that destiny is the substance of our hope. If we question and examine the deepest hope of the human heart and the deepest dynamic in our shared history, it may become clear that we are, in our heart's core, people who hope for a Christ, a God-man, a unique person who brings salvation.

Questions Leading to Transcendental Christology

The very idea of a God-man, a unique person who brings salvation, is easy to misinterpret. In fact, reflective Christians today can worry whether their faith in the event of Christ is intellectually sound or really childish acceptance of a primitive, mythic view of God and the world. The worry arises from two troublesome questions about the event and person of Christ.

The first question concerns its uniqueness. What does it mean to say that the one event of Christ is decisive for all human history? Such talk could be interpreted to mean that at a certain place and time the transcendent God arbitrarily intervened in the process of history. To be sure, that is a childish way of thinking about God and the world. The world has its own structure and internal dynamics, which God created. God is the transcendent creator and does not act as a creature in the world alongside other creatures. If the transcendent God is personally present in the history of the world, this presence is effective in and through, not in place of, the worldly reality which God creates. It is to this worldly reality that God means to be present; it is to human persons that God gives divine life. And so we need to understand how the unique event of Christ is truly part of our history in the world and at the same time special, indeed unique. How can we articulate an understanding of our human history and its relation to God which makes credible the idea of a unique event in salvation history?

A second troublesome question is about the personal reality of Christ. What does it mean to speak of a person who is human and divine, a God-man? We could imagine it to mean that God appears in the world in the guise of a man, as God "dressed up" as a man. Or we could imagine a strange being who is a mixture of the divine and the human, a being semi-divine and semi-human. Is Jesus Christ really human, a man who lived and died in genuinely human freedom? At issue here is not merely the Church's doctrine. The formula of Chalcedon does not describe a figure taken from primitive mythology. The Word made man is true man, "perfect both in his divinity and in his humanity." The issue is understanding. We need to reflect on what it means to be a human being. Can we express an understanding of human being and its relation to God which makes credible the idea of a real human radically united with God, the idea of a God-man?

These questions about the unique event and person of Christ move us beyond a Christology which is purely historical. As the previous essay has shown, we must regularly return to historical testimony about Jesus Christ so that general doctrine about him may preserve its historical basis and we may keep in touch with his actual message. But if we are to make credible the developed doctrine of the Church and appreciate the full significance of Christ's message through the centuries, we need to complement historical Christology with an essential Christology, which makes intelligible the idea of a God-man.

Traditionally, theologians developed an essential Christology by reflecting on the person of Christ in terms set by the early Church. Through a succession of councils at Nicaea, Ephesus, and Chalcedon, the Church rejected misconceptions of Christ and carefully formulated the classic doctrine about Christ which is reflected in our creed. Against those who could not accept that the transcendent God truly becomes incarnate in Christ, the Church affirmed the divinity of Christ. Against those who could not accept that it is truly man in whom God becomes present with us in history, the Church affirmed the genuine humanity of Christ. Christ embodies the full and final revelation of God's saving love and of human fulfillment in God's love, because in Christ God and man are unsurpassably united. A classic formula from the Council of

Chalcedon (451 A.D.) articulates this carefully elaborated doctrine about the person of the God-man: "one identical Son, our Lord Jesus Christ . . . perfect both in his divinity and in his humanity . . . two natures without any commingling or change or division or separation . . . united in one person." But such traditional formulae will not provide an adequate response to contemporary questions about Christ. To be sure, the formula of Chalcedon is a decisive achievement in the history of the Church's understanding of Christ, and it will always be an authoritative source for the Church's continuing reflection. But just because the formula of Chalcedon is concerned with the truth about Christ, we must also recognize the limitations of the formula. Then we can renew our reflection and articulate our faith in Christ in a contemporary form.

A first limitation of Christology based on the formula of Chalcedon is its focus on the person of Christ in his unique individuality. It does not suggest how the event of Christ fits into the process of human history as a whole. As our question about uniqueness suggests, we need a Christology which shows how the unique event of Christ is truly part of our common human history. A second limitation of traditional Christology is that it describes the person of Christ in philosophical concepts like "nature" and "hypostatic union." Such concepts are far removed from the ideas we use today to interpret our experience. As our question about Christ's true humanity suggests, we need a Christology which interprets the person of Christ in relation to what we today understand ourselves to be. In sum, to express and appreciate anew the meaning of Christ we need an understanding of the God-man which is based on a reflective appreciation of what it means to be a human being. This reflection is what we have already seen described in chapter two as an anthropology.

An approach to Christology through anthropology is one of Karl Rahner's major contributions to contemporary theology. Rahner interprets the event and person of Christ in relation to the essential structure of the human person. Because he reflects on the essential conditions of all human experience, conditions which transcend any one, particular kind of experience, such a Christology is called transcendental Christology (*Foundations*, pp. 206–12).

Hope and History

The first stage of such a transcendental Christology shows that it belongs to the very nature of human persons to hope for salvation and to look in history for a savior. The notion of a unique event of salvation must be shown to fit a proper understanding of human history. In our earlier chapter on anthropology we saw Rahner's analysis of the fundamental dynamics of human experience. God creates the human spirit as transcendence in history. There is at the heart of human life a dynamic orientation to the Mystery of God. Now we must develop an understanding of human life as essentially a life of hope, hope for definitive meaning and fulfillment in union with God.

What most poignantly reveals the hope at the heart of life is the limitation we feel in all our experience. Not only in suffering or frustration, but even in our most satisfying moments we are aware of limitation. There is, for example, a peculiar loneliness amidst the sure love we experience in celebration with close family or dear friends. This special loneliness does not arise from lack of love, and it does not inhibit genuine joy in love. Rather, loneliness in the very experience of love points to the boundless capacity of the human heart and the restless desire that our love have unconditional, timeless meaning. In fact, in varying degree we are conscious that all our experiences are limited, only partially fulfilling, passing moments in a life story which itself is but one among countless stories in human history. To live, to take seriously our experience in the world, is to hope that our lives culminate in a unity which draws the fragmentary moments of our experience together with the lives of others with whom we share a common history.

It is because the human spirit is a boundless capacity measured by the Mystery of God that in everything apart from God we experience limitation and must live in hope. The hope at the heart of life is hope in God as the ultimate Thou who embraces our history in self-giving love. God, the one creator of all, can draw all things together in unity. God can guarantee the ultimate meaning of human life in the world by allowing our lives together to share in the infinite life of God. Indeed, God, the goal of our hope, is also the origin and support of our life in hope. We live in hope of fulfillment in union with God because the self-giving love of God summons and energizes our hope.

But human history as a whole is clearly incomplete. The Kingdom of God has not been established. Living in hope, we must look in history for an event that could assure us explicitly of God's saving, self-giving love. We look for an event in which God pledges his love definitively and unambiguously. We may call the event in which God pledges and guarantees his self-giving love absolutely an event of absolute salvation. What would its elements be?

First of all, it would be the event of a human person, a savior. God's love can only be effective in history when a person freely accepts his love. Second, a savior would be united with God in a radical way, in a union which is unsurpassable and irrevocable. Unless God is present in the savior in a union which is unsurpassable and irrevocable, God's self-giving love is only effective in history in a tentative, still open, ambiguous way. Finally, the life and destiny of the savior would reveal human fulfillment in union with God. The savior would be a human person who surrenders everything to God in death and in death is accepted by God. Because the savior in his person is the absolute pledge of God's acceptance of humankind in self-giving love, we may call the savior the absolute bearer of salvation. Presently we will explore the notion that an absolute bearer of salvation is, in fact, a God-man. But at this point it may be helpful to indicate how the savior is decisive for the whole of human history.

We always tell stories from hindsight. Though we begin at the beginning ("Once upon a time"), we must know the ending first. Because we already know that the incidents of the story lead some place, it is a simple matter to locate the beginning and arrange the incidents in sequence. A mother can respond to her child, "Your father and I? Well, it all began . . . ," because the mother knows the meaning of "it," the story of the parents' relationship. But the story and its meaning depend on the end. In fact, the parents' original relationship might never have developed or might have remained one of casual acquaintance, but in the end, the relationship turned out to be—rather, their love freely made it to be—a courtship which culminated in marriage. The end, the decisive pledge of love in marriage, determines and reveals the meaning of the parents' history. The end makes the story.

With the image of courtship and marriage and the principle that the end makes the story we can understand how the savior is uniquely decisive for the whole of human history. As we have seen, God creates the human spirit as transcendence in history and graciously empowers humankind to live in hope of saving fulfillment in union with God. Because of the self-giving love of God, the whole of history is fundamentally a dramatic dialogue between God and humanity. The true significance of the divine-human drama of history, God's "courting" of humanity, remains tentative and ambiguous until the drama reaches a decisive culmination, a "marriage moment." The savior, in whom God definitively pledges his self-giving love, is that decisive culmination. The savior may be described as the marriage moment in the courtship of

God and humankind. Because of the savior the meaning of the historical relationship between God and humanity is no longer tentative, for God is irrevocably committed to us in self-giving love. Of course, the dialogue between God and humankind continues. History as a whole has not reached its complete fulfillment. But the true significance of history is determined by the irreversible victory of God's love in the person of the savior. In the savior time reaches its fullness, the fulfillment of humanity has begun. The savior, then, is decisive for the whole of history, the cause of salvation, because in and through him the goal of our hope becomes a real part of our lives and history.

To be sure, all human activity is significant in the achievement of salvation. What shapes our common history from the very beginning is God's intention to share divine life and love with all humanity. God is at work in the whole of human history. But God's self-giving love has real effect only in real history. And real history moves toward a real goal, a decisive culmination. It is only in relation to that real goal that human history comes to be definitively a history of salvation. Therefore, human salvation in union with God, salvation worked out in real history, is uniquely dependent on the savior, who is the decisive culmination of history—and, indeed, of all the material universe (*Foundations*, pp. 178–203).

The Person of Christ

In the first stage of transcendental Christology we have seen that the idea of a unique event of salvation fits with a proper understanding of our human history. Human life is, at least, life in hopeful anticipation of a savior. Now, in the second stage of transcendental Christology we focus on the unique personal reality of the savior. Our purpose is to explain the idea of a savior who is a God-man.

The savior, we saw, is the human person in whom God's irrevocable union with humanity in self-giving love is decisively achieved and revealed. There are many ways to say what this implies about the person of the savior, but they all come down to this, that in the person of the savior God and humanity are radically one. We can say that the savior is a person graced by God in an absolute way: God is present in the savior and the savior is one with God, not conditionally, not just as a matter of fact, but absolutely. We can say that in the person of the savior God expresses himself definitively as God with us! The human reality of the savior is established by God as God's very own human reality, for nothing but a reality of God himself can definitively express God. We can say that in the person of the savior there is the unsurpassable and irrevocable offer and proclamation of God's self-giving love! In the person of the savior there is a perfect and inseparable union of what is offered and proclaimed with the one in whom the offer and proclamation exists. In the human reality of the savior, God himself is decisively present, expressing himself as God decisively with us, because the human reality of the savior is the human reality of God, the human reality which God creates as his own.

In classic Church doctrine, the technical phrase used to express the radical union of God and man in Christ is "hypostatic union." "Hypostasis" means a concrete, individual reality or substance. Specifically, "hypostasis" refers to the reality of the Word of God. Christ's human reality exists only because it is the human reality of the Word of God. The hypostatic union, therefore, is the union by which Christ's human reality is substantially united with the Word of God, belongs essentially to the Word of God. The union of man and God in Christ is not conditional, but substantial; it is a union rooted in the reality ("hypostasis") of the Word, God who becomes man in Christ.

Actually, the classic doctrine of the Church gives us the key to understanding the idea of a God-man. Christ is truly human and truly divine ("perfect both in his divinity and in his humanity"). In Christ the authentically human and the divine are not opposed or in competition. Rather, the human and the divine are distinctively themselves precisely in their relation to one another ("without commingling . . . or division . . . united in one"). To be sure, it is by God's creative, self-giving love that the human and divine are united in Christ. But in our own experience we can verify in a way the process of creative love by which two persons are united in a radical way and, in their union, retain their distinctiveness.

When two persons are in love their joy reveals that they are fulfilled at heart through their love for one another. Gratuitous love brings them to life in a fully human way. But their life in love does not subvert their freedom or suppress their individuality. It is precisely their distinctive selves which they present to one another, and it is by gratuitous love that they share what they are. In the union created by love, distinctiveness goes together with nearness, freedom goes together with dependence. Human freedom becomes truly free and fulfilled when it is caught by the love of another.

We can understand the relationship between human persons and God in a similar way. If a human person has at heart a dynamic orientation to union with God, then the human person is brought to life in a fully human way when caught by the love of God and drawn into union with God. As with friends, so with God. Dependence on the love of God does not subvert our freedom and nearness to God does not suppress our distinctive individuality; rather, we are most truly our unique selves in loving union with God.

Perhaps a better analogy for the union between God and human persons is the relationship between parents and children. Parents do more than share love with their children. The creative, risk-taking love of parents brings the children to life in the first place. Parents give children the life which can mature into a free acknowledgement and acceptance of parental love. In a similar way, the creative love of God creates and sustains the human freedom with which God means to share divine love.

With the principle that love creates union in diversity (as friend with friend and parent with child), we can understand the idea of a savior who is radically united with God, a God-man. According to the Christian anthropology which this book proposes, human nature is transcendence to God in freedom. Because human being is defined by the mystery of God, authentic human existence means radical surrender of oneself to the mystery of God. Moreover, God is not just the origin and distant focus of human transcendence: God creates humankind for union with God. Hence human nature is at heart a capacity for personal union with God. A human subject achieves the fulfillment of its very being by freely giving itself up to union with God. And it is the creative, self-giving love of God which sustains a human person and enables the person to become one with God. And so we can think of Christ's human reality in its radical union with God as the uniquely perfect fulfillment of human being.

Of course, a human person comes to be in and through a personal history. The union of God and humanity is a historical process. The radical union of man and God in Christ is a union acted out and achieved in the personal history of Christ. The story of Jesus is the story of the man in whom God himself becomes, because God creates this man as his very own. But it is a story, a history: it is the story of a man in the destiny and deed of whose life a unique relationship to God the Father culminates in the self-emptying death of the cross and then his resurrection as Lord.

In sum, we can understand the idea of a God-man if we accept that it is the very nature of the human person to be, by God's creative and self-giving love, united with God. Of course, to interpret the unique person of Christ in relation to the very nature of the human person is a radical approach to Christology. We fully appreciate the radicality of Rahner's analysis when it leads us to ask why there is only one hypostatic union. As a matter of fact, we know ourselves to be sinners, and we know the experience and confession of the disciples of the risen Lord to have been that Christ is unique, the one mediator between God and man. But the crucial point is that all humanity is summoned to beatifying union with God. As we saw, the unique deed and person of the savior is the decisive moment which reveals what is in process throughout the whole of human history.

Christ, the Word Incarnate

Thus far we have tried to make sense of the unique person and destiny of Christ by looking at the event of Christ from the perspective of the human person. But, of course, it is Christ who makes sense of us. The question about human fulfillment which at heart we are, the question which we live in hope, is a question for which God provides the answer. In Christ God reveals the true meaning of the world and human history. For in Christ the Word of God becomes man, and through the Word Incarnate we know that God means to become "all in all." Let us turn finally to consider the event of Christ from the perspective of the becoming of God in history (*Foundations*, pp. 212–28).

It may help to begin by reflecting on the process of "embodiment" in our experience. By "embodiment" I mean the process by which the human spirit makes itself effectively present through creating an expression of itself. The process of expressive embodiment is basic to our experience with one another, because the human person is an embodied spirit (spirit-in-world). We come to be who we are for one another through expressions of ourselves (words and gestures, etc.). A handshake, for example, is an embodiment through which I express and make effectively present for another my good will. The gesture is something I create. But in the gesture there is a unity between the self and the embodiment in which the self comes to explicit expression. Except through some gesture like a handshake I am not effectively present as who I choose to be for the other. Such gestures, therefore, are not mere external signs. They are symbols, expressions in which I embody what I choose to be, and through which I succeed in becoming what I choose to be, for another. Indeed, through symbolic gesture I do more than touch the other; I succeed in bringing to life what I mean to be.

The process of symbolic embodiment becomes more complicated as the relationship to be expressed and achieved becomes more complicated. When, for example, the self-giving love of spouses extends itself creatively and expresses itself in the begetting of children, the expressive embodiments of their marital and parental love are free human beings. The children will embody the loving spirit of their parents to the degree that the children freely choose to appropriate that spirit. But in one degree or another the children are expressive embodiments of the self-giving love which they accept or reject.

Now the process by which God becomes human is a process of embodiment, of effective presence through self-expression. In the incarnation God creates a human reality as God's very own. In this human reality God expresses God's own life and thereby becomes decisively present in our world as God with us. Let us reflect briefly on the confession of faith that in the Incarnation God becomes human.

First, then, God *becomes*. Strange. The transcendent God—all-perfect, therefore not subject to change, eternal—really becomes. The becoming of God is not a becoming in God as God is in himself, for God is all-perfect. But God does become what God was not, in and through another. God becomes by creating the human reality of Christ as God's very own human reality.

To acknowledge the true becoming of God in the human is to confront the mystery of God's creative, self-giving love. Why does God do this, why does God become human? By choice, by will—that is, out of love. The only necessity for God to become in and through an other is the necessity of utterly gratuitous love. The apparently strange idea of God's becoming is really the idea of God's self-giving love.

Second, God becomes in his *Word:* "the Word became flesh" (John 1:14). Now the Word of God is God's own expression of himself, "the image of the invisible God" (Colossians 1:15). So God becomes in and through his self-expression. The act by which God creates the human reality of Christ as his own human reality is an act of self-expression.

The notion of self-expression can help us understand how God really becomes in an other. On the one hand, this becoming in an other is real becoming, because it is utterly free. God has his self-expression within himself: "the Word was with God" (John 1:1), so that God does not "need" to express himself outwardly. On the other hand, when God

freely creates another as his very own, this act of creation and unification makes sense: it is an act by which God himself becomes because it
is an act of self-expression. God becomes effectively present with us in
the world, God becomes God-in-the-world, by creatively expressing, by
embodying his will to be God with us: God in his Word becomes God in
the Word Incarnate. Christ, the Word Incarnate, is the effective self-
expression in and through which God becomes God with us.

Finally, the Word of God becomes *human.* Our understanding of the
human person is crucial here. The human person is transcendence to
God, summoned to live by divine life, in union with God. Thus, God
becomes by expressing himself in a human reality who is created to embody divine life, to be Son of God. When God speaks and spells the
Word which he is for us, what becomes is a human united with God.

Of course, as we have seen, we must not isolate God's deed in
Christ. The becoming of God in the Word Incarnate is the decisive
manifestation of God's will to share divine life in the Spirit with all humanity. The sending of the Word is inseparable from the sending of the
Spirit. The Word Incarnate is the decisive manifestation of God's will to
share divine love with all humanity. Because Christ is the decisive
manifestation, the sacrament, of God-in-the-world, the world as a whole
has a sacramental character. The world does not reflect God simply by
pointing to God as its creator. No, our one world, with its evolution and
history, is the place and the process in which God himself means to
become "all in all," in Word and Spirit.

It is a glorious vision, this Christic sacramentalism which Karl
Rahner articulates in his transcendental Christology and his meditation
on the Incarnation. In it the mystery of God and the mystery of human
existence come remarkably close. One may question, as we noted earlier, whether such a Christology does justice to the surprise of God's
saving, self-giving love. But perhaps the question is troublesome because it is too abstract. How, in fact, are God and humankind close?
The final answer can only be God's love, victorious in the Word made
flesh. But the dynamics in the embodiment of love—what a challenge is
there! The story of the Word made flesh moves to the self-emptying
love of the cross. And so the account of our faith in Christ can never be
presumptuous but remains always an account of our hope, hope in the
self-giving love which is always a surprise. To accept the good news of
Christ and a sacramental vision of the world is the marvel of hope sustained by self-giving love.

QUESTIONS FOR DISCUSSION
AND SUGGESTIONS FOR FURTHER READING

A reader of this chapter encounters Rahner's strong concern to let the teaching of the Council of Chalcedon operate as some kind of norm in theological reflection. In what ways does such a formula function in your own Christology? Is it the end of a certain line of thinking, or can it be viewed rather as a kind of beginning in an ever-renewed reflection on the mystery of Christ? In his early essay on "Current Problems in Christology," *Theological Investigations* 1, pp. 149–200, Rahner explores how a modern Christology might be developed in the context of the limitations and difficulties of classical, Chalcedonian Christology. He raises the more general issue in "What is a Dogmatic Statement?," *Theological Investigations* 5, pp. 42–66.

The notion of savior is an important one in a transcendentally inspired Christology. How would you explain your own understanding of salvation to a non-believer? How much of the human person and community would share in that salvation? Would earthly existence become something preliminary or all-important because it can be "saved"? Rahner offers his own reflections on the Christian meaning of salvation in both spiritual and systematic essays. A touching example of the former is "The Comfort of Time," *Theological Investigations* 3, pp. 141–57; the more systematic approach is well exemplified by "History of the World and Salvation-History," *Theological Investigations* 5, pp. 97–114, and the article "Salvation" in *Sacramentum Mundi* 5, pp. 405–9, 419–33, 435–38.

Rahner claims that concrete human living embodies a transcendental hope and that the incarnation is the embodiment of God's response to that hope. This may lead us to reflect on the meaning of symbol in our Christian lives. What is a symbol? Is it a central concept in your way of expressing the meaning of Christian life? With "The Theology of the Symbol," *Theological Investigations* 4, pp. 221–52, Rahner presents his understanding of symbol as a dynamic process which is at work in the life of God and Christ, in the life of the Church, and in our experience of ourselves as embodied spirits. Many readers find it helpful to approach this rich essay by reading first its third section on the body as symbol.

9

On Being Christian—Together

MICHAEL A. FAHEY

This essay discusses the Church as the collected gathering of all those blessed with faith to see God acting in Jesus Christ. Seven specific questions about Church are addressed, among them the founding of the Church, the diversity of church organizations and traditions, belonging to a particular church, and scripture and church teaching.

Riding subways or buses in our busy cities affords countless opportunities to indulge in that fascinating pastime, people watching. And if we also keep our ears open, especially near youngsters, we can learn much about the kind of beings we humans are, persons marked with an insatiable curiosity, always posing questions. Children in their own uninhibited way are ever bent on finding answers to every imaginable sort of question prompted by commercial advertisements or graffiti. "Mommy, what is a 'mortgage'?" "How do people give blood?" "What is the Salvation Army?" Staring at a disabled youngster, a child might even blurt out: "Why does that boy walk funny?" Asking questions and searching for answers are part of being human and something we never completely lose. Effective teachers often describe their job less as providing the right answers and more as helping students to formulate the right questions. As we grow older we reflect on the importance of asking the right questions; we also beat our breasts when we realize how we have offended by not asking a question ("I never thought to ask . . .").

About Church there are a myriad of questions to be asked, some silly, some complicated, many difficult even to formulate. And to understand the writings of any thinker, including Christian theologians such as Karl

Rahner, it is important to understand what questions they are asking in one particular book or at one particular stage in life. A theologian as profound as Rahner has raised many questions about Church, about sharing a vision of faith in Christianity. He has written monographs about the Church and sacraments, the role of bishops in the Church, individual freedom and Church, the dynamic or charismatic dimension of the Church. Numerous articles treat a wide panoply of special questions on the Church. Here, rather than reviewing every question that Rahner has ever posed about Church, I intend instead to restrict myself to those questions about Church that he asks in his book *Foundations of Christian Faith*. According to my calculations Rahner poses seven specific questions about Church. For many of us these questions may not be the most burning ones about Church. They may even seem odd questions, especially if we open this sizable book, skip hundreds of pages and begin to read at the section entitled "Christianity as Church". (pp. 322–401). This book can not be read as a detective story where we peek at the ending to solve the riddles. When we approach Rahner's *Foundations* it has to be chapter by chapter, in sequence, and with pencil or marker in hand, perhaps with a glossary for difficult theological terms nearby.

I say that I counted seven questions that Rahner raises in *Foundations*. Your curiosity perhaps is awakened and you ask, "All right, well, what are they?" Could we postpone listing them for a moment and focus first on some terms, some vocabulary, some general reflections too on "Church books" and on the goal of this book in particular?

The Aim of Ecclesiology

When theologians talk about Church they are not normally referring to a church building, the little church around the corner facing the village green, nor do they mean, as often is the case in popular usage, "those in charge": bishops, pastors, popes, elders or ministers. For theologians Church means above all the collected gathering of persons who have been blessed with faith to see God acting in Jesus Christ. The invitation comes from God, but, as Rahner writes, "we ourselves are the Church, we poor, primitive, cowardly people, and together we represent the Church" (p. 390). Because it is rooted in our own weaknesses we have to accept the Church "with its inadequacies, with its historical dangers, with its historical refusals, and with its false historical developments."

This community called Church is a spiritual reality: Its borders are not fully definable in empirical terms, it is not totally visible. At least in the first half of "Christianity as Church" Rahner refers to Church in the sense of the worldwide Church as it existed prior to the splinterings into confessional groups either at the Great Schism between East and West or at the Reformation. Hence the word Church is not meant to be identified exclusively with Roman Catholicism, Orthodoxy, Anglicanism, Lutheranism or other local or international Christian bodies. Throughout this essay the word Church (capital "c") refers to the total gathering of believers in Christ, whereas church (small "c") refers to a specific local or worldwide embodiment. This helps to remind us that Church does not refer to a church building, nor to the hierarchy, nor to a particular confessional body. In short, Church is less an object that sociologists can study than it is a reality of faith best understood from the inside by saints and penitent sinners.

Theological reflection about the meaning of the Church's life is known technically as "ecclesiology": reflective investigation (*logos*) about the assembly (*ekklēsia*) of believers in Jesus Christ. Theologians in turn who devote their skills to the study of this *ekklēsia* are known as ecclesiologists. A small number of persons in our day have achieved some prominence in this discipline: Henri de Lubac, Yves Congar, Hans Küng, Avery Dulles, John Zizioulas, to name a few. Even in a long list of ecclesiologists one would scarcely place Karl Rahner among the foremost. His interests have been too encyclopedic, his writings have wrestled with too many questions. As a result, he has never presented a fully developed study on the theology of the Church—an ecclesiology. Others have analyzed his works dealing with the Church and suggested what would be the grand lines of his ecclesiology. One such collaborative study discovered a consistent method amid many developments and shifts in his own thinking (see "A Changing Ecclesiology in a Changing Church: Development in the Ecclesiology of Karl Rahner," *Theological Studies* 38 [1977]: 736–62).

Because ecclesiologists, like all specialists, focus on one specific aspect of Christian revelation, they need frequent reminding to keep all the elements of faith in proper perspective so as to respect what Vatican II in the Decree on Ecumenism has called the proper order or "hierarchy of truths." It would be easy for ecclesiologists to succumb to the temptation of focusing so exclusively on the reality of Church that it appears to be the core or the central mystery of Christianity around which all Christian doctrine orbits. Rahner has consistently warned of this danger, and he repeats this with emphasis as he takes up the question of Church in *Foundations*. The Church is not the central aspect of God's revelation. The core always remains the absolute mystery of God's self-communication to our world in the humanity of Jesus of Nazareth. Even in an interview published on the recent occasion of his seventy-fifth birthday, Rahner stressed that the center of his theology is God as mystery and Jesus Christ as the historical event in which God turns toward humankind (see *America* 140 [1979]: 177–80).

Rahner's Goal

Rahner's treatment of the Church in *Foundations* is controlled by the very specific, comprehensive goals envisaged by his book. Throughout he is trying to help readers appreciate the reasonableness of believing in Christianity today. As he continues in his argumentation he reasons further that one can justify commitment to one particular family of Christianity, in his own case, the Roman Catholic church. This overall objective explains why Rahner concentrates on such and such a particular question and not on others. Forgetting his particular goals, some reviewers of *Foundations* have registered general disappointment and frustration with this chapter, which makes up almost twenty percent of the entire book.

In this chapter on Church Rahner is primarily involved not with an abstract transcendental analysis of mind and heart, but with the historical, contingent, or what he would call the categorical aspect of human experience. Rahner's method is not simply to explore fundamental theology in an exclusively transcendental way by an analysis of our thoughts and loving commitments. He certainly does analyze human thinking and willing in the same transcendental method used by Immanuel Kant and restated in neo-Thomism by Joseph Maréchal. But, attuned to the advances of philosophy since Hegel's reflections on history, Rahner is sensitive to the changes that have developed in Christianity in time. Hence his discussusion of the Church attends to the *history* of this community of grace. These themes are already adumbrated in Rahner's fifth chapter in *Foundations*, which might have been translated more literally as the "History of Salvation and the History of Revelation."

Even the title of the section "Christianity as Church" is especially indicative of Rahner's goal. The accent is decidedly more on Christianity than on Church. He argues that Christianity will always appear from one

age to another in some sort of churchly form. Against those who argue
that it is possible today to have Jesus without Church he insists that the
memory of Jesus as Lord exists only within the Church. Because his
emphasis is on Christianity, on Christology, on God's self-communication, he foregoes many of the traditional questions that are justifiably
raised in manuals of ecclesiology. His book is not intended as a
"Summa" of Christian theology.

As we begin to enumerate the seven questions about Church that
Rahner raises, it is helpful to recall that each question could be ap-
proached from two perspectives, either first-level or second-level reflection. Second-level theological reflection is that detailed, highly specialized, sophisticated exploration of the topic from a scientific perspective
that makes use of primary sources, original languages, close attention to
literary forms, and specialized historical data. Not many persons are
trained to do this high-level scientific investigation for more than one or
two areas of concentration. First-level reflection, the method that
Rahner proposes throughout *Foundations,* is no less rigorous but relies
rather on analysis of reflective self-presence. Such reflection draws upon
my own preconceptual experience in faith and emphasizes this rather
than the material content of all the institutional elements of Church
teaching. This first-level reflection focuses upon my own existential
structure, and sees what light can be shed upon faith from my own
status as a human being, as a person gifted with certain capacities that
can be regarded as conditions of possibility for God's speaking to me.

1. The Origin of the Church

What then are the seven questions that preoccupy Rahner in his long
section devoted to Church? The first question is basic and down-to-
earth: Is there an intimate connection between the teaching, healing mission of Jesus of Nazareth and the subsequent community known as
Church, be it the Church of the second or the twentieth century (pp.
326–35)? The same question could be formulated in another way: Did
Jesus actually found or institute the Church? Since we do not have direct
access to the mind of Jesus, and since we lack anything resembling a
personal interview, we can not construct our answer on the basis of
direct responses. Yet the question of Jesus' intention is very pertinent
and the question forms a natural link with Rahner's previous discussions
in his long chapter on Christology. Did Jesus plan the Church or did it
just happen? If the Church just happened, as the Roman Empire hap-

pened to follow upon the Roman Republic, then obviously this would alter the Church's status, at least for believers.

This question about Jesus and the Church would be quite involved if we were to treat it at second-level reflection. But without going into highly exegetical research, Rahner can make use of a general consensus among New Testament scholars. Biblical researchers point out that because the New Testament writers were totally convinced of the resurrection of Jesus and because they believed that God was acting in Jesus from the very beginning of his public life, these apostolic writers "retrojected" some events which might have occurred in the post-resurrection period into the public ministry of Jesus of Nazareth. This is a sort of telescoping of time that seemed from the perspective of faith thoroughly justifiable and legitimate. Some material which may actually have occurred after the resurrection is placed earlier in the Gospel accounts of Jesus' ministry (e.g., Simon Peter's confession of faith in Jesus as the Messiah, or the account of the transfiguration of Jesus). One can not take the chronology of the gospels unquestioningly at face value. Furthermore, Jesus of Nazareth's own self-awareness, his own consciousness of who he was as Son of God during the early years of his ministry, may actually have developed in stages that are somehow blurred in the final redaction of the gospels.

But one of the most useful ways to state the connection between Jesus of Nazareth and the community called Church would be to establish that Jesus even before his death envisaged the survival of his teachings and made provisions for coming generations especially by training disciples. Even granted that the New Testament writers rearranged, expanded, interpreted events in the life of Jesus from their own subsequent faith perspective, still the sources seem to indicate as historically unquestionable that Jesus did form a circle of twelve around himself; that he did make predictions about coming persecutions; that he did give instructions to Simon Peter about the need for him to strengthen the brethren in the future (Luke 22:31 ff.); and that he did expect some persons to be charged with special responsibilities to safeguard his message.

The gospel accounts of the Last Supper and the institution of the eucharist further attribute to Jesus a keen awareness of the dread events that were to come. During these last days of his life, Jesus is recorded as speaking about a time that would follow. All this said, it is commonly held by biblical and historical theologians today that some central institutions connected with the Church only gradually developed and that much of the shaping of the early Church took place after the death and resurrection of Jesus under the subtle inspiration of the Holy Spirit. The original Church, that is, the apostolic Church, gradually came to use some institutional structures (at least in some local churches) selected from a wide range of possible choices. In other words, Jesus had left some basic provisions for Church, he promised the sending and abiding presence of the Holy Spirit, but many choices about what community structures, what oral traditions would be emphasized were worked out only gradually in the first generations. For us today it is not always easy to judge whether this particular structure is of divine, irreversible command (*juris divini*) or whether it is a human prudential decision (*juris humani*). Even with institutions of this second kind it is unclear sometimes whether the choices are now irreversibly part of the pattern of Christianity, whether they are binding on generations to come.

The answer to the first question whether Jesus of Nazareth founded the Church is for Rahner a resounding "yes," although this does not imply that Jesus foresaw a particular juridical organization for a definite community, nor that he foresaw the eventual worldwide totality of such communities. Still, from the time of Jesus' death and resurrection, there were always some who saw Jesus as absolute savior. Believers saw Christ as the expression *par excellence* of God's tangible and irreversible offer of love to humanity. Ultimately, one might argue, it is only of secondary importance whether this or that element of Church life during the apostolic age is traceable back to a specific decision, statement, or gesture of the historical Jesus. Even today, much of what shapes Church structures goes back to concrete choices or decisions chosen by the Church from a genuine range of possibilities.

Beyond the basic provisions given the Church by Jesus, the founder left all else under the inspiration of the Spirit who would guide the free choice of the first generations of Christians. To decide what can and cannot change, one must decide what is essential for faithfulness to the gospel, continuity with the apostolic community, and correctness of teaching. This discernment cannot be easily accomplished.

2. Unity amid Diversity in the New Testament

Rahner's second question might be formulated quite simply: Is it true that the individual authors of the New Testament, writing after the

Church had already existed for a generation or more, conveyed views about Church that are different and perhaps even incompatible (pp. 335–42)? This amounts to asking whether there are different or divergent theologies of the Church, different ecclesiologies, in the New Testament. For his answers Rahner relies here also on a general consensus of New Testament scholars and on his own assessment of the data. Differences there certainly are, but not incompatible ones. There is a unity amid diversity. It is true that different accents are notable in the New Testament. For instance, Matthew's Gospel expresses the role of the Church in ways somewhat different from Mark and Luke and certainly from St. Paul's epistles. There is a difference in the vision of Church in John's Gospel from that of the First Letter of Peter. While these are different ecclesiologies, however, they are complementary rather than incompatible. The differences are rooted in the practical problems facing the various nascent churches that produced the New Testament writings.

As Rahner reflects on this question, he draws heavily though without direct citation on the research of various German New Testament scholars from the last ten or twenty years: Hans Conzelmann, Wolfgang Trilling, Rudolf Schnackenburg, Anton Vögtle. He is attracted to Conzelmann's idea that Luke in his Gospel and in the Acts of the Apostles sees Christians as persons living in the "time of the Church," the period between the ascension of Jesus Christ and the second coming of Christ at the parousia. The time of Israel, in Luke's view, led to the time of Jesus, the "center of time," after which follows the time of the Church.

Scholars have seen in Matthew's Gospel the conviction that the Christian community is in fact the "true Israel." Such a view is not strong in Mark's Gospel, which is written for a non-Jewish audience. Biblical theologians and others will stress these differences, but in fact there is a basic harmony and unity of vision about the nature of Church. As a matter of fact some contemporary writers who are specially sensitive to the presence of certain kinds of charisms or forms of spirituality in the various separated Christian churches today would reason that this may be due in part to the fact that some churches stress one gospel or cluster of epistles, one ecclesiology in preference to another New Testament ecclesiology. This may be somewhat oversimplified, but there is an element of truth here. Beyond what Jesus himself taught during his lifetime, the New Testament records the vision, the aspirations and long-

ings of different local churches. Added to this, there is a clear
development in the New Testament, a gradual move with time toward
more institutionalization. The roles of certain persons in the community
become more formalized. A trend toward what has been called "early
Catholicism" becomes observable, with more attention given to
bishops, supervision of doctrine, entry into ministry by laying on of
hands.

Still, despite these various strands or different accents in the New
Testament, we are dealing with a commonly shared view that there is
only one Church founded by Jesus Christ, a Church that is both visible
and invisible, having an earthly and a heavenly mode of existence, gradually moving toward formal structures. By the second century these
structures were well established in some churches. But not all the elements in these structures are necessarily of divine origin, they are the
product of human forces and evolving, shifting history.

3. Outside Church No Christianity

The third question haunting Karl Rahner in his investigation of
Church is posed in somewhat technical terms, but the concern is crystal
clear. The translator renders this section of the book as "Fundamentals
of the Ecclesial Nature of Christianity"; I would prefer to translate the
title as "Basic Remarks on the Church-Relatedness of Christianity."
The question: Is relationship to Church an indispensable quality of
Christianity (pp. 342–46)? Here again Rahner's answer is a resounding
"yes." He is arguing pointedly against several theologians who gained
some notoriety in Germany by suggesting that we can have Jesus without a Church: Jesus yes, Church no! Church-relatedness is essential to a
Christianity which is not our own invention or the projection of our own
desires but a community pre-existing under grace before our entry into
it. The Church is not just a useful religious organization, but a spiritual
reality that offers institutional mediation of salvation and grace.

From this perspective stressing the impossibility of salvation in isolation, one could reinterpret the old adage of St. Cyprian of Carthage:
"Extra Ecclesiam nulla salus," outside Church no salvation. In other
words, Church is something that springs from the essence of Christianity as God's self-communication to humankind made manifest and
effectively expressed in Jesus. Why is Church-relatedness indispensable? From the reflective point of view that he uses in first-level proce-
dures, Rahner aims to show that Christianity must be related to Church

because human beings are persons whose interior, social, historical experiences require shared interpretation. Further, given the distinct possibility of distorting the message, or of being caught up in our own subjectivity, the Church must exist endowed with some authority to discern the true from the sham. Christianity would be a fragile and dangerously threatened organization if all depended only on my subjective interiority. Rahner is arguing that for Christianity salvation is quite distinct from the kind of redemption that might be understood by other religious traditions in which it occurs in subjective interiority rather than in the concrete historical interplay of persons. First-level reflection points to the appropriateness of God's addressing my subjectivity, my personal freedom, but always in the context of a community that keeps in check the possible distortions of my own subjectivity.

This question about Church-relatedness may be articulated here in terminology that is foreign to us. But as a question it makes eminent sense especially if we happen to enter into dialogue with those Christians tempted to flee association with Church in order to attain the unspoiled Jesus Christ. The living Christ must be encountered in a community that loves and shares or not at all, as Peter Schineller has pointed out in chapter 7 while treating the Christological implications of Matthew 25:31–46.

4. Belonging to a Particular Church

The fourth question that Rahner raises is also the most delicate and most difficult to articulate. His formulation could give the mistaken impression that he is quite insensitive to the institutional commitment of other Christians. The question at hand deals with that justifiable, antecedent trust that each Christian normally possesses toward his or her own particular church, a church body with its own particular history, spirituality, sacramental system, and governing structure. Rahner's question could be stated in other words: How can I justify to myself my commitment to this one particular Christian church, one which I see as embodying the message of Jesus, preserving the apostolic traditions, and patient of reform (pp. 346–69)? In other words, how in this ecumenical age can I justify my allegiance to this particular church? The question is not meant to be interpreted as an exercise in ecclesiastical one-upmanship, pitting one church against another in apologetical fashion. For those who are Catholics the question will inevitably be answered one way. But the question could be, indeed must be, asked by

other Christians too. Rahner speaks of an indirect method for showing
the legitimacy of the Catholic church as the Church of Christ. From
what he writes later in this section and from what we know of his
publications related to Church unity, it is clear that he does not mean
that the Catholic church and only the Catholic church is the Church of
Christ. Such a view would contradict the teaching of Vatican II, which
refused to repeat Pius XII's earlier formulation in his encyclical *Mystici
Corporis* (1943) that the Church of Christ is identical with the Roman
Catholic church. Vatican II in its debates over the Dogmatic Constitution on the Church, *Lumen gentium,* specifically replaced the word "is"
with the formula "subsists" to eliminate any pure and simple identifica-
tion. The final official text reads: "This Church . . . subsists in the
Catholic church, which is governed by the successor of Peter and by the
bishops in union with that successor" (*Lumen gentium,* no. 8).

Rahner's question is not raised to convince the unbelieving members
of the scientific, intellectual community, nor is it raised to confound the
vast number of Christians outside the Catholic church. His question is a
form of thinking out loud for himself and before an audience of fellow
believers generally within the same historical family of faith. In dialogue with other Catholics, Rahner is able to offer some intellectual re-
assurance about the reasonableness of this specific Christian church
which is his home. Whatever underpinnings he does provide are not intended as a substitute for a personal act of faith nor as a sure recipe for
producing grace.

How then can a member of a specific church (in Rahner's case the
Catholic church) articulate an untroubled confidence in a specific confessional tradition to one's own satisfaction, and to the edification of a
wider circle of friends and well-disposed associates within a different
Christian church? His way of describing the procedure may sound par-
tisan or narrow-minded, but the method itself as we shall see can be
used, indeed must be used, by an Orthodox, Anglican, Lutheran Christian. It comes down ultimately to an invitation to adult Christians to
give an account of their Christian hope and faith.

To proceed with this experiment, Rahner suggests three criteria that
will support my personal confidence in a particular church: continuity,
fidelity, authority. I can justify my association with a particular church
if I perceive that it is in very close historical continuity with the original
gospel. Also I will need to be convinced that this church of mine faithfully preserves and fosters the basic substance of Christianity, and that

there exists within it some authority capable of acting as a check to my own subjective distortions.

The first criterion of continuity will be examined in a historical reflection. In a simple and uncomplicated way I look at the Catholic church, if that is my spiritual home, to see if I can recognize it in a close relationship with the gospel origins. As a Catholic I will normally be convinced that the major teachings of Jesus' message are preserved in the Catholic church and that the Apostolic structures that begin in the New Testament are embodied in this church. My own judgment might even lead me to conclude that other Christian churches are lacking in certain structures I judge critical to the fullness of New Testament ecclesiology. Of course, other Christians from other historical forms of Christianity will perceive the gospel and apostolic traditions amply reflected in their own experience of community.

To explain the second criterion for reasonable allegiance to a confessional church, namely fidelity to the basic substance of the gospel, Rahner proceeds as a Catholic and as one who lived in Central Europe in close cultural proximity to Lutherans and some Calvinists. Hence his reasoning has a particular flavor that may not be attractive to North Americans. For he applies the criterion of fidelity to the Catholic church and finds that it is faithful to the core of Christianity as summarized in the Reformers' triple affirmation: *sola gratia, sola fide, sola scriptura* (literally: grace alone, faith alone, scripture alone). By these three "alone's" or "only's" the Reformers were trying to express their conviction that salvation is achievable only by God's grace, only by saving faith, and is guaranteed by promises enshrined only in sacred scripture. Rahner's judgment would seem to justify the recent suggestion in ecumenical circles that the Catholic church could give official approbation to the Lutheran confessional statement known as the Augsburg Confession (1530), whose 450th anniversary is now underway.

Finally, the third criterion of authority plays a role in how I would prove to my satisfaction the reasonableness of allegiance to my particular church. Catholics appeal to the double authoritative source of scripture and official teaching. Historically the Reformed churches have placed greater stress on scripture, whereas the Catholic church, especially in the last several centuries, has put greater emphasis on the ministry of teaching, especially the official teaching associated with the ministries of bishops and the pope. Already in this brief discussion of authority Rahner is alluding to the next two questions he will raise, namely, the role of scripture in the Church and the possibility of an official, authoritative teaching in the Church.

In discussing why it is intellectually honest today to belong to such a community called the Catholic church, Rahner seems toward the end of this section to have some misgivings that his remarks might be interpreted as derogatory or uncomplimentary to Protestantism. So he goes out of his way to state with vigor that Protestantism kept alive gospel truths that seemed gasping for breath in Catholicism. A Catholic can not maintain that Protestant Christianity lacks grace, justification, sacramental liturgies, the abiding presence of the Holy Spirit. He goes so far as to suggest that the separation between Catholic and Protestant, though much in need of repair, might have originally been permitted by the mysterious designs of divine providence in order to assist the Church to live its vocation to be the Church of Christ more faithfully.

5–7. Scripture, Teaching Office, and the Individual

Three final, interrelated questions remain in Rahner's exploration of Church. Question five points to the concrete form of objective authority in the Bible: What kind of doctrinal authority is attached to those writings called the Word of God (pp. 369–78)? Sacred scripture, we are told, is a singular and preeminent way in which God's revelatory self-communication to humanity becomes explicit and thematic in history. Here Rahner draws upon some of his earlier writings about the development of the canon of scripture, that authoritative listing by the Church of what writings actually comprise the Christian Bible. The process interests him because it shows the Church in action, capable of recognizing itself in certain writings of the apostolic community, capable of adopting the Jewish canon of scripture (the Old Testament) to its own new covenant.

His interest in the origin of the canon, the list of writings said to be inspired by the Holy Spirit, focuses on the Church's power to distinguish. The Church's explicit awareness of what particular writings actually formed the Word of God grew as the Church itself was taking shape. The Church had the confidence to state without hesitation that these writings called New Testament and the Jewish Bible, now reread as a foretelling of Christ and his Church, were more than word about God, but actually God's Word spoken to a still living community. The Bible emerges as the privileged source of objective authority outside my own subjectivity. And the best way to describe the New Testament is to label it the Church's book. For the New Testament resembles a family album of photos. Only members of the family circle experience the full impact of the memorabilia. They perceive relationships and situations that are inaccessible to the outsider. Since the New Testament is a family album, the Church's book, it is a tangible norm for Christians in which are recorded the original Church's earliest insights about Jesus Christ. According to Christian belief scripture is a collection of writings inspired by the Holy Spirit so that it enjoys a normative character unmatched by any other source in the Church.

Rahner also tries to penetrate more profoundly into what Christians mean when they say that scriptures are "inspired," literally that scriptures are "breathed into" by the Holy Spirit, with the result that God is believed to be truly the author of scripture, who inspires the human authors to write as his agents. The fact that one can possess a collection of writings, the Word of God in the words of men, illustrates how two realities can be blended into one finished product: God's grace and human freedom producing a single achievement.

A second concept is associated with scriptural inspiration, that of inerrancy. Inerrancy argues from the belief of inspiration that the scriptures teach only saving truth free from any element of error. What God wanted recorded in these sacred writings for the sake of our salvation possesses a guarantee of truth. Before the use of historical-critical method for the study of the Bible, biblical inerrancy was often seen in a rather sweeping fashion, which suggested that every detail of the biblical text possessed some significant element of truth, whether it be some numerical figure, a reference to astronomy, animal physiology, geography, or what have you. In more recent times biblical scholars insist that the term inerrancy applies first and foremost to the saving truths of salvation, and that affirmations about other matters have to be assessed in light of the literary genre of the authors and the degree of scientific knowledge available to them.

Expressed briefly, the Church's book, the Bible, has an unchallenged supremacy in the life of the Church. All other formulas, whether creeds, council texts, dogmatic affirmations or statements of the teaching office (magisterium), stand under the Word of God and must be evaluated in the light of that primary source of light and truth. Scripture emerges therefore as the expression of the early Church's living consciousness of faith, a reality that unites in creative tension the inevitable pluralism in the Church's changing structures throughout history.

Rahner's sixth question focuses on the thorny question about magisterium, a word usually translated now as official teaching, or teaching
office. Rahner's question is quite simply: Is there an absolute, formal
and binding teaching office in the Church (pp. 378–88)? Perhaps this
question is the most characteristically Catholic one in his whole discussion. The question assumes importance here because the concept magisterium is frequently used by Catholics to argue that there is an objective
norm in the Church for testing the spirits against faulty interpretations
and infidelities to the gospel. Not surprisingly, most of the recent international and national bilateral theological dialogues between Christians
have had to address this question.

This official teaching, especially when it explicates the gospel, can be
seen as absolute and binding authority for the conscience of an individual Catholic, although as Rahner stresses such an obligation has to be
freely accepted to be human and purposeful. There is no question of
simply appealing to an extrinsic sort of authority capable of making
decisions for the individual. Authority's force and vigor flows from the
on-going presence of Christ's authority in the Church. This Church is
seen as an expression of the ongoing presence and historical tangibility
of God's ultimate and victorious power in Jesus Christ. Because the victory of Christ is believed to be final and effective, the Church as a
whole is convinced that it will not totally lapse into error. Such a
complete lapse into error would contradict the victory of Christ for humanity. Either the presence of Jesus Christ lives on visibly in the memory and actions of believers or the presence of the risen Christ ceases to
be a reality for the world.

Is there such a thing within Catholicism as a special teaching office
which can make not only disciplinary or prudential judgments but even
doctrinal decisions? This teaching ministry, if it exists, would guarantee
that the Church can be protected from erroneous doctrines of major import. Rahner notes that the Church cannot be Church if it does not have
some assurance of authority to declare some crucial teaching erroneous
and unorthodox. In a Catholic perspective, the entire college of bishops,
the whole episcopate in communion with the Bishop of Rome who exercises the Petrine ministry as successor of Peter is seen as mediating au-
thoritatively the orthodox understanding of faith. Rahner has in other
writings stressed that this ability to teach and decide does not reside exclusively within a closed group. Rather, he has written, it is present
within various voices within the Church, present in different ways, in

different accents, but notably in the believing community's special instinct to recognize the authentic from the inauthentic in the life of the Church, that charism technically known as the *sensus fidelium*.

The final question raised in exploration of Christianity as Church is: How as a free individual can I live a full Christian life within the Church that includes a highly profiled, organizational, juridical framework (pp. 389–401)? In the light of norms that are external to me, such as scripture and official authoritative Church teachings, how can I effectively continue to accept Christianity as sign of the infinite, mysterious offer of God through Jesus Christ to my own personal freedom?

Those who have followed Karl Rahner's long career as a theologian will recognize here a theme which goes back to the days before World War II. For years he has asked how an individual in a community setting can preserve the sacred domain of the personal and free. His answer is not complex. Freedom is preserved by consistent conscious attempts to appropriate personally one's faith commitment. The Church is not the only setting where challenge exists. In every area of life, such as in learning to speak a particular language, learning to read, developing specific tastes in music, art, literature, even choosing a career, we receive the basic elements from a community of persons, friends, family, nation, from a cultural heritage. Then we shape this given into something personal. Life is filled with the constant interplay between what is taught and then personally appropriated.

Individual Christian living can therefore co-exist quite healthily with ecclesial Christianity. Personal appropriation of a gift from God molded into a harmonious unity is no more unlikely than having body and soul live in union, or freedom and external forces blended. Every influence in life is nurturing and limiting at the same time. We need not fear limitations. We learn to appreciate the contributions of family and friends to our personal development without being blind to their limitations and weaknesses and sinfulness. So too with the Church, as Rahner writes:

> For this reason we are obliged to see the church in its concreteness, in its finiteness, with the burdens of its history, and with all its negligences and perhaps even false developments, and *in this way* to accept this concrete church without reservations as the realm of our Christian existence: with humility, with courage and sobriety, with a real love for this church and a willingness to work for her, and even with a readiness to share her burdens in ourselves and in our lives, and not to add the weakness of our own witness to the burdens of this church. (*Foundations,* p. 390)

Questions for Discussion

Karl Rahner closes this remarkable chapter on Christianity as Church by noting that the most real thing about the Church itself is precisely its ability to offer "the liberation of man and of human existence into the absolute realm of the mystery of God himself" (p. 400). His investigation ends where it began, facing the incomprehensible mystery of God's self-communication. If we understand properly God's desire to speak to humanity, how can we exclude from this audience any non-Christians or nonbelievers? Must we not see all persons in the ultimate depths of their existence as addressed by God's Word?

In our analysis of Rahner's discussion, we have seen him pose seven comprehensive questions: about Jesus' role in organizing the Church, about the different ecclesiologies in the New Testament, about the necessary Church-relatedness of Christianity, about the comprehensiveness of his own Catholic church, about the role of scripture, authoritative teaching, and personal freedom in Christian life. As we follow his lead through the book, we will doubtlessly form additional questions. When that happens, Rahner's method is becoming personally appropriated.

Several questions might be raised about Rahner's procedure in this section of *Foundations*. In particular, do his seven questions, especially questions one, two, and five, make clear enough how his first level of reflection is at work? How would you yourself be inclined to address each of the topics in question?

Furthermore, how satisfying do you find his answer to the question whether Jesus founded the Church? And would it not be possible to pose question four on the legitimacy of adherence to the Catholic Church in a more felicitous way, with less appearance of exclusivism?

There are important questions, too, about ministry and office in the Church. How, from a Catholic perspective, can we really think of a Church which has the Bishop of Rome and the entire College of Bishops jointly at its head? Could Rahner not have drawn upon more recent studies on the role of Peter in the New Testament and on the development of papal and episcopal ministries in the ancient Church, and in a way that would illuminate the contingent factors in Church life? Could he not have pointed out, as he has in other writings, that the much misunderstood notion of magisterium is not exclusively identified with a specific group or ministry in the Church?

Just to ask these questions, however, is to appreciate the value of Rahner's method and to continue a process he himself initiated.

SUGGESTIONS FOR FURTHER READING

A stimulating recent statement of Rahner's ecclesiology may be found in *The Shape of the Church to Come*. This lively description of the future of the Church appeared first in German in 1972 with a title that may be literally translated as "Structural Changes in the Church as Challenge and Opportunity." It was occasioned by Rahner's involvement in the West German Pastoral Synod in the early seventies.

"Church and World," *Sacramentum Mundi* 1, pp. 346–57, is a striking analysis of the Church's mission in the world today. It contains much material that is not found in other writings by Rahner.

"The New Image of the Church," *Theological Investigations* 10, pp. 3–29. Basically an address delivered first at Coblenz, West Germany, in January 1966, this essay contains a convenient summary of Rahner's ecclesiology in the days that followed the Second Vatican Council.

"Basic Observations on the Subject of Changeable and Unchangeable Factors in the Church," *Theological Investigations* 14, pp. 3–23. In this lecture delivered first in 1971 Rahner discusses what elements in the Church could be changed and what are completely unchangeable. Some of his views are adjusted slightly in "Open Questions in Dogma Considered by the Institutional Church as Definitively Answered," *Journal of Ecumenical Studies* 15 (1978): 211–26; also in *Catholic Mind* 72 (1979): 8–26. This address delivered at the International Congress of Jesuit Ecumenists in Frankfurt in 1977 contains some of Rahner's most recent thoughts on *jus divinum* and *jus humanum*. It also marks an advance over *Foundations* for its views on the ecclesial nature of Protestant churches.

10

The Realism of Christian Life

JOHN CARMODY

Rahner's reflection on the daily life of Christians is distinguished both by his humanism and by a sober realism. He sees the Christian sacraments as distinctive help for that life, the way grace is embodied and shares our history at key moments. The traditional Catholic sacraments are here interpreted in this context.

K ARL Rahner's theology never wanders far from concrete Christian life. Analyses that at first seem abstract or merely speculative turn out to blaze new light on prayer or pastoral care. In the eighth chapter of *Foundations,* he is deeply concerned about personal, sacramental faith, so he labors mightily to overcome the cultured despiser of religion in us. By turns he is sober, hopeful, absorbed with death, lilting with life. The hallmark, though, is his humanism. No matter how churchy the topic, Rahner stays close to our searching, our marriage to the absolute mystery of God's love. Let us plunge into his realism.

Sober Realism

Through the previous essays we have seen something of the interaction between Christian anthropology and theology, something of the ongoing exchange between our human constitution, which makes us listen for a directive revelation, and God's self-giving, which is for the Christian most manifest in Jesus. Clearly, this interaction supposes that our lives proceed with a measure of freedom—that we have some say about what we become. If we use our say well, a real, mysterious God will come into view, calling us beyond our present achievements, challenging us to grow. Our lives, therefore, become engaged increasingly with something or someone we cannot control. Perhaps this is best seen from our endpoint.

Death caps our time. It is our finishing, our summation. And, at death, it is unmistakable, undebatable, that we are not in charge. Our freedom, therefore, is the chance or capacity to respond well to a situation of being limited, being a creature. As it takes up this task, human freedom often grows alert to a peculiar fuzziness at the borders. Things fall away somewhat, because none of them explains itself fully. Through success or failure, in business, schooling or personal relations, reality seems to include a "more," an invitation to think it a greater whole. Accepting this strange realism, our freedom steps toward Augustine's God: the quiet for our restless hearts, the depth more intimate than we are to ourselves. Aware and unaware, we move through the years testing whether our most basic task is not to say a simple, sundering word of response to this God. Like Hammarskjold in his *Markings,* we notch the trees toward this clearing, this place and time when we realize we have freedom in order to return love for love.

In this perspective, Christian life is essentially just human life, though faith interprets human life by giving Jesus a special weight—a primacy among our resources for saying how time should unfold. Speaking of this fusion of common humanity and allegiance to Jesus that characterizes a Christian pilgrimage, Rahner says:

> The ultimately Christian thing about this life is identical with the mystery of human existence. And hence we can readily say that the ultimate and most specific thing about Christian existence consists in the fact that a Christian allows himself to fall into the mystery which we call God.

Why is this desirable? Because the Christian

> is convinced in faith and hope that in falling into the incomprehensible and nameless mystery of God he is really falling into a blessed and forgiving mystery which divinizes us. (*Foundations,* p. 430)

From the outset, then, we should underscore that the Christian should be doing what all other human beings try to do: grow, endure, understand, love, end well. There are moments of pleasure and joy in this, of course, but there are also sufferings and difficulties. In fact, for those who meet life directly, without averting their gaze or refusing to put their bodies where they may be clawed, the sobriety of Christian spirituality can be a blessed relief. Contrasting it with the remorseless upbeat of advertising and pop psychology, one can hear an inner imp say, "Three cheers for grimness." Life is hard: confusing, demanding, disappointing. One does not have to live long to know what sin or breach of promise means. If the Buddha did not become serious about life until thirty or so, because his parents sheltered him in luxury, he only became enlightened when he left this never-never existence and encountered disease, old age, and death. The years themselves finally force us to be serious about this strange gift we have of existing in bodies that can reflect, existing as awarenesses condemned to search and probe. In this sense there is a certain sobriety to Christian realism: our lives are not likely to be smooth and easy, we are sentenced to the pain of pressing on.

That is not to say that Christian faith is not radically hopeful. By the enticements of that grace which is everywhere, ingredient in all human searches, God moves us to a curious expectancy, keeps alive at least a bit of passion that one day all things be well. Social life, now so mottled and venal, just "must" somehow, someday, be better. The Church, often scandalously leaden, just "must" dazzle somewhere as a pure nimble bride. We ourselves, who are through many periods of the life cycle the worst burdens, also "must" come to that single exhaustive yes or no our present fracturedness never allows. We depend on this "must," this deep-down hope. Reflecting it toward the gospel Christ, we look ahead to what resurrection might mean for our town, our loves, our world. But it remains a thing of darkened glass, part of our surrender to the God we cannot control. Unless the grain of seed fall in the ground, unless we suffer the pluralism and sunderings of non-angelic life, we can't really glimpse what a resurrection or Spirit-given-fulfillment might mean. God has crafted better than often we would wish. The very harshness of life, the high odds that something bad will occur—these are prime agents in our maturing.

Christian Striving

Like many who have reflected on human maturation, then, Rahner stresses what we have to undergo, our "passion." He would agree with T. S. Eliot that our greatest action is our passion. This does not mean we cannot and should not act. Personally and socially, our freedom makes us responsible to grow, promote our neighbors' welfare, husband and mother the good earth. It does mean that God's "majority," God's mystery ever greater, dominates a Christian spirtuality. We have not the primacy, the priority. We have not chosen life or the conditions under which we pass through time. Has God chosen us, God set the conditions?

If you doubt the primacy of passion, remember death. At the end of our time, at least, it is pellucid that we must undergo what the mystery has set us. None of us escapes death. As the philosopher Martin Heidegger (a great influence on Rahner) has shown brilliantly, death shapes the horizon of all our time. Indeed, as our time grows gravid we become more sensitive to a primal option. Shall we side with Dylan Thomas, refusing to go gentle into that good night, or shall we side with traditional faith, trusting that we lose this form of life for something better, something compatible with the Eastern Orthodox prayer, "You are a good God, and you love humankind"?

On the way to death, in hope of resurrection, what we do and what we suffer comprise a story, a narrative in which we are both tellers and tales. The special theme of interest here is the tension between where we now are and where we feel called to be. Unless one is virtually dead to conscience (and very few people are), there is a sort of energy or dynamic that comes from a sense that we could or should be better. This might show, among other places, in our work. Artists, for example, can never long be satisfied with what they have achieved up to any given point. The poem or painting wrought today may please them tomorrow, but by the day after tomorrow they likely will have thoughts and an itch to do better, to surpass the day before yesterday's child. So too in business or family life. Besides the gross ambition of making more money, people in business can possess an almost aesthetic desire for a smoother operation, a more efficient cash and energy flow. Besides their simple, sometimes prayerful pleas for peace, parents can long for better handling of their children—greater success at understanding them, making them happy, helping the circle of family joy to expand.

The core of this energy or dynamic, in a theological interpretation, is the lure of God's love. The mystery calls us beyond where we now are, invites us to grow or transcend. For Paul this meant maturing to the measure of Christ. For John it meant more intimate union with the vine, so as to bear more fruit. The classical writers on prayer speak of passing from purgative through illuminative to unitive way—from cleansing to understanding to cleaving to God in love. Perhaps we should say, more simply, that what God has done in Christ sets us an agenda to grow. By the promptings of the Spirit, we are gentled towards a greater integrity, a purer resonance to God. Increasingly, we come to suffer from our present dividedness and superficiality. Increasingly, we see how idolatrous or sinful we are.

Idolatry, of course, sets some limited good in the place we should reserve for God. It is perhaps the capsule of sin, the heart of the estrangement we feel within ourselves or experience socially. The "morality" which the Christian learns in a world of grace is therefore in good measure an anti-idolatry. Our main responsibility, summarized in the twofold commandment to love God and neighbor, is to keep the core of our freedom consonant with, open to, the absoluteness that God's love uniquely carries. When our core is open, many of our moral problems, and many of the pains in lifelong striving, fall away. For when the eye of our intention is simple, there is a coincidence, a union of love of God and neighbor. Never perfectly, but nonetheless with increasing success, we can find God in all things: friendships, work, civic duties, play. There will always be some fragmentation, some wearying sense of "busy-ness." Few of us will become mystics proper, constantly feeling a oneness with God. But bit by bit we shall come into our own humble inheritance, our own simple version of Confucius' golden mean, the classical Greeks' insight that virtue is a matter of balance.

It is a paradox, of course, this Christian balance. Not only do we never attain it once and for all, but it depends on giving up again and again the things through which we move—so that we have no lasting treasure but the incomprehensible God. Paradoxically, human freedom only increases by giving itself over to the one legitimate treasure, the one nonidolatrous object of worship or concern, God himself. Rahner has demonstrated this brilliantly, working out the philosophy of the creator-creature relation with a sure existential touch. He has shown that creatures become themselves by union with God rather than distance from God, by opening themselves to mystery rather than turning from it in false independence. Much like the story of the prodigal in Luke 15, therefore, our stories tend to feature a return to our senses in which we realize that some of our self-assertion was foolish. We thought to become hot stuff, movers and shakers, and what we gained were castoff husks.

So, we must learn how Christian striving centers true freedom in God's love. There can be many variations on this centering, and one should not pontificate about just how it ought to proceed. If, for instance, an oppressive or patriarchal culture has made women by and large powerless and diffident, then their striving may not fit the classical paradigms of giving up "pride." As Valerie Saiving Goldstein argued years ago, women may have first to become more assertive and active—have first to develop selves rather than renounce them. But the basic striving, the central theme playing through all human stories, will never wander far from an increasing repose of one's freedom in gracious mystery, an increasing effort to approach the threshold of death with a passion that makes one happy in God's world yet eager to meet its source.

The Core of the Sacraments

What we have developed so far amounts to the Christian's share in the moral or spiritual or religious life—which ultimately are much the same. We are moral if we act in light of conscience. We are spiritual because we wonder about this light. Religion shows that the light comes from mystery, leads into holy love. Knowing and unknowing, we race the light through time. This is the human condition, the reflective life imposed upon all born to question. The Christian "difference" is found in whatever distinctive help Jesus and the Church may offer.

Traditionally, theologians have located such distinctive help in the sacraments, taking them as a Christian program for good living. What, then, are the sacraments basically about? The word *basically* is important, for many Christians discuss the sacraments superficially, with a yawn or a sniff. Worse, they associate the sacraments with inhibiting laws, scruples, or extrinsic ceremonial. Their catechesis, with little fault of their own, has never become something adult, something up to the measure of the rest of their intellectual and moral development. It has failed to be in a modern key what it was in the early church: a "mystagogy"—an absorbing initiation into the living presences of God's beautiful love. It has failed to generate a religious humanism.

If we take a basic view, however, the sacramental life is just the operative form of incarnational grace. By this I mean that what happens in the eucharist or the other sacraments depends directly on God's having to communicate the divine love-life by taking flesh and sharing history. What Rahner emphasizes about this choice is that it has made grace *irrevocable*. As he sees it, from the time of Jesus the heart of faith does not doubt our success or the world's. Once and for all God's love has been given and received. Once and for all the covenant has been sealed, to be opened and fully displayed in what we anticipate as "heaven."

The church is the community constituted by this irrevocable, definitive gift God has made in Jesus Christ. It exists to publish the glad tidings, the tremendous import, of the Christ event. When Christians gather to remember their Lord, invoke the Spirit of his presence, and celebrate his death until he returns, they actualize and express their community. If they are realistic, if their scriptural words and consecrated signs bear them a humanizing love, then the world for which they publish will find them eloquent indeed.

Symbolic expression, it follows, is essential to Christian communal life. In Rahner's own words: "The sacramentality of the church's basic activity is implied by the very essence of the church as the irreversible presence of God's salvific offer in Christ" (*Foundations,* p. 413). The sacraments are but expressions of the Church's basic nature. In fact, we must insist that the Church, like Jesus, is itself a basic sacrament—an elemental form that grace uses to petition entry and give us new hearts of flesh. Far from being a thing of laws or pompous decrees, the living Church is just a social or institutional body for God's love. In keeping with our materiality and history, the Church acts to make present the ongoing story of salvation, the ongoing drama of the mystery's revelation and self-giving. To be a member of the Church is at bottom to be a worshiper, an acclaimer, a yea-sayer to what God did in Jesus of Nazareth who became the Christ. It is to live in a priesthood that has reason to think bread and wine, oil and water, sex and prayer can carry God's love. Ecclesial life is a gatheredness for this purpose—for saying thanks, expressing gratitude through fraternal and sororal service. It is coming together to try to return love for love.

At core, Christian sacramentality depends on and expresses the definitiveness of God's love. The Church is a community centered in this definitive love and serving it; the individual sacraments are acts through which the Church expresses what it is, gives form to grace for the world. In traditional theology, this understanding of sacramentality led to the conclusion that there is something unfailing about the sacraments. One can find in them God's irreversible grace. Regardless of the merits of the minister, or even of the recipient, the sacrament itself is a form of divine love. Were this not so, the Church could not express itself as the definitive community of salvation.

To be sure, there are dangers in this line of reasoning, and often enough Christians have succumbed to them. If "unfailing" is misunderstood, confession or communion can easily become mechanical or rushed. At ebb tide, I once saw mass, rosary, and stations of the cross dispatched in twenty-five minutes. A church in New York used to have flashers that went off at the last word of the consecration.

The unfailing or objective character of the sacraments is therefore but half the story. It has to be balanced by a quite fallible and subjective side, where what the ministers and recipients have in mind is all-important. Unless they have a personal faith trying to come up to the personal love that God offers, it all rings worse than hollow. As the sabbath was made for men and women, so were the church's sacramental words and signs. They must be slow, beautiful, loving. We must give them soul-space. Even a Rembrandt is unimpressive if set in the middle of knickknacks. The sacramental ways of God instinctively seek peace and simplicity as well as full-bodiedness. Elijah's small still voice has a lesson too few liturgists have learned.

Initiation, Calling, and Forgiveness

The core of Christian sacramentality is the irrevocable love of God which the gathered people formally express through their consecrated words and signs. Whether or how Christ instituted all seven of the sacraments that Catholics administer is a matter for ecumenical theology to clarify. There would seem, though, to be no insuperable difficulty in holding for these seven if they do indeed express the Christian community's essential mission. On the other hand, there can be an order of dignity or priority among them, such that the Reformers' stress on baptism and the eucharist receives its due. Each sacrament has its own richness, its own variations on grace, however, so by considering them all we can find God in more ways and places.

Today baptism and confirmation are frequently called the sacraments of initiation. This is a designation with solid roots in Christian history, but it also owes something to the work of historians of religion, from Van Gennep on, concering "rites of passage." These historians, basing themselves especially on anthropologists' observations of archaic ("primitive") societies, have noted that it is usual for groups to ceremonialize the key moments in the life cycle: birth, puberty, marriage, and death. Each of these times is what Victor Turner has called a *limen:* a threshold to a deeper relation with the sacred. For Christian society, baptism and confirmation have been one's initial access to community participation in the sacramental life of grace. Baptism clearly has overtones of dying to sin and rising to newness in grace, on the model of

Jesus' passover. Perhaps its stronger motif, however, is that here one formally becomes a member of the Christian "gathering" ("synagoge"). From the outset of explicitly Christian life, therefore, the social dimension is to the fore. Following Jesus is not an individual venture, not a heroic warfare waged alone. Christians are members of one another, for they are baptized into the one body of Christ.

Confirmation advances on this initiation, stressing that the new life is not only a cleansing from sin, a turning from idolatry, but also an infusion of the Spirit for the sake of mission. Because of its social character, the new life entails witnessing to God's love. Such witnessing is a natural outward aspect of inner Christian being. If I have been baptised and am striving to live up to God's love, then what I do in front of others inevitably testifies to what I believe and value. In this way simple honesty, to say nothing of prayer or self-sacrifice, is a social and even political act. Confirmation, though, impels us into the world more self-consciously. If the Spirit, as Paul says, moves in our depths to make our prayer, so too, as John says, it gives us inspiration to witness to Jesus and stand by our faith. This witness need not be grandiose, as though we were Daniel in the lions' den. When mature, it blends seriousness, humor, and self-deprecation. The seeds of confirmation, that is, flower in a clear-eyed realization that what we do in our work, with our friends, before society influences God's credibility. If we have had a parent or friend who has witnessed to Christian love, if we have known someone who really was surprisingly good, then we can appreciate what this sacrament ought to nurture.

In a sacramental theology such as Rahner's, orders and marriage bring God's love to bear on "states in life," ritualizing what we believe about priesthood and conjugal sharing. One of the most attractive aspects of this theology of orders is that it helps us to see how the holiness of the church depends on those who hold power and bear the most visible ministries of grace. For the people of God, whether power is in the hands of holy persons or serious sinners could never be something indifferent. Lovingly, then, that people sacramentalizes the strength promised those who lead it. By laying on hands, the church palpably impresses its reliance on the Spirit. With potent imagery, it makes orders entail prostrations of humility and songs of joy.

As Rahner goes out of his way to say (*Foundations*, p. 417), there is no theological reason why orders and marriage cannot be given to the same person. Further, as a study commissioned by the Catholic Theological Society of America concludes, there seems no great theological obstacle to conferring orders on qualified women. Consequently, a large body of Catholic theologians now hold it desirable to ordain women, single or married, and married men. In their actual exercise, orders amount to mediating God's love. The church should embrace whatever human experiences can facilitate this mediation—and embrace them with alacrity.

The theology of Christian marriage spotlights the biblical theme of God's covenant with humanity, and the evangelical theme of Christ's union with the church. Sharing time and life, spouses can gain a good inkling of the God who, according to Exodus 3:14, is known by being with us. So, unless this God is irrelevant to Catholic priesthood, marriage could indeed enrich Catholic orders. Similarly, women's experience of menstruation, gestation, lactation, and motherhood could amplify the resources on which priestly mediation draws. "States in life," then, run together more than they flow apart. As a state in life, orders shapes the ministrations of love by providing formal training, functions, and status. Marriage, virginity, or the single life shape the ministrations of love by their impact on where one can serve and what experiences one can draw on. 1 Peter 2:9, we recall, makes priesthood an ingredient in all Christian life. The more basic "state in life," then, is where baptism places us. Orders and marriage simply bring out the needs for grace, the possibilities for service, that come with accepting church power or joining with another to make "one flesh." We may hope this simplicity prevails in the shape of the church to come.

Penance and anointing apply Christian sacramentality to human weakness, both moral and physical. To the end of our days we are sinners—people incompletely penetrated by God's love. It was a prime ministry of Jesus to forgive sinners, and a prime scandal to his contemporaries. Jesus' God, of course, was an "Abba"—a "Daddy" full of paternal care. How could such a God not urge his prime minister to seek out what was lost, to touch what was most dejected and burdened? No more than a nursing mother could forget or abandon her child could such a God not mourn those fighting the love that would give them joy. The church has been wise and Christlike indeed in expressing itself through a sacrament that forgives sins. Seventy times seven, the biblical hyperbole has it, God forgives us. There is joy in heaven, we read, when sinners repent. If the sacrament brims with these directive emotions, it is a vehicle of peace.

Anointing, too, brings forgiveness, but its special function is to prepare our surrender to God, our acceptance of God's last invasion, at death. We begin to die from the moment of our birth, and recent philosophy has meditated profoundly on what it means to be cast through time toward death. As death starts to creak in one's bones, the carriers of grace, its material forms, grow more precious. Often old people are intensely grateful for the small gifts of a warm sun, a cooling breeze, a bracing cup of tea. They have learned the lesson that psychologist Erik Erikson makes the "work" of old age: to love life in face of death. This is "wisdom," Erikson says, and anointing might be seen as the church's formal instruction in it. By balming the body, and praying for the spirit, the church tries to stir up our thanksgiving and hope. God knows the burdens of human flesh. God has endured the agonies of abandonment and giving up the life we know. Could this God not understand the frailty to which time hollows us? When my father died, after years of hollowing by cancer, anointing seemed to have left him almost transparent. I saw him early on New Year's Day as an El Greco portrait—gaunt yet beatific. Since then I haven't feared death, for it is as though he has somewhat anointed me—with a hope that my sufferings, whatever they may turn out to be, will also be purifying, will also make for a beautiful ending—and beginning—in love.

The Eucharist

The six sacraments we have briefly studied are somewhat "occasional," directed to special times and needs. By contrast, the eucharist is at the center of Christian life, a sacrament for all times and needs. Biblically, it is clear that the Lord's Supper recapitulates absolutely fundamental aspects of Jesus' work and intention. There is, first, the central motif that in giving his body and blood for us Jesus links it with his death. Insofar as death is the summary act, in which we surrender everything to God, this action of Jesus has unique significance. In instituting the eucharist he tells us that he dies for us—that his surrender to the Father is "for us and our salvation," as the liturgical creed has it. He secures the Kingdom by seeing his mission through to the cross. The community we call Church rests on this self-gift, which the eucharist memorializes. If we anticipate a messianic banquet, when God's triumph will break through fully, we also ought to recall that our joy depends on Jesus' having "descended into hell."

It follows that we may not separate the eucharistic meal from Jesus' death and resurrection. To be sure, breaking bread together, nourishing life by feeding on Jesus' body and blood, offering ourselves in grateful return—these sacramental facets deserve full development. At times in the past the emphasis on sacrifice was so heavy that they were neglected. A balanced view reminds us that joy and sorrow cross—that Jesus lived to die, died to rise. Uncrossed optimism disserves both human experience and Jesus' own life. If we face life's harshness at the eucharist, as in baptism, we can catch something of the gratuity, the absolute wonder, of resurrection and the vision of God.

I once heard William Leonard, a pioneer among Jesuit liturgists, explain this indelibly. He was a prisoner of the Japanese during the Second World War. When liberation came, he sensed as never before what Christ must have meant to the first century. That century was in bondage to despair. Suddenly, the resurrection burst open its prison walls. Out of sin and hopelessness came unexpectable glad tidings: "Behold, I make all things new." At least on occasion, the eucharist should shock us with this novelty, this nearly incredible news, that we've been set free by Jesus' love. Faith says Jesus is present at our supper, to draw us deeper into the relations he bears the Father and the Spirit. He is present to repair his body and serve its fuller growth. Truly, then, the eucharist epitomizes all that we confess and need. Truly it is the sacrament of sacraments, the ecclesial act *par excellence*.

Christian Humanism

The sacraments should make us intimate with nature, society, self, and God. Unless they do, they are not humanistic, for these four "poles" define our world. Can Christian faith intensify their beauty? For instance, can it accept the criticism that often it has read Genesis as a warrant to ravish the earth, and so been a cause of pollution, despoliation and ecological ruin? Can it reform, purify itself, and become nature's friend? Yes, if it emphasizes its sacramentals more and lets them explain our earth—through its baptismal water, oil of chrism, bread, wine, wax, fire, music, and gold. If God creates nature, nature itself is sacramental. As Maximus the Confessor spoke of a "Cosmic Liturgy," we can celebrate quasars, black holes, mitochondria, polypeptides, and mesons. For galaxies and subatomic particles alike explode with our God's power. Evolutionary eons and historical centuries alike come to an Omega in Christ. This is praise, not hard science, but it has enormous potential for our future ways to live. There is an ecological revolution latent in sacramental reform, had we only spiritualized senses to grasp it.

The same holds for faith's relations with the self, society, and divine mystery. Renewed, brought up to date, sacramentalism could be humanizing, liberating, for each. Penance, for example, could greatly assist the fight for a healthy self-love. Depth psychology shows that self-love is crucial to each generation's chances for peace. By facilitating forgiveness, and reconciling us to our inevitable moral ambiguity, penance could powerfully help tame the furies of violence, the outbursts of disgust.

Analogously, the community organization at work in good liturgy holds half the response to the Marxist demand that oppression cease. If Christ died for the sake of justice, serious Christians cannot pray to God until they have been reconciled to their brothers and sisters. Only the faith that does justice is pleasing to God. What the prophets dinned at Israel more than holds true today. A certain radical politics is inescapable from confessing that no Caesar is Lord. A certain subversion follows inevitably if one cannot serve both God and mammon. The kingdom of God suffers violence; the violent bear it away. Materialism, capitalism, consumerism—these know in their marrow Christ is an enemy. His "violence" is a ceaseless "No!" to their sway. Socially, faith is only humanistic if it liberates people from injustice. That this is growing clearer in Christian theology today is one of its happiest portents.

Finally, all the sacraments reach out to "the God who gives himself as man's own in eternal and incalculable love" (*Foundations*, p. 430). In other words, all the sacraments dramatize our faith and hope that the wild abyss is a loving parent, a tenacious spouse. In ecstatic times we glimpse this God's beauty, the splendor ever ancient ever new. In trying times we contend with her darkness and quiet. Because Jesus was ecstatic and bereft, we know our own way will take many turns. "For every thing there is a time, for every time a purpose under heaven"— who learns this but painfully? If the master suffered for his obedience, so will the disciple. If the master gained glorious fulfillment, the disciple may not suffer in vain.

The soul's deepest hunger is to contemplate God. Through dark nights and clouds of unknowing, it follows fragile spoor. Faith in Jesus spares it few hardships in hunting. Jesus unsettles as much as secures. But because of Jesus' Spirit there is great expectancy, great hope. As Hopkins saw:

morning, at the brown brink eastward, springs—
Because the Holy Ghost over the bent
World broods with warm breast and with ah! bright wings.

Questions for Discussion

The next essay deals with Christian hope more expressly. Before turning to it, however, let us pause to open discussion of two further questions. I suggest that they may prove central to helping a theology such as Rahner's reach its richest interpretation of Christian life, its richest experiential yield for faith, in the years ahead.

The first question concerns the place of prayer, both individual and social. Paul tossed off the injunction to pray always, and exemplary Christians such as Rahner's mentor, Ignatius Loyola, spoke of finding God in all things. But for many of us prayer is not a natural, congenial, comfortable communion with the mystery we love. For many of us the sacraments are not lively, not grave and beautiful, because we have not contemplated how the Spirit impregnates them, what it gives us to sense and taste. Does a full theology of Christian life not have to become a theology of prayer?

In works other than *Foundations,* Rahner has dealt with a full range of ascetical and mystical issues. His *Spiritual Exercises, Theological Investigations* 3 and 7, and *Visions and Prophecies* come to mind. They suggest that we contemporary Americans do not pray comfortably because little in our culture nurtures relaxed contemplation. William Johnston's *The Inner Eye of Love* is a recent work that could redress some of our imbalance. It mediates well medieval and Asian insights about interiority. But the first steps in prayer are really not recondite. To begin to contemplate God one need not master yet another book. It is enough to take any signal human experience and turn it toward the mystery lovingly. Simply staying with a Florida sunset, a child's sickness, financial worries, a flash of love—simply offering this to God's quiet gives the Spirit access to one's depths. Prayer is just lingering love of the mystery, as close as a groan or a breath. Christian theology has a serious obligation to shout this from the rooftops. How can each of us do his or her part?

A second question: in prayer, work, social action, must we not find a contemporary version of the traditional *imitatio Christi*—a contemporary reproduction of Christ's way? Liberation theologians such as Jon Sobrino in his *Christology at the Crossroads* argue this point eloquently, with special attention to its politics. On any grounds it is pressing. We are Christian inasmuch as we walk Jesus' path, reproduce Jesus' "mind," bear forth Jesus' love. Rahner emphasizes that grace sets us in Jesus' relation to the Father. Christian life today deeply needs to recover the parabolic speech, spiritual freedom, and political commitment that translated this relation for first century Palestine.

Jesus was alert, poetic, radical. He hungered and thirsted for justice. *Imitatio Christi,* then, is a clarion call to feel, suffer, and rejoice. It is a choice for life. "God's glory is human beings fully alive," the Greek Father Irenaeus said. Echoing in Rahner's realism, his words set us a pressing agenda. Jesus was sent that we might have life, and have it more abundantly. We have to make this message ring, to liberate its spirit from the dead letters. Can we? A world of grace is only surpassing good news if it is lovely in human limbs and faces. An absolute savior is only credible when people we know glow with health. Each day two ways stand before us, life or death, blessing or curse. Which shall we choose?

SUGGESTIONS FOR FURTHER READING

The article on "Faith," *Sacramentum Mundi* 2, pp. 310–13, is a brief but rich sketch of the way to faith; it situates God's call in the midst of our human striving in a world held by Mystery.

The Church and the Sacraments is a short book in which Rahner exposes his basic notion that the Church is the primal sacrament and the individual sacraments are unfailing self-expressions of the Church largely geared to critical occasions in the life cycle.

In "Considerations on the Active Role of the Person in the Sacramental Event," *Theological Investigations* 14, pp. 161–84, Rahner moves sacramental religious experience away from an individualistic conception, to show its relations to the person's existence in a whole world of grace.

The Dynamic Element in the Church is a brief book showing the charismatic nature of the Christian community; it also has a difficult but very rewarding essay on the experience of the Spirit that is at the heart of contemplative prayer such as Ignatius Loyola's *Spiritual Exercises.*

Finally, two outstanding examples of Rahner's spiritual writing are *Encounters with Silence* and *On Prayer.* The first is a series of meditations written in the late thirties, while the second comprises the Lenten Sermons preached in St. Michael's Church in Munich in 1946.

11

The Hope for Humanity: Rahner's Eschatology

WILLIAM M. THOMPSON

Traditional teaching on the "four last things"—death, judgment, heaven, hell—has been significantly reshaped by Rahner's emphasis on the instinct for fulfillment in all human experience. This essay presents his interpretative principles, showing how they relate to his thought on Christ and humanity and also drawing out their practical implications for Christian life in the present.

I remember hearing once from a New York psychoanalyst that after reading an essay I had written on the doctrine of hell, he could at last reconcile his scientific training with his religious faith. For him the notion of hell was the great stumbling block to faith. What the psychoanalyst did not know was that my study had been greatly influenced by Karl Rahner. Although Rahner has never done a sustained treatment of humanity's ultimate destiny, individually and collectively, he has contributed brilliant essays on possible approaches to the subject, and it is here that his contribution lies. If you will, he has been most concerned with the conditions necessary if modern people are to make the ideas of eschatology their own. He seems very early in his career to have become aware of how difficult it is for modernity to give credence to the various doctrines that comprise Christianity's eschatological faith: the resurrection, beatific vision, purgatory, hell, heaven, the final judgment, the communion of saints, the bodily resurrection, the transfiguration of the world.

Rahner has written in various places about some of the difficulties which we moderns have with beliefs about a final destiny. He points to our secular experience of the world today. It is an experience of the world as "worldly," as finite and human, and thus apparently the result of inner-worldly causes and human planning. No doubt, our modern consciousness of planning our own future implies a certain eschatological aspiration: We experience ourselves as hoping beings, as goal-directed. Yet this is a secularized eschatology, and it is no longer immediately evident how this can be reconciled with the Christian belief in an afterlife which transcends human self-making and is the gift of God.

Allied with this is the problem of demythologization, which becomes even more urgent in the area of eschatology. It would seem that the traditional afterlife statements of Holy Scripture and tradition are particularly prone to the colorful imagery characteristic of mythology. However one might try to explain this abundance of mythological imagery, Rahner is acutely aware that people today cannot easily assent to statements which seem to have no anchoring in empirical human experience. As we will see, his unique contribution to eschatology probably lies here, in his attempt to probe how, given our moorings in the present, we can speak at all of the "last things," the absolute and final future.

Finally, there is the fact that in the history of theological reflection, eschatology has undergone a kind of privatization and interiorization. Instead of being a proclamation about the hope for the world and humanity as a whole—and thus something relevant to society at large—it has become strangely reduced to a proclamation about the individual's private destiny. Attention was concentrated upon the immortality of the individual soul, and the cosmic and social perspectives of scripture were lost from sight. One might look to the growing individualism of the western mind as a partial explanation for this privatization of eschatology. A further factor might be the historic tendency of Christianity towards a dualism in which earthly society is devalued in the face of the supernatural. Every religion which believes in a supramundane revelation runs the danger of denigrating the mundane. The earth and our linkage with it through body and social responsibility are replaced in the Christian imagination by a fascination for eternity and our linkage with it through "soul." But for our contemporaries this means that eschatology all too easily becomes an otherwordly utopia and opiate for the people, fostering a kind of indifference to the misery of this world. Rahner is aware of this, and some of his finest work has been concerned precisely to show how a properly understood eschatology should rather foster a healthy but critical worldly secularity and social involvement.

Preliminaries to Rahner's Eschatology

Perhaps the most basic insight to be considered is this: Eschatology is not idle speculation about a simply unknown future, nor does it indulge our desires for uncontrolled fantasy; rather, it is directly concerned with our present, insofar as our present reaches out toward our future. Inasmuch as the various Christian creeds profess the *expectation* of what is to come, we may say that the tradition recognized this, for that expectation is something present, a hope present within us, and not simply something yet to come. We are *now* beings oriented to the future; we are eschatological in our very being itself.

It is the presentness of eschatology which makes it important for our salvation. Were it simply concerned with a future wholly extrinsic to our present existence and thus in no way known by us now, it could be of no import to our attempt to achieve salvation in this world. It is also this presentness which protects Christian eschatology from the charge of promoting a devaluation of the world. For if it truly illuminates our present, it can lead us to deeper commitments and to a renewed affirmation of the importance of the "now."

We are aware that the traditional treatment of eschatology, at least in relatively recent theology, hardly recognized how eschatological assertions should bear upon our present. By treating eschatology as a doctrine of the last things and by placing it simply at the very end of the study of theology, the classical treatment reinforced the notion that eschatology simply concerns itself with what awaits us at the end. Further, a look at the Catholic church's teaching on this matter reveals that the treatise on eschatology is still in its beginnings. What we find is a very unselfconscious series of apparently unrelated statements, with the possible exception of Pope Benedict XII's definition concerning the direct vision of God. Evidently Christianity has had to wait until humanity became conscious of itself as historical, as essentially future-oriented, before the treatise on eschatology could come into its own. This new era was largely initiated by non-Catholic theologians, especially by Albert Schweitzer's and Johannes Weiss's discovery of the eschatological element in Jesus' message. This was carried further by Rudolf Bultmann's attempt to reinterpret the last things existentially and by C. H. Dodd's notion of realized eschatology. Yet this attempt to avoid the one-sided supernaturalistic eschatologism of Orthodox Protestantism has too quickly led to an equally one-sided radical rejection of eschatology's futurity, something theologies of liberation are reacting against. Nothing less than a rethinking of the foundations of eschatology seems called for, and this is precisely what Rahner has attempted.

Interpreting Eschatological Claims

To my knowledge, no theologian has produced anything equal in scope or balance to Rahner's famous essay on the principles for interpreting eschatological claims, "The Hermeneutics of Eschatological Assertions" (*Theological Investigations* 4, pp. 323–46). A reading of such recent books as Edmund Fortman's *Everlasting Life After Death* or John Hick's *Death and Eternal Life* reveals that such a hermeneutics is still needed if we wish to avoid not only an exaggerated fundamentalism but also an overcautious, almost rationalistic humanism. As we shall presently see, Rahner tries to travel a middle way.

A basic principle of interpretation is that eschatology really has to do with the future, with what is yet to come, with a God-yet-to-come and his gift of life. Only if there is such a real future is eschatology worth speaking about, can it have any relevance to humanity in its own right. This position sets itself against a radical existentializing of the last things in the sense of Bultmann or a one-sided and exclusive emphasis on realized eschatology. These latter two emphases tend to forget our essentially temporal makeup as moving toward the future; they reduce us to abstract personalities who do not actually become through a temporal process. One implication here is that if the future is a real future, then it entails a certain readiness on our part for the unexpected, the surprising, the uncontrollable. This latter element is often missing in radical existentialistic reformulations of eschatology. Yet, granting this renewed stress on eschatology as future, it still remains necessary to articulate principles for interpreting the eschatological assertions of revelation, principles which would be derived from that revelation itself. Without them we continually run the danger of reading our own uncriticized presuppositions into divine revelation, and in this way we unwittingly limit what in fact God wants to communicate to us. As an example, Rahner singles out the fundamentalist's tendency to read eschatological assertions the way he reconstructs some past event he has observed. This ends up de-eschatologizing humanity itself: In its present existence it is unaffected by the future, because the future is only what is yet to come and not that which is at hand in its futurity.

We gain another basic principle of interpretation by relating two key insights. The first is that scripture has not revealed to us the day of the end of time (cf. Mark 13:32; Revelation 1:7). This does not merely mean that we cannot fix an exact date for the end; it has salvific and theological significance. The end's character of hiddenness is essential to it. Only in this way can the revelation of the last things be one of mystery. For revelation is not making known what was once unknown; it is the approach of the mystery as such. This also provides us with a criterion for distinguishing genuine eschatology from false "apocalyptic." Both employ colorful imagery, and so this cannot be the difference between them. Rather, apocalyptic understands this imagery as a spectator's report, and so excludes the character of absolute mystery and hiddenness found in genuine eschatology. (It might be well to point out that Rahner uses "apocalyptic" as a technical term for the view which considers eschatological statements as previews of eternity, rather than as imaginative, faith-inspired extrapolations from our present Christian experience. Whether scholars of the classical apocalyptic literature, such as the books of Daniel, Enoch, and Esdras, would agree with Rahner's choice of words is open to question. These scholars tend to view the classic apocalyptic literature as a profound expression of hope in God which employs language in a *symbolic* way. It's probably safe to say that we just don't know how literally that literature understood the language it employed. In any case, Rahner uses the phrase *false* apocalyptic, and we will follow that usage here.)

Secondly, if human beings are essentially historical, if they only live by moving through time, then they cannot really understand or orient themselves without both a retrospective view of their past and a prospective view of their future. "Anamnesis" and "prognosis" are basic aspects of being human. To say we are prognostic means that we understand our present only to the degree that we grasp it as moving toward the future. The existentialist tends to demythologize and even repress this dimension of futurity. The key point is that if the presentness of our being is our being-referred-to-futurity, then the future is an inner moment of our actual being as it is present to us now. "And so knowledge of the future, in so far as it is still to come, is an inner moment of the self-understanding of man in his present hour of existence—*and grows out of it*" (*Theological Investigations* 4, p. 331).

The future, then, is indeed something known and present, but in a hidden way. The content of our eschatological knowledge must accordingly be that element of the future still to come which is necessary for our present existence. Knowledge of the future is knowledge of the futurity of our present: *Eschatological* knowledge is really knowledge of the possible fulfillment of our present. This approach preserves both the real meaning of the revelation of the last things and their hidden character. For on this account the eschatological future remains uncontrollable and hidden and yet also present, something we really look forward to, something in the presence of which we hope, dare, trust, and surrender ourselves.

This means that we can rightly presume that our knowledge of the future, even our revealed knowledge, is limited to what can be derived from our understanding of the possible fulfillment of our present experience. For a Christian this means that eschatological revelation is identical with God's revelation in Christ. Eschatology is thus not a preview of events yet to come, but the understanding of the future accessible to us through our faith in Christ, something we need for our spiritual freedom and faith. Eschatology transposes Christian anthropology and Christology into the terms of their fulfillment. More specifically and technically, we can say that eschatology is the revelation of the fulfillment promised by God's trinitarian self-disclosure and graceful self-communication in the crucified and risen Lord. To the extent that we are able to engage in such a forward-looking draft of our existence, our eschatology will be sound.

On this view of the matter, we may draw some basic implications at this point. Because eschatological thinking involves a forward-looking draft rather than a direct vision of the future, the future remains hidden and thus is able to confront us precisely as the absolute mystery. This also enables us to understand better the colorful eschatological imagery employed in the scriptures: "fire," "lightning," "thunder," the "judgment seat," etc. Imagistic thinking flows from the imagination, and this is precisely what must be at work when mystery as such is in question rather than simply empirical objects observable to the senses. Further, we are able to avoid both a false apocalyptic view of eschatology as well as a totally existential and demythological interpretation. Both suppress the hiddenness of the mystery, the first by attempting to unveil it, the latter by reducing it to our present. To paraphrase Rahner, extrapolation from the Christian present into the future is eschatology; interpolation from the future into the present is apocalyptic; reduction of the future into the present is radical existentializing.

We might grasp the usefulness of this approach even better by dwelling on some of its less obvious implications. For one, since eschatology can be nothing more than a description of our Christian situation in terms of the intrinsic future possibilities of the present, all presumption about the future is ruled out. This means that any assertion of the certainty of salvation for an individual before death or of someone's actual damnation tries to unveil the hiddenness of the future. Interestingly, Rahner thinks that eschatology is based on the certainty of Christ's gift of salvation as an actuality—and not a mere possibility—at least in the case of the Church's martyrs and saints. But damnation can only be seen as a possibility. The possibility of damnation is enough to rule out presumption, for it forbids individual Christians to identify the triumph of grace in history with their own salvation. For another, since eschatology is concerned with persons in their totality, it will try to speak of the fulfillment of the whole person as understood by theology and by faith. Thus, the person is both an individual and a member of society, and correspondingly eschatology will be both individual and universal. This enables us to relate what might otherwise appear to be disconnected beliefs about resurrection, heaven, and beatific vision on the one hand, and final judgment and the communion of saints on the other. Further, as humanity is both corporeal and spiritual, so eschatology will rightly speak of the resurrection of the flesh and not only of the spirit.

The Hope for the Individual

Although Rahner's main contribution lies in providing us with an overall orientation for the interpretation of Christian hope, in various places he has sketched a forward-looking draft of this hope for the individual. What destiny awaits each one of us? Can we live our present more fully if we realize that we are moving towards a future which opens up to God himself? We cannot, of course, radically separate the final hope for the individual from that of collective humanity; each of us is a collective and social being. But if we cannot separate, we can discriminate—unless we choose to empty persons of their individuality. In Christian anthropology and Christology, each human being is redeemed quite individually by Christ. An eschatology for the individual attempts to transpose into the form of fulfillment our present experience of being a Christian individual; it extends into the future our present capacity to be an individual. It is in this light that we should understand the traditional doctrines concerning death and eternal life, heaven and the bea- tific vision, the so-called intermediate state of purgatory, and hell ("the possibility of eternal loss," as Rahner calls it).

Again, the key insight is that we are dealing with an extrapolation from our present Christian experience into the future. The problem, then, is our insight into our own present and lived experience of Christ and salvation. It is here, on the level of the analysis of Christian experi- ence, that Rahner's theology pays high dividends. Few theologians have described with as much power the depth of Christian experience. For example, we already know something of eternity because we already ex- perience the radically unconditioned character of our love, our hope, our decisions, our openness to the mystery. We already experience in some way eternal life; only because of this can we speculate about it and ex- tend it into the future in the form of fulfillment. Even within time we have experiences which transcend time's passing away. Thus we are led to a notion of eternity not as time's prolongation, not as a succession of acts following one upon the other, but as the conquering of time, the final and definitive validity of human existence achieved through the ex- ercise of our freedom. Such a notion presupposes a *kairotic,* biblical "once and for all" far more than a linear conception of time. Ultimately it is based upon God's unconditioned, time-conquering, free bestowal of his own love. In this light, then, the Christian belief in a personal sur- vival beyond death only articulates under the guise of completion our experience of already being more than death, of truly transcending the passage of time. This also clarifies why we can dread death so much, for it is felt as a contradiction to our present experience of being eternal.

This notion of "eternity" is the key to understanding Christian belief in heaven and hell: Eternity *is* either the entrance into God's presence through love or a final state of closure against him. "Heaven" is per- haps the more inclusive term pointing to the mystery of ineffable happi- ness which ensues from our final closeness to God. Less inclusively, the term "beatific vision" highlights the intellectual dimension of this hap- piness. We recall that each human person is simultaneously oriented to God through transcendence and destined for God's graceful self-com- munication. Heaven with its beatific vision can therefore be said to be the experience of transcendence and grace in the mode of their comple- tion. But the beatific vision does not annul the divine mystery, for the mystery is not merely the limit of our finite knowing but its ultimate and positive goal, as we have seen repeatedly in earlier chapters. We will see God face to face, it is true (1 John 3:2, 1 Corinthians 13:12), but in the manner proper to us as finite creatures.

Coming now to the difficult question of hell, we must remember that the scriptural and traditional assertions are not to be read as previews in a literal, empirical sense. What we have is rather a case of "threat discourse," expressing the ultimate possibility of human estrangement from God in all the dimensions of a person's life. Such language aims at bringing out the relevance of revelation to our lives now, a claim of utmost seriousness whose refusal entails terrible consequences. In this light discussions about the "fire" of hell—whether real or metaphorical?—still move within the preview mentality. "Fire," "eternal loss," and similar images do not indicate that we can reduce the loss of God to a merely psychological state, but rather that a real and objective loss of God is in question. Once again the key notion we must grapple with is that of eternity. Because human freedom is the will and possibility of positing the definitive, there *can be* an eternal hell, a state of the definitive achievement of one's decisions in history, removing the possibility of the further revision of those decisions. This would be a state of ultimate closure to God. Perhaps, with Thomas Aquinas, we should envision this eternal capacity of closure on our part in a way which protects God from the charge of being a vindictive punisher. This would entail thinking of hell as the intrinsic possible result of our own inward obduracy.

For traditionalists, the difficult aspect of this theory is the notion that hell is only a possibility, and thus not truly on a par with God's triumphant grace, which at least in some cases is an actuality (the Church canonizes; it does not condemn to hell). We simply have no clear revelation from Jesus on this matter. The nature of his threat discourses has to do with a radical summons to the Kingdom, not with whether some are actually lost. A similar restriction applies to the teachings of the Church. To go beyond this minimum is to exchange eschatology for false apocalyptic. On the other hand, what enables us to believe in the actual salvation of the saints and martyrs is the event of Christ, proclaiming that God's grace has truly begun a transformation of human history. Apparently we need to maintain in dialectical tension both the redemption of all by Christ *and* the real possibility of eternal loss. No faithful Christian doubts that God wants to redeem him or her in Christ. But we also need to come to terms with the radically closed heart and mind of a Nazi torturer, a Papa Doc Duvalier, and an Idi Amin.

The doctrine of purgatory still needs much more reflection. Purgatory essentially concerns the notion of an "interval," some kind of maturation after death in which the finality of one's decisions penetrates the whole breadth of one's many-leveled being. We already experience such an interval in the tension between any radical decision we have made and our attempts to integrate it into all the aspects and actions of our lives. A similar interval exists between an individual's eternal fulfillment and that of the world as a whole; between, also, individual fulfillment and the full "glorification" of the body. We should not apply temporal categories here: The purgatorial interval does not imply that final decisions of the past are undone, but that they penetrate all levels of the personality. We are on the level of the eternal, and not the temporal.

The Hope for Humanity and the Earth

In the faith of the Church the individual is never isolated, but a member of a community, a historical and bodily being immersed in the world and coming to be through this world. A collective eschatology, then, transposes into the terms of future fulfillment what we already experience and know of our social and bodily existence. Such doctrines as the resurrection of the body, the final return of Christ, and the communion of saints are traditional expressions for this social eschatology. The doctrine means that "the history of the human race as a whole is moving in its history towards a fulfillment of the human race which will end history" (*Foundations,* p. 445). Here again it is the notion of the eternal as the definitive and final which is crucial; Rahner takes this to mean that history will end, for were time to go on indefinitely, every moment would lose its value, always being about to be postponed to an endless future.

One way to understand this is to recall that matter is not simply a condition for the human spirit, an element that can be set aside once spirit has done its work. Rather, matter is an intrinsic element for the human person as spirit in the world. We can never set aside our bodies: For better or worse they are the medium through which we express our mind and heart. If this is so, then matter must somehow share in spirit's transcendent dynamism. Insofar as matter is our connatural surrounding, it too will know eternal fulfillment. This is one way, but perhaps a rather obscure one, of understanding the earth's eternal consummation.

A related but alternate route is Christological in its orientation. We have seen the principle that ultimately all eschatological statements should be translatable into Christological ones, for Christ ultimately reveals the full destiny of humanity. Pursuing this, we could say that just as one would be lapsing into a kind of Christological spiritualism were one to deny Christ's glorified body, so one would be guilty of an eschatological spiritualism were one to deny the material transfiguration of the cosmos. Jesus remains for all eternity the God-man, and this means that God is a God with the world, with flesh, and conversely, that the world and flesh share in the eternity of God. To believe in Christ's glorified body, then, is to believe in the world's transfiguration. Perhaps we would do well here simply to remember the image offered us by the Book of Revelation: "I saw . . . a Lamb that seemed to have been sacrificed" (Revelation 5:6). Here the seer of Revelation is speaking of the glorified Christ, for the Lamb is said to be at God's throne. And yet it is a glorified Christ in whom the flesh remains, for "it seemed to have been sacrificed." So also does our flesh remain.

The Eschatological Attitude of the Christian and the Church

In his more recent writings, perhaps under the pressure of political theologians, Rahner has concentrated on what he calls the "eschatological attitude." This question brings us directly into the way in which Christianity's eschatological belief illuminates, motivates, and even transforms our present Christian existence. We should not lose sight of what we have already said about the traditional doctrines of the afterlife; those doctrines give content to our eschatological attitude, they assure us that the future toward which we move is not an empty void but the holy mystery which has drawn near to us in Christ. But now we simply want to explore the power of those doctrines to light up our present existence, to motivate us for our worldly tasks even now.

Understanding the eschatological attitude is a matter of grasping the mutual relationship between the absolute future of God and the "utopian" future which we ourselves plan and attempt to enact in history. We recall: Against the radical existentializers Rahner maintains that there is a real and veiled future constituted by God. As the *absolute* future, God cannot be identified with any specific event among the many events of the world. The Divine is the ground of the world as a whole, determining the world's future consummation. A "utopian" future would refer to what at the present moment is yet to be achieved but will actually come about within the world. And here we can imagine several possibilities: (1) that which comes about because of a predetermined evolutionary pattern (viz., reproductive fertility will issue forth in the continuance of the race) and (2) that which results from human creativity and freedom (the genuinely "new"). What stems from human ingenuity is more properly the utopian future, of which humanity has only recently become aware in a self-conscious way.

Basically it is because Christianity is a state of radical openness to the mystery of the absolute future, which *is* God, that we have an eschatological consciousness capable of transforming our lives. This means that we can only really affirm God—know God—by shattering every idol, every answer which threatens prematurely to halt our questioning and to truncate the genuine fulfillment of life. The revelation of Christ does not annul this stance of radical openness, but only confirms or promises us that God *really* wants to be our future. This Christian attitude toward the absolute future imparts a radical dimension to our utopian future, for the only way in which we can maintain ourselves in this state of readiness and openness is to engage ourselves positively and critically towards an ever fresh future within society itself. Belief in the absolute future should, if you will, generate historical utopias. It liberates us both *for* a stance of critique and openness on the one hand and *from* a hysterical quest for novelty on the other. It stands between the postures of presumption and despair.

Perhaps we can understand the point better if we clarify what an eschatological consciousness does not mean. Fundamentally it is opposed to any "ideology," any closure to reality's wholeness, any conversion of something partial into something absolute. We can imagine at least three forms of ideology. Ideologies of "immanence" absolutize finite aspects of our experiential world—for example, nationalism, rationalism, materialism, etc. Ideologies of "absolutism" idolize one's grasp of the absolute and so rob the relative and finite of their value—for example, supernaturalism, quietism, chiliasm, etc. Finally, ideologies of "transcendence" simply absolutize the empty and formal process of surmounting the first two forms of ideology, so that the present becomes devalued by relativism and the transcendent future is simply an empty void allowing anything and everything. This last ideology again suggests the value of actually attempting to sketch a forward-looking draft of eschatology. Only in that way can there be a real norm protecting us against relativism or a feverish revolutionary attitude. This may well be one of Rahner's main contributions to political theology, which often tends to use the concept of the "future" in an empty and formal way.

The positive side of the eschatological attitude, the actual utopian planning in which the Church and the individual should engage, carries us beyond the scope of this essay and into the realms of ethics, ecclesiology, and practical theology. For the individual, utopian planning requires a capacity to discern the ever new will of God in the unique here and now. For the Church itself, Rahner has offered proposals for a new practical theology concerned with utopian planning and has even sketched a draft of his own in *The Shape of the Church to Come*. Here his balance is worth highlighting. Some theologians have seen in the Church's eschatological faith primarily a summons to de-idolize the finite and temporal, including the structures of the Church itself. This has come to be known as the "eschatological reserve," and its basic stance is to recognize that all is provisional. Now this tactic is entirely appropriate, particularly in highly industrialized and developed countries, where materialism is all too common. However, in the so-called third world this attitude may foster indifference and inactivity, a kind of subtle acceptance of a problematic *status quo*. A third-world situation more clearly calls for sagacious commitment to utopian planning and attempted change. Both tactics—that of reserve and that of planned intervention—are legitimate postures flowing from the Church's eschatological faith. If we can grasp this, we are on the way to comprehending what is meant by the mutual relationship between the absolute future and the utopian future. To decide prayerfully which tactic to adopt rests for individuals on their capacity for discernment and for the Church as a critic of itself and society on its function of pastoral discernment aided by the science of practical theology.

Questions for Discussion

As we have repeatedly seen, eschatology flows from an extrapolation into the mode of fulfillment of what we already experience and know as Christians. Of necessity, such thinking is highly theoretical, and for that reason we should link our new formulations of eschatology with those of the great tradition, maintaining a kind of constant critique of ourselves. This theoretical factor is the central nerve in Rahner's entire theory and the aspect of his reflections most open to further development. Here we see the importance of reading Rahner's eschatological theories in the light of his anthropology and Christology. From these foundations we can attempt a forward-looking draft; through them we can protect ourselves from the charge of mere subjectivism. But it would be worth exploring what other eschatological drafts might flow from different views of anthropology and Christology. For example, what might eschatologies based on an evolutionary, or process, or an American pragmatically oriented anthropology and Christology entail? How might they differ from the one presented here? How could each illuminate the other?

Furthermore, insofar as a sound eschatology rests on a sound understanding of our present Christian existence, isn't there a richer source for our eschatology than we often realize in the writings of the saints and mystics? Presumably they have lived and grasped Christian experience at its depths. In a true sense they reveal to us what we can be. And many of the key mystical themes surface in eschatology: the ineradicable mystery of God, even in eternity; the beatific vision as a trinitarian relationship and indwelling in the believer; final union with God as union also with all creation; the enduring presence of Jesus' glorified humanity, even in eternity; eternity as bliss, love, and ecstasy, a matter of intuitive rather than conceptual knowing, etc.

Moving to our actual draft of the future, the key issue to negotiate is eternity. We recall: Eternity is not time's prolongation or continuing succession, but time's conquering. Our experiences of conquering time, such as love's unconditionedness and the finality of our decisions, are transposed into the terms of their fulfillment: Eternity is absolute finality, absolute conquering of time. Eternity must be understood to some extent in terms of a mystical ecstasy. This eternal finality toward which all creation tends enables us to grant a radical seriousness to our world here and now, the place in which our actions and decisions achieve their radical finality, particularly at death, the limit moment of our temporality. But is this notion of eternity the only one consistent with what we know of Christian existence now? Must our "pretastes" of eternity be conceived as experiences of finality, as Rahner maintains, or might they not tend toward a kind of limit in the final achievement of selfhood, of integration and unification? If eternity were not so much "finality" as a limit toward which we tend, then it could be conceived in more processive and dynamic terms. To understand eternity in continuous terms, however, would require exploring whether God is static or dynamic. It would also bring us back to anthropology, to the question whether human beings remain dynamic even in eternity. Would this devalue life before death, since that life would always remain open to revision, or would it rather grant life before death only a relative importance?

Finally, I suspect we all need to be reminded that our belief in the absolute future should generate historical utopias. Still more we need to reflect on what this means for our daily living. A combination of eschatology and utopia has in fact always existed in Christianity. Rahner's great contribution here is in refusing to reduce eschatology to utopian thinking, in stressing their mutuality and distinctiveness, and in emphasizing the legitimacy of the varied postures of utopian commitment. You yourself may wish to consider what forms of utopian imagination are consistent with eschatological faith. The chiliastic or ideological tendency may be ruled out, but can we be more precise about forms of utopia consistent with our faith? The monastic tendency with its modern variants (interest in contemplation, mysticism, the oriental religions) might be a form of utopianism highlighting the eschatological reserve. Might not some of the currents stemming from political and liberation theology provide us with a new form of utopian commitment and secular planning? This is certainly an area where further reflection is called for, and Rahner's clarification of the issues clearly outlines the framework in which such thought can fruitfully go forward.

SUGGESTIONS FOR FURTHER READING

The article on "Eschatology" in *Sacramentum Mundi* 2, pp. 242–46, is rather technical and condensed. It contains important observations on why eschatology needs to be reinterpreted, on Rahner's differences from Bultmann and Dodd, and on some questions Rahner has not yet fully treated (viz., the "cosmic powers," the persistence of evil, etc.).

"The Hermeneutics of Eschatological Assertions," *Theological Investigations* 4, pp. 323–46, is Rahner's most detailed treatment of how to interpret eschatological statements; perhaps his most important contribution to the field.

Rahner's best–known discussion of death is found in *On the Theology of Death*. Here he discusses the death of Jesus and of Christians and also propounds his theory of how Jesus through his death enters into a new and cosmic relationship with the world.

"The Eternal Significance of the Humanity of Jesus for Our Relationship with God," *Theological Investigations* 3, pp. 35–46, is a fundamental article which is suggestive for the question whether Jesus' humanity remains the salvific means of God's presence even in eternity.

"The Question of the Future," *Theological Investigations* 10, pp. 181–201, is the best overview of Rahner's views on the eschatological attitude, the relationship between eschatology and utopian planning, and the different kinds of utopia.

12

An Ethics of Faith

JAMES F. BRESNAHAN

Our fundamental option of response to God's self-gift is expressed in concrete historical acts. Whether those acts can be considered good or bad relates to how they fulfill the basic moral ideal: love of God and love of neighbor. This essay suggests how traditional Catholic natural-law thinking may be revised and renewed by Rahner's theology; it also examines the complementarity of the essential and the existential dimensions of ethics.

KARL Rahner's impact on systematic theology is widely acknowledged, but he has only begun to influence the field of ethics. Ethicians analyze human action to determine when it is to be called good and when evil; above all, they try to develop arguments to explain and support their analysis. Particularly if they work within religious traditions as Christian ethicians (or moral theologians) they intend their work to have practical consequences in the lives of their readers. This practical orientation leads them to be preoccupied with problem areas in human living. How can sexual activity be used or abused? Can medical technology be made to serve rather than suppress human interests? Will economic and political power be employed selfishly for a few or altruistically for the increasing millions of deprived persons populating our planet? Rahner seldom touches directly on these staple topics of ethics, and when he does take up one or another of them, he hesitates to infringe on the professional ethician's territory. He limits his contribution to deeper issues which lie behind all that ethicians do but which they frequently do not choose to explain. Rahner elaborates a theory of the human person and of freedom.

In my view, Rahner's thought on freedom and the person will increasingly change the way ethicians, especially Roman Catholic ethicians, develop their descriptions of the moral life and the guidelines for decision and action based on such descriptions. Let me try to highlight the most important elements in Rahner's thought that may reorient natural-law thinking and perhaps make it more adequate to the contemporary challenge faced by ethics. Before doing that, however, we ought to have clearly in mind what this challenge to ethics really involves for all of us.

Challenge to Ethics: The New Moral Perplexity

Rahner himself speaks over and over again of the new way people today experience their freedom. This experience gave rise to Karl Marx's analysis of work and alienation and to Sigmund Freud's theories of the inner structure of personality lying below the level of consciousness. In philosophy, early glimmerings of the experience caused Immanuel Kant to turn systematic reflection on human knowledge away from human beings as objects of observation toward a new concern for understanding the structures of conscious thought and choice within the subject. Among Catholic thinkers, this new experience of freedom led the Belgian Jesuit, Joseph Maréchal, to initiate a style of thought in which Rahner shares. Maréchal sought to recast the more objectively oriented philosophy of Thomas Aquinas in the light of Kant's turn to the subject. He inspired his fellow Belgian Jesuit, Gérard Gilleman, to make an early but important sketch of Aquinas's ethics reshaped through attention to the contents of self-awareness in action. The result was Gilleman's *The Primacy of Charity in Moral Theology*. Rahner's own contribution to ethics derives from this new understanding of freedom and seeks to express it for the Church today.

Rahner points out repeatedly that our era is the first to realize that it has the power to "build the earth," as Teilhard de Chardin would say, or destroy it. The most inspiring and yet also appalling aspect of this power is that it can build or destroy not merely a stage set on which we act out our lives but the very world of which we ourselves are part. Increasingly it will be our own decisions that determine the shape of the world in the future. Our awareness of this power makes us aware of moral dilemma on an unprecedented scale. Whenever we attempt to do good, we seem inevitably to do evil as well, and sometimes prodigious evil.

Examples are ready to hand. Can we make use of atomic power in any truly peaceful way? But can we sustain human civilization without using it? Can we continue to develop and employ the myriad forms of modern technology without consuming the resources of the earth, especially fossil fuels, that only a few decades ago seemed inexhaustible? And can we use technology without plunging third-world populations into a misery made worse by rising expectations? On the other hand, can we preserve humanity without this technology, indeed without increased efforts to make the scientific advances from which it flows? These kinds of moral dilemma, social in nature, have their impact on every aspect of our individual human lives as well. Can we sustain intimacy in family life and friendships and still use the systematic planning and bureaucratization of life that has been common in our recent culture? That planning, it seems, has given us leisure and energy to make intimacy our conscious goal and yet it also threatens intimacy itself.

This experience of our freedom as power which produces moral dilemma has precipitated a crisis in contemporary ethics. Ethical reflection is supposed to help us understand and solve moral dilemmas. Yet today ethics, including natural-law thinking in ethics, does not seem able to produce readily understandable, or at least widely acceptable, solutions to the dilemmas we face. It is not that we know what we ought to do about these perplexities but haven't the heart or energy to take on the tasks. No one can prove that our era of history is more morally debased than any previous era. In spite of the Holocaust, in spite of the Gulag archipelago, in spite of the frantic use of free-fire zones and massive carpet bombing in Vietnam, we do have evidence of a widespread and active concern among many people today to feed the hungry of the world, to succor those who are oppressed, to humanize the lot of all who are now hopeless. Moral sensitivity may even have increased by comparison with past ages. But we do not seem able to employ our power in ways that we agree may be more effective than destructive in the long run. The challenge comes directly from our experience of our own freedom in action.

Natural-Law Ethics

Rahner's contribution to ethics is made primarily within the Catholic natural-law tradition. Interestingly, James Gustafson has argued in *Protestant and Roman Catholic Ethics: Prospects for Rapprochement* that natural-law thought is also likely to have increasing influence on Protestant ethics. The natural-law idea itself has a long history. It originated in Greek and Roman Stoic philosophy. It was adopted and adapted by medieval Christian theologians to explain the rational order of moral life, individual and social. It was further developed for that purpose by later Catholic theologians and secular philosophers. At the heart of this tradition is the conviction that the moral ideal and moral obligation are rooted in being, in the structures of being called human nature. So the central claim of natural law is that morality can be discussed reasonably and explained at least in part by investigating that nature.

It is a common conviction for all exponents of natural law that moral obligations are not arbitrarily imposed from outside human life—whether by some divine command or by the arbitrary preference of human beings autonomously opting for one or another set of values. The positive implication of this view is that the natural structures built into human being reflect the wisdom of their source; thus, if human action seeks reasonably to conform itself to these structures, it will be humanly successful (as wisely intended by the creator) and so morally good. When human action arbitrarily contradicts these structures of human being, it is destructive of humankind and the world, and so morally evil.

For the natural-law thinker, therefore, the structures of nature reveal obligation; every "is" is pregnant with an "ought." The natural-law tradition has always expressed the conviction that ethical reflection can and must locate basic, immutable dimensions of human being; by doing so, it can provide reasonable guidelines for morally good action. With all of this Karl Rahner continues to be in agreement. He endorses the continued development of what he calls "essential" ethics, that is, an analysis of the essence or nature of the human person in order to develop guidelines that categorize some acts as good, or at least permitted, and other acts as evil.

Nonetheless, Rahner has criticized premodern forms of natural-law thinking for being too willing to discuss human action in the same terms it used for the action of other, non-human beings in the world. This kind of thinking tended to be excessively cosmos-centered and insufficiently oriented toward the uniqueness of human being and human action. Despite its emphasis on freedom of choice, the older view failed to focus adequate attention on the human person. Thus it failed also to recognize the distinctively creative power of human freedom when it takes the form of love and its distinctively destructive power when it is a refusal to love. The person was not understood enough as creative of human history. Nature was treated as if it were static and ahistorical; human action encompassed and constrained by nature was considered merely as the creaturely execution of a divinely preformed destiny. In no real sense did human action share in the divine creative action. The accent was on the destructive power of acts that violate the norm of nature. In no real sense was freedom a risk-taking venture participating in God's own risk of creating a world of persons who are able to respond to God and who respond not merely by producing good or evil acts but by making themselves good or evil.

Rahner's Revised Natural Law

What Rahner asks of natural law is that it accept a new portrait of the person and freedom, which brings with it a new orientation in method and an enlarged conception of the human nature which is to be analyzed.

First, with regard to method, Rahner urges that the overly objectivistic conception of human beings yield to a reflective interpretation of the person's own experience of structured freedom. The structures of nature are to be found not primarily by empirical observation but by looking *within* the immediacy of conscious self-experience. Anne Carr and William Dych have already discussed the importance of this shift to experience throughout Rahner's theology. It is especially important in ethics. This starting point in reflection on experience means that henceforth the search for nature, the structures which provide human freedom with its moral ideal and its sense of obligation, will begin by looking within the human person's immediate experience of the self acting morally, within subjectivity. There the core of nature is to be found, the most basic structure of the being of the person which, because it grounds freedom itself, must not be violated. Empirical observation of human beings in action will still be used, but subordinate to this reflection and its findings.

Rahner clearly displays this new point of departure for ethics throughout the early chapters of *Foundations of Christian Faith,* even though his emphasis there is on the basic imperative of human experience, the call to respond in faith to Mystery. This experience of freedom and responsibility can properly be called moral experience or, with Rahner himself, global moral instinct—the moral experience of the self in action on which ethics reflects and which it interprets in order to develop a systematic, conceptual theory of good and evil.

In *Foundations* Rahner suggests how this moral experience can be a point of departure for understanding the basic moral ideal and obligation: human response to the self-offer of God which is at the heart of conscious personal existence. As he argues there also, the human person experiences this basic moral ideal as one that must be worked out through acts in space and time, acts that are always ambiguously related to the consciousness of responsibility, because the person is conscious not only of being free but also of being determined by physical, psychological and social influences. These determinisms are recognized from within experience itself as being among the structures which encompass freedom: nature in the older sense.

Description of Rahner's methodology already indicates the second feature of a natural law which accepts his portrait of the person and freedom. Natural law ethicians must enlarge their conception of what is included within nature. It is the nature of a *person* that must be analyzed. One must first analyze the grounding structure of the person as such that makes freedom itself possible; then, in this light, one must also discover and interpret the structures of human nature which encompass that freedom, limit and channel its exercise. The task of essential ethics, analysis of the moral quality of acts, must now be pursued with explicit attention to the unique character of the freedom which operates within the structures surrounding it. Natural-law ethicians are now to deal explicitly with what grounds and empowers as well as limits the unique activity of the person in freedom.

Rahner sees the basic structure which grounds freedom in the human person as a dynamic drive toward incomprehensible Holy Mystery. He argues, in detail that need not be repeated here, that this structure of being makes the actual performance of self-conscious and objective thinking and acting possible. Here one discovers what he means by freedom. In its most basic sense, discovered at the heart of personal activity, freedom means responsibility for shaping one's own self and striving to do so. Freedom is a capacity to do this in accordance with the other structures of nature or to refuse to do so. But freedom is capacity for moral action first at the level of that grounding structure of the person, then at the level of the structures which encompass, limit, and channel freedom. We begin to see that an enlarged meaning of nature and a reflective methodology sharply accentuate the conscious and self-disposing character of every choice that one makes within the structures encompassing freedom (nature in its older, more restricted sense).

When natural-law thinking absorbs this new accent on freedom and its grounding structure, it must pursue the task of essential ethics differently than before. Ethicians will continue to look for what is unchangeable in nature, a core nature that limits and channels the person's freedom so that acts which have the effect of trying to change this core nature will be declared immoral. But ethicians will also have to acknowledge the possibility that some dimensions of what has been considered in the past to be unchangeable nature do not pertain to this core, are peripheral structures in the being of the person. The particular form they have taken in the past might be changed by freedom without harm to what remains unchangeable. Nature cannot be thought of simply as ready-made and wholly immutable; at least what many ethicians in the past have designated as unchangeable cannot be so regarded.

This shift in expectations really depends for its full development on whether or not Rahner's portrait of the person is accepted, especially in its emphasis on the truly creative potential of human freedom. For if freedom can be creative in any true sense, then it can really bring into being something new in the world, something new even in what has previously been thought to be unchangeable nature. In the next section I will examine how Rahner explains the creativity of freedom. But one of his examples may clarify our point here.

In discussing the contemporary controversy among Roman Catholics over contraception, Rahner has considered the meaning of authority and obedience vis-à-vis dissent from Pope Paul VI's reiteration of the traditional prohibition in *Humanae Vitae*. As is his custom, he avoids entering directly into an ethical argument for or against contraception. But he does note as a preliminary point that those who dissent from the prohibition display intrinsic plausibility when they take the position that human freedom can be creative, can even change the physical structure of the sexual act. This contradicts the assumption of at least some of the defenders of the prohibition. Physical structure as observed is not necessarily an immutable boundary which human freedom can attempt to change only at the risk of an evil act. One must show, of course, that changing this physical structure would maintain or enlarge the scope for the freedom of the person to express itself creatively. And Rahner notes that at least some of the dissenters have made arguments in that direction.

At this point, we have seen briefly how Rahner's new methodology and emphasis on the potentially creative character of human freedom helps natural-law ethics to rethink nature as the grounding structure of the free person. In effect, Rahner has moved natural-law thinking into history. We cannot attempt a complete account of how this historically conscious thought may develop in the future. But let me sketch the principal features that a renewed natural law may display on the basis of Rahner's reflections on the person and freedom.

The Basic Moral Ideal: One Love for God and Neighbor

Looking more closely at Rahner's portrait of the person, we will be struck by his emphasis on love. This category sums up the true meaning of human freedom and the true destiny of the human person. All of us must exercise freedom by striving both to love God and to love our human neighbor. The distinctiveness of this norm as it emerges from Rahner's reflections is its emphasis on the primordial unity of the one, centered human self. This unity is the element within moral experience that holds the forefront of attention. It is a complex unity, but its different elements are intimately intertwined in the experience of the centered personal self; they constantly interact with one another and mutually condition one another. The basic moral ideal and obligation, love of God and love of neighbor, is grounded not in two separated loves, insulated from one another, but in a unified reality, one loving expression of the one freedom of the one human person. The moral ideal and obligation which emerges from Rahner's interpretation of moral experience has two facets that can be explained and understood only so long as this unity is accentuated.

First, then, we must examine the ideal and obligation of love at its most basic level in the person. We have seen that the moral experience of the self engaged in moral striving may be called global moral instinct. Rahner qualifies that phrase by calling it a global moral instinct of reason. Moral striving can be interpreted by reason, though always in an incomplete way and with language derived from experience of objects outside the self. Rahner also insists that this ethical interpretation of global moral instinct is made even more difficult by the fact that reason and freedom always mutually condition one another. A person's commitment and involvement in love is always a project underway that conditions reason; we know what we want to know by reason of our love. Ethics depends on its own subject matter, love in action, for the accuracy and validity of its reasoned theorizing. And if the ethician's involvement is not all it should be, that will affect adversely the ethical theory he or she produces. Given these qualifications, however, we can follow Rahner's interpretation of the basic moral ideal and obligation at its most basic level: love is first of all loving fundamental option, the disposal of self in response to incomprehensible Holy Mystery.

Fundamental option, as we saw in chapter four, is Rahner's term for the exercise of freedom in its most basic sense as the responsible shaping of one's very self. Fundamental option must be distinguished, therefore, from its product and expression, freedom of choice, which is more accessible to our reflection because freedom of choice produces the moral acts of which we are conscious. Fundamental option is a dimension of the self in action as immediately aware of self; it is accessible to systematic reflection only in and through the acts which it produces through freedom of choice. Yet, all acts produced by free choice have moral significance only insofar as they are embodiments of a fundamental option. Acts produced by free choice are morally good only insofar as they are fitting expressions of fundamental option as love. Thus, in order to grasp the original meaning of love as the moral ideal, we must distinguish loving fundamental option from the acts in which it is expressed and embodied. What are the primary characteristics of this option?

For Rahner, love at the level of fundamental self-disposing freedom is first of all a personal response to a personal Being. Love is primordially the answer to a call. The human self is called to surrender itself into incomprehensible Holy Mystery by reason of the grounding structure of freedom itself, the central structure in the nature of the person. The dynamic outreach toward incomprehensible Holy Mystery which enables all conscious knowing and free decision must be interpreted as an inner word addressed to the self by the Mystery from which the self originates. The self finds itself drawn toward a Holy Mystery from which it must originally have come.

Rahner emphasizes two characteristics of this innermost summons empowering all self-awareness and self-disposing response. First, it is a created word to the human self expressing the hidden creative intent of Mystery. The "come" contains a "let be," Holy Mystery's self-sharing gift of being. Second, this creative word expresses the inner reality of Holy Mystery as personal, as what is most intimate and incommunicable in Being. The "come" also contains, therefore, a demand that the

human person come to know what is intimate and incommunicable in itself by responding in kind, by imaging in the self this creative "let be,"
by accepting the gift of being co-creative of itself with Holy Mystery.

The answer to this call takes place first of all at the level of fundamental option. The answer is love when it is a "yes" to the very
structure of the person, to the innermost grounding of freedom itself, to
the nature of person as such. The self co-creates itself with Holy Mystery. The person surrenders self to the out-reaching dynamism at the
heart of personal Being. The self says a personal "yes" of love by
giving over the whole of one's heart and being to Holy Mystery; in this
way the self becomes fully the image of the creating Holy Mystery.

At this point we can grasp more clearly why Rahner has accented the
creative potential of freedom taking the form of love and why he makes
this the primary subject matter of a revised natural-law ethics. Loving
human freedom at the level of fundamental option participates personally in the divine creative action, shapes a self as something truly
new and unique in all the world, yet does so in at least implicit dialogue
with the Holy Mystery. We see now more clearly why Rahner emphasizes the risk of human freedom. All that has been said about loving
fundamental option necessarily implies the real possibility that the self
will utter a "no," will refuse the deepest personal relationship, will
negate the self's very ground of freedom. Rahner always asserts, however, that this love-refusing and self-destructive "no" is necessarily less
powerful than a love-affirming and self-co-creative "yes." The tragedy
of a human person's self-depersonalization at this level of fundamental
option cannot overcome the creative power of Holy Mystery at work in
the world through the hearts of all who answer "yes."

How does this interpretation of love at the level of fundamental option relate to ordinary ethical reflection? Rahner emphasizes from the
beginning that the fundamental option of our love must realize itself in
the conditions of bodiliness, sharing the world of space and time with
other human beings. Different kinds of acts must be examined to determine whether or not they truly express a loving, co-creative "let be."
Essential ethics does this, as in the past, by analyzing the structures of
bodiliness and sociality (nature in the older and narrower sense) and
asking how they limit and channel the sharing of creative love with
other human beings. But Rahner's understanding of loving fundamental
option reminds such ethical reflection to recognize that the creative experiment of freedom may lead to discovering possibilities for change in

what had been considered immutable structures of nature. These structures are meant to enable our loving fundamental option to be effectively creative; they channel and limit for that reason. And so they are unchangeable in any particular form only insofar as they are necessary to sustain the creative thrust of love.

But there is another task for a revised natural law that accepts Rahner's understanding of the basic moral ideal, the love of God and of neighbor in unity. Rahner spoke of this task in his early writings as "existential ethics," deliberately contrasting it with essential ethics. An essential ethics can only deal with the moral quality of acts in the abstract, as related to anyone's freedom. Can contraceptive sexual intercourse, for example, or the use of economic power by paying wages, be a fitting expression of loving fundamental option? Existential ethics, as Rahner originally explained it, has the additional task of showing how the fundamental option of love is related to a particular concrete choice by an individual or a group acting in concert. How does someone come to choose a certain life work or profession, for example, or how do two people determine that they should marry each other, and not anyone else?

An existential ethics cannot explore the unique appropriateness of the *content* of a particular act for a given person. That would move ethical reflection back into its essential function, since the content of the act can only be discussed in abstraction from the unique individual's effort to love. But existential ethics can explore how the individual or group comes to sense the appropriateness of a particular act within its conscious moral experience or global moral instinct. We can try to discern and explain the signs that an act is appropriate, signs that an individual or group may use to resolve doubts and come to a decision.

Rahner's call for an existential ethics to complement essential ethics really focuses the attention of revised natural law on a dimension of moral experience that is discussed throughout the early chapters of *Foundations*. In experiencing freedom and responsibility we also experience their limits; we recognize the influence of psycho-physical and social determinisms that not only limit and channel the expression of loving fundamental option, but may also prevent it. A person or a group of persons, even though striving to love, may act in a way that really does not embody loving fundamental option at all. Accordingly, the existential dimension of ethics must also seek to recognize the signs of disunity between love of God and what ought to be its expression in

love of neighbor. While Rahner himself has not developed these implications fully, I think they can be called the exploratory task of existential ethics and that they will lead to a renewal of ethical reflection in its
essential moment.

For now, however, let us turn to consider in a final section how Rahner's analysis of free personhood and its basic moral ideal, love of God
and love of neighbor in unity, fit within an explicitly theological context. How does a renewed natural-law ethics, focusing on moral experience in its complex unity, relate to a faith that accepts the Word of God
in history? How can we reflect on moral experience as an experience of
the moral exigencies of faith in Jesus Christ?

Jesus Christ as the Source of the Basic Moral Ideal

Rahner's contribution to a revised natural-law ethics, as it has been
discussed to this point, could be called a philosophical one. It has dealt
with human reflection on moral experience, on global moral instinct,
which relies on reason. But from Rahner's perspective, this interpretation of moral experience is also a reflection on the experience of faith,
on global moral instinct which relies on reason *and* faith. Indeed he
argues that human reflection on moral experience is demanded by faith,
authorized by the Word of God addressed to a personal partner in dialogue. What is apparently "only" philosophy finds its true home within
theology.

Briefly, this may be expressed as follows: Rahner's portrait of the
human person and freedom finds its fullest expression in Jesus Christ, at
least for the explicit Christian believer. For all who believe in Christ,
the basic moral ideal of love of God and love of neighbor in unity finds
both its exemplification and its historical origin in Jesus Christ, the one
who lives out his mortal life in love, who gives it up for his friends, and
who through being raised from the dead confirms the absolute, final validity of the basic moral ideal and obligation.

It is relatively easy to show that Jesus Christ *exemplifies* the basic
moral ideal and obligation for the Christian. Christ is the appearance
within human history of a person who sums up the moral ideal which
believers also recognize by reflection on their own moral experience. By
reference to Christ and the historical efforts of Christians to live as
Christ did, ethical reflection on moral experience can identify with
greater accuracy what love really implies. The concrete character of the
risk and venture of freedom becomes clearer. In Jesus Christ we have

new insight into the situation of human malice and the need for love to be lived out under contradiction and even to self-surrender in death. Above all, Christ makes clear the real power of human love to triumph through the bearing of the cross.

This means that a revised natural law functioning as an explicitly theological ethics should pursue essential and existential ethics with all the richness of meaning that reference to scripture and the tradition of Church life in Christ make possible. And, explicit Christian faith will urge this ethics to take critical account of any deficiencies in love within moral experience which tend to diminish the accuracy and adequacy with which moral experience is interpreted. The stance of faith urges ethics to be critical, to be an ethics grounded in faith, exploring love by seeking continual conversion both in heart and mind.

It is more difficult to show that Jesus Christ is the *source and origin* of the basic moral ideal and obligation discovered within moral experience. This demands a theory of freedom under grace, a theory of grace as the grace of Christ, and above all an understanding of grace as a dimension of immediate self-consciousness. Rahner's theory of the supernatural existential, which chapter five has discussed, supplies this need. If all humanity can be understood as moving towards the full truth about itself in Christ, then the consciousness of freedom and of the basic moral ideal is part of that movement in the grace of Christ.

But the most difficult issue for a revised natural-law ethics functioning within faith is to determine whether Jesus Christ is the exemplar and origin of the basic moral ideal and obligation for *all* human beings, even those who have not known Christ in a way that leads them to accept him with explicit faith. The ideal of natural law has always been to make moral argument in a way that is meaningful to and makes claims upon all human beings. Does attachment to the Jesus Christ of history compromise that? Rahner's theories of the supernatural existential and of faith that can be anonymously Christian suggest the answer. Again, these have been discussed in earlier chapters. I will note only their implication for ethics.

These theological theories, based on God's universal salvific will for all human beings and its focus for all in Jesus Christ, propose that every human person who reaches awareness of the basic moral ideal of love knows Christ, the exemplar of this ideal, even if not by name. Any human person who is in fact living out this moral ideal at the level of fundamental option, however inadequately the person may express this basic love in acts, is actually empowered to do so by grace that is grace of Christ, shaping the person in the likeness of Jesus. Consequently, an explicitly Christian revised natural-law ethics can pursue its essential and existential tasks with a radical openness to the moral experience of non-Christians and to their versions of ethics. Christ as embodiment and source of the moral ideal will be found there, though in forms which need further interpretation. Indeed, Christ may be found in ways that historical Christian ethics in the West has neglected. For instance, Gandhi's non-violent search for truth or Hinduism's profound reverence for all living things can summon explicitly Christian ethics to renewed reflection on how love can be creative in action.

At the same time, the mission of Christian natural law will be what Rahner claims every Christian mission should be. It will be an effort in all humility to announce the full meaning of what non-Christians already aspire to in their moral life and, if they are truly persons of good will, what they are already achieving—love of God and love of neighbor in unity, fashioned in the likeness of Christ.

To that end, a revised natural-law ethics must be an ethics grounded in faith, exploring love, but above all living in hope. Even as a rigorously reflective philosophical-theological discipline, this ethics can function in hope if its practitioners really accept the capacity of human freedom as love rooted in the grace of Christ to accomplish infinitely more than can be done by human malice. A Christian natural law taking inspiration from Rahner should regard itself as the bearer of good news, news about freedom as love, glad tidings about the venture of human freedom. The Christian optimism of this ethics will finally dominate its sober, sometimes soberly pessimistic, realism about the prophetic and difficult demands that love makes on human freedom. Love under grace can accomplish its creative task if it perseveres in being a self-surrender even in death into incomprehensible Mystery. This ethics should reflect the confidence of St. Paul whose preoccupation was with him who "being rich, became poor for our sakes, that by his poverty we might be made rich" (2 Corinthians 8:9).

QUESTIONS FOR DISCUSSION AND SUGGESTIONS FOR FURTHER READING

After reading this introduction to Rahner's ethical thought, one might naturally ask whether our moral perplexity today is really a question of moral dilemma or whether it is only a failure of nerve in people who know well enough what they should be doing but just do not do it. Furthermore, is a theory of the human person and freedom really necessary in order to discuss the moral quality of our acts? Could ethics not be done simply as a search for logical consistency in one's moral arguments about different kinds of acts? Stimulus for this discussion may be found in Rahner's collection of basic essays, *Meditations on Freedom and the Spirit,* which shows from several perspectives the connection between Rahner's theological anthropology and his ethics.

One might also ask whether natural-law thinking can really transcend its preoccupation with the ready-made structures that encompass human freedom. Can it realistically permit Rahner's accent on the creative potential of freedom as love to reshape traditionally received moral norms? Here you might profitably consult again some of the readings suggested at the end of chapters two and four. "The Experiment with Man," *Theological Investigations* 9, pp. 206–24, is an important essay concerned with humanity's capacity to plan and shape its own reality; it treats the relation between freedom and the "nature" or "essence" of the human. On a more explicitly Catholic issue, Rahner's essay "On the Encyclical 'Humanae Vitae'," *Theological Investigations* 11, pp. 263–87, offers a valuable discussion of the 1967 Doctrinal Letter of the German bishops, and then asks how individual Christians may consider themselves justified in conscience when they deviate from the papal teaching; it also assesses the significance of actual practice among Catholics since publication of the encyclical.

This chapter sees Rahner proposing the unitary love of God and neighbor as the basic moral ideal. How can this ideal escape being so subjective that it separates the fundamental option of love from its embodiment in acts of free choice, thus turning ethical reflection away from serious concern with good and evil acts? "Reflections on the Unity of the Love of Neighbor and the Love of God," *Theological Investigations* 6, pp. 231–49, is Rahner's classical essay on the theological aspects of this question.

Can Jesus Christ really be the origin and embodiment of the basic moral ideal for Christians? What of those who have never heard of Christ, or who have heard of him only in ways that seem to make him incredible? This far-reaching question suggests a review of the topics treated in chapters six and seven on Christology, together with the readings indicated there.

Finally, it would be important to consider how Christians as a community relate to ethical discussion and political planning in society at large. Among several important essays Rahner has written on this subject, "Church and World" in *Sacramentum Mundi* 1 has already been recommended at the end of chapter nine. Another would be "The Function of the Church as a Critic of Society," *Theological Investigations* 12, pp. 229–49, which argues the need for the Church not only to be self-critical but also to serve as a critic of society, a function which should be exercised by Christians in general as well as by the official Church.

Basic Bibliography

Collected Works of Karl Rahner

Theological Investigations 1: *God, Christ, Mary and Grace*. London: Darton, Longman & Todd, 1961; New York: Seabury Press, 1974.

Theological Investigations 2: *Man in the Church*. London: Darton, Longman & Todd, 1963; New York: Seabury Press, 1975.

Theological Investigations 3: *The Theology of the Spiritual Life*. London: Darton, Longman & Todd, 1967; New York: Seabury Press, 1974.

Theological Investigations 4: *More Recent Writings*. London: Darton, Longman & Todd, 1966; New York: Seabury Press, 1974.

Theological Investigations 5: *Later Writings*. London: Darton, Longman & Todd, 1966; New York: Seabury Press, 1975.

Theological Investigations 6: *Concerning Vatican Council II*. London: Darton, Longman & Todd, 1969; New York: Seabury Press, 1974.

Theological Investigations 7: *Further Theology of the Spiritual Life 1*. London: Darton, Longman & Todd, 1971; New York: Seabury Press, 1973.

Theological Investigations 8: *Further Theology of the Spiritual Life 2*. London: Darton, Longman & Todd, 1971; New York: Seabury Press, 1973.

Theological Investigations 9: *Writings of 1965–1967 1*. London: Darton, Longman & Todd, 1972; New York: Seabury Press, 1973.

Theological Investigations 10: *Writings of 1965–1967 2*. London: Darton, Longman & Todd, 1973; New York: Seabury Press, 1973.

Theological Investigations 11: *Confrontations 1*. London: Darton, Longman & Todd; New York: Seabury Press, 1974.

Theological Investigations 12: *Confrontations 2*. London: Darton, Longman & Todd; New York: Seabury Press, 1974.

Theological Investigations 13: *Theology, Anthropology, Christology*. London: Darton, Longman & Todd; New York: Seabury Press, 1975.

Theological Investigations 14: *Ecclesiology, Questions in the Church, The Church in the World*. London: Darton, Longman & Todd; New York: Seabury Press, 1976.

A Rahner Reader. Edited by Gerald A. McCool. New York: Seabury Press, 1975.

Books

The Christian Commitment. New York: Sheed & Ward, 1963.

The Church and the Sacraments. New York: Herder and Herder, 1963.

The Dynamic Element in the Church. New York: Herder and Herder, 1964.

Encounters with Silence. Westminster, Md.: Newman, 1960.

Meditations on Freedom and the Spirit. New York: Seabury Press, 1977.

On Prayer. New York: Paulist, 1968.

On the Theology of Death. New York: Seabury Press, 1973.

Spirit in the World. New York: Herder and Herder, 1968.

The Shape of the Church to Come. New York: Seabury Press, 1974.

The Trinity. New York: Herder and Herder, 1970.

Revelation and Tradition. With Joseph Ratzinger. New York: Herder and Herder, 1966.

Encyclopedias, Dictionaries

Theological Dictionary. By Karl Rahner and Herbert Vorgrimler. New York: Herder and Herder, 1965.

Sacramentum Mundi: An Encyclopedia of Theology. Edited by Karl Rahner et al. 6 vols. New York: Herder and Herder, 1968–1970.

Glossary

Absolute savior (absolute bearer of salvation): the person in whom we have the unambiguous pledge of God's irrevocable commitment to us in self-giving love. Because such a person embodies the offer and acceptance of God's self-gift in an absolutely decisive way and inaugurates the Kingdom, he must be one with God in a union which is unsurpassable and irrevocable. *See* pp. 111ff.

Absolute future, God as: in Rahnerian thought this refers to the *total* future yet to come, a future which is both humanity's achievement and God's gift. "God" should be understood inclusively: God-with-humanity-and-world. The redeeming creator will not be finally separated from the redeemed creation. *See* pp. 163ff.

Analogy: the way certain attributes (or predicates) are affirmed of a subject. Analogy involves a resemblance in the significations of a single word when it is used in reference to different subjects, but also allows for differences in meaning dictated by the various subjects. For example, the fundamental dependence of creatures upon God allows for God to be named—for attributes to be predicated of God—from the things which God creates, without at the same time suggesting that one knows how these predicates are realized in God, except to say that in him they are realized more profoundly. Analogical predication is thus distinguished from equivocal predication (where the meanings of the same word are totally different) and from univocal predication (where the meanings remain the same throughout successive predications). *See* pp. 42ff.; also *Foundations,* pp. 72f.

Anonymous Christianity: the theory that God's grace in Christ is offered to and affects all persons, even non-Christians; the saving love of God which Christians know explicitly reaches non-Christians in an anonymous, hidden, or implicit manner. Rahner argues that true faith can be implicit in loving action, enabled by the grace of Christ and shaped in the likeness of Christ, even though not explicitly aware of Christ as its origin and exemplar. *See* pp. 102f.

Anthropology: the study, derived from both philosophical and theological sources, of human experience, of the totality of the human person or of humanity in its most universal characteristics—as knowing, responsible, historical spirit. *See* pp. 18, 110.

Apocalyptic: from the Greek for "revealing/uncovering." Biblical scholars limit the word to refer to those Jewish and Christian writings which "reveal" God's plan for history's end. (Examples are Daniel 7–12 and parts of the Book of Revelation.) Rahner, quite differently, is referring to the mentality which claims to be in possession of an actual "preview" of the world's end in a literal, observable sense. *See* p. 157.

A posteriori: that dimension of human experience which designates its character as fundamentally historical, categorical, situated in the flow of events as they follow one upon the other in time. *See* p. 34.

A priori: that dimension of human experience which designates the prior givenness of human transcendence as knowledge and freedom open to the infinite of being, a transcendence which is mediated through the *a posteriori* or historicity. *See* p. 34.

Autonomy: the condition of belonging to oneself, of being and acting on one's own; for Rahner, human autonomy develops in direct proportion to our dependence on God. *See* pp. 46f., 56ff.

Beatific vision: traditional theological imagery (based on 1 Corinthians 13:12) for the final state of fulfillment of personal creatures through immediate relationship to God. *See* pp. 67, 160f.

Canon of Scripture: the authoritative list of which books comprise the Bible. The Church believes that Sacred Scripture is composed of Israel's inspired books, called the Old Testament by Christians, and a New Testament. Sacred Scripture is the Word of God, inspired by the Holy Spirit who is seen as the principal author of the Bible. *See* p. 132.

Categorical: pertaining to that dimension of human experience which is historically particular and concrete; the specific content of everyday knowledge and decision-making, as distinguished from its transcendental openness to the wholeness of being. *See* pp. 23f., 123.

Causality, divine: the way God influences the existence or nature of another. *See* pp. 56f.

Chalcedon, Council of: ecumenical council of the Church in 451 which responded to the Eutychian heresy and defined that Christ is one person in two natures, which are united unconfusedly, unchangeably, indivisibly, inseparably. *See* pp. 109f.

Chiliasm: historically, the belief that Christ in person will return and rule on earth during the millennium, or thousand-year period, before the world's end; more broadly, any feverish movement claiming to have arrived at the end or final view of things. *See* pp. 164, 167.

Christology from above (descending Christology): starting from a doctrine of the triune God, this approach shows the possibility and significance of God becoming human in time through the incarnation of the Word. *See* pp. 93ff.

Christology from below (ascending Christology): focusing upon the man Jesus of Nazareth, this approach traces the real history of Jesus and finds the fullest presence of God in human history in Jesus. *See* pp. 93ff.

Christology of saving history (historical or categorical Christology): the study of Jesus Christ that looks especially to the New Testament history of Jesus and retraces the path of the first disciples to faith in him as the Christ and Risen Lord. *See* pp. 93ff.

Christology, transcendental (a priori or essential Christology): this approach examines the experiences and necessary structures of the human person which enable that person to believe in and respond to Jesus as the Christ and Son of God. *See* pp. 12, 93f., 110ff.

Church: the collected gathering of persons who have been called to accept the Lordship of Jesus Christ, and who have responded in faith by receiving baptism. *See* pp. 121ff.

Church (usually not capitalized): within the worldwide Church a number of local eucharistic communities exist which are particular manifestations of Christianity. These are called "churches." The term is also used to designate the various confessional groupings that have come into being, especially since the major splinterings of the Church during the Great Schism between East and West and the Reformation. These traditions, such as the Catholic church, the Orthodox church, and the Anglican church, are marked with different ecclesiastical doctrines and structures. *See* pp. 121ff.

Church-relatedness: the indispensable churchly or ecclesial nature of Christianity, based on the interpersonal, social aspect of salvation in Christ; Church-relatedness is reflected in the ongoing historical and structured community of faith. *See* pp. 128f.

Concupiscence, inner and outer: concupiscence, for Rahner, is the inevitable tension between human nature and the human person, between what we have actually become through the exercise of freedom and what it is possible for us still to become. Also, ethically, it is the psycho-physical and social determinism of which the human person is aware in moral experience inasmuch as they can both impoverish and empower the responsible exercise of freedom as creative love. **Essential ethics** reflects on inner and outer concupiscence in order to understand what is changeable and what is unchangeable in human nature and, accordingly, to support freedom as creative love. *See* pp. 174f.

Conscience: traditional term for human beings' awareness of responsibility for their commitment and action, either in love (good conscience) or in refusal to love (bad conscience); conscience strives to judge what acts are appropriate to this commitment. *See* p. 172; also **Fundamental option** and **Global moral instinct.**

Creation: the act by which God brings into being all nondivine reality, or the reality so brought forth. *See* pp. 46f.

Creator: God as the one on whom the whole being of the world radically depends through all of time. Since God freely establishes and continues all finite beings and Himself constitutes the infinite difference between God and things, creation is not simply a beginning in time, but the utter dependence of all things upon God as upon their absolute and permanent source. *See* pp. 46f., 142.

Creatureliness: not simply the createdness of all things, but the fundamental structure of the human relationship with God in radical dependence. This dependence is experienced in every act of transcendence, whether knowledge or love, and in the consequent openness to revelation and the directions of grace. *See* pp. 45ff., 142.

Ecclesiology: that branch of Christian theology which provides reflective investigation (*logos*) about the Church (*ekklēsia*) and its connection with the central belief of Christianity, God's self-communication to the world in Jesus Christ. *See* p. 122.

Ephesus, Council of: ecumenical council of the Church in 431 which responded to Nestorianism and declared that Mary is truly *Theotokos,* the "God-bearer" (in Western terminology, the "Mother of God"). *See* p. 109.

Episcopate (or episcopacy): the collegial or collective body of bishops, as in a nation (episcopal conference) or in the Church universal (worldwide episcopate). In some churches, such as Roman Catholicism, bishops are understood to possess the fullness of the priesthood and to be principally responsible for exercising pastoral office. The term is related to the New Testament concept of *episkopē,* a unitive ministry of vigilance and supervision (cf. 1 Timothy 3:1). *See* p. 134.

Eschatology: from *eschatos* (furthest), this is the branch of theology treating of the last things, such as death and the afterlife. *See* pp. 153ff.

Ethics, essential: Reflection on the moral content of an act considered abstractly, as capable of being performed by anyone, to determine whether this act is fit to express love or not. **Natural law** carries out this reflection by asking whether the act violates the permanent basic structure of the person. *See* p. 172.

Ethics, existential: Rahner's term for reflection on the process by which an individual person or group of persons discerns the unique concrete form of loving action which is fitting for this person or group at a particular moment in their history. *See* p. 179.

Existential: a generic term applied to those characteristics or capacities of human existence which make it specifically human and distinguish it from other modes of existence. Self-awareness and freedom are examples of such existentials. *See* pp. 7, 27; also **Supernatural existential.**

Existentiell: an adjective referring to existence in the concrete and to the ways in which the structures of human existence are given concrete content. "Existentiell Christology," for example, is a person's lived faith relationship to Jesus Christ as distinguished from general concepts or doctrines about him. *See Foundations,* pp. 59, 305ff.

Experience, moral: a general term designating immediate self-awareness in which the conscious subject knows itself to be free and responsible, involved in continuing moral activity with a history of success and failure in expressing love. *See* pp. 173f., 176.

Experience, transcendental: the experience of transcendence, that is, the conscious process of reaching beyond all the individual elements of experience both singly and as a totality. It is a necessary and intrinsic dimension of all experience of the finite world. *See* pp. 5f., 19f., 23f.

Freedom: the transcendental openness of human nature toward the self-realization of the person by means of historical choice; like knowledge, freedom has both categorical and transcendental dimensions. *See* pp. 22f., 52ff., 174f.

Fundamental option: Rahner's term designating our most basic expression of ourselves in freedom. In this option we strive to shape ourselves with either a loving yes or a love-denying no to the Holy Mystery toward which we are drawn in all conscious free acting. *See* pp. 52f., 141, 177f.

Global moral instinct: Rahner's term for the moral experience on which ethics reflects systematically, seeking to interpret it, though always inadequately, in conceptually articulated ethical theory. *See* pp. 173f., 176.

Grace, created: a divine gift, other than God but above our natural powers, freely given to us by God. For Rahner, created grace—for example, any "actual grace"—is a consequence of God's self-communication. *See* pp. 66f.

Grace, uncreated: God's own life, as freely present in the recipient of divine self-communication; God's indwelling in human life. *See* pp. 66f.

Guilt: the condition of sinfulness, with emphasis on the subjective awareness of the sinfulness. *See* pp. 54ff.; also **Sin.**

Hierarchy of truths: a term employed by Vatican II to indicate that there exists a relative order of importance among the doctrines and creeds of the Church. *See* p. 122.

Historicity: the primordial character of human existence as temporal—set in the present, deriving from the past, and moving into the future; in a broader sense, historicity may refer to time, space, culture, and history as the context in which human persons are fundamentally situated. *See* pp. 27, 79.

History: while history is quickly defined as a record or chronicle of world events, modern philosophy tends to speak more of historicity, the place in the individual's life and personality where the world of time and geography, of economics and art meet an individual man or woman. The historicity of God's presence, of grace and revelation, is most clearly seen in God's becoming a limited individual person, Jesus, son of Mary and Joseph, born in Nazareth, circa 4 B.C. *See* p. 79.

Homoousion: technical term used by the Council of Nicaea (and in the Nicene Creed) to affirm that in the Godhead the Son is one in being with the Father. The original Greek term means "of one substance"; the Latin equivalent is "consubstantial." *See* p. 109.

Horizon: the co-presence in all human experience of the fullness of being —God—as the source and goal of human knowledge and freedom, the unlimited context of all limited human experience. *See* pp. 9, 20f.

Hypostatic union: the union in which a genuine human subject (body and soul, mind and will) belongs to the second person ("hypostasis") of the Trinity. The human nature or reality of Jesus does not exist simply in its own right, but precisely as the human reality in which the Word of God becomes man. The existence of the man Jesus, therefore, is rooted in and sustained by the very reality ("hypostasis") of the Word. *See* pp. 110, 114.

Incarnation: Christian belief that God became enfleshed and fully expressed himself humanly in Jesus of Nazareth. "The Word became flesh and lived among us" (John 1:14). *See* pp. 116ff.

Incomprehensibility (of God): the endless intelligibility of God which can never be exhaustively grasped (comprehended) by a finite intellect because of the everlasting disproportion between the infinite, self-communicating God and the finite, contemplating subject. Rahner emphasizes that the beatific vision—the destiny of grace—does not remove this incomprehensibility, but discloses it in all of its depths: God is seen and loved as inexhaustible. *See* pp. 39ff.

Inerrancy: a theological term used of Holy Scripture to assert that since the Bible is inspired it must be inerrant or without error. *See* p. 133.

Inspiration: a theological term rooted in an image found in 2 Timothy 3:16 related to the books of the Bible. Scripture is said to be in-spired (literally, "breathed into") by the Holy Spirit. The word asserts that God is the author of the Bible, even while using human writers as instrumental agents. The term is also used analogously of prophets, saints, ideas. *See* p. 133.

Institutional mediation: Christianity confesses Jesus Christ as the unique mediator between God and human beings. Because of the close sacramental presence of Christ in his Church, however, writers speak of sacraments, holy or ordained persons, and even institutions as "mediating" the grace of Christ. The term follows from the incarnational principle that since God became human in Jesus Christ, all earthly realities can be bearers of divine grace. The term also stresses the community dimension of salvation in Christ. *See* pp. 128f., 134.

Intelligibility: the self-disclosure of reality to intellectual awareness; the truth of being, which grounds the fact that things can be understood. Intelligibility is called final when the infinite being which is the context or horizon of all finite reality not only explains itself, but gives coherence and intelligibility to all finite things. *See* pp. 35ff.

Jus divinum: a term used to describe what is seen in the life of the Church as of divine right, divine law, divine institution, or divine ordination. Its counterpart is *jus humanum,* what is of human or churchly decision. For instance, that Israel's scriptures were meant to be complemented by additional New Testament writings is seen by Christianity as something *de jure divino.* The decision in the early Church to divide the pastoral office of ministry into bishops, priests, deacons, is often seen as being *de jure humano.* The difficulty of discerning what is *juris divini* and what is *juris humani* can sometimes be extremely difficult. *See* p. 126.

Knowledge, thematic: that mode of consciousness of the self and the world which has been objectified in concepts and expressed in word. *See* pp. 4f., 21.

Knowledge, unthematic: consciousness of the self and the world occurring within and identical with one's actual, lived relationship with the world and experience of it. *See* pp. 4f., 21.

Magisterium (or official teaching): the Church in the exercise of its responsibility and ability to teach the Gospel authentically. In popular Roman Catholic writings and some ecclesiastical documents the term is often used more restrictively to refer to a group (bishops and Pope) who have primary responsibility for pastoral teaching. *See* pp. 134f.

Myth: talk of God which takes the form of a human story inasmuch as it represents the transcendent God active in history as one being among others, as part of the created world. In a positive sense, it is an inescapable dimension of all religious discourse, which can only speak of God in terms derived from experience in the world. In a negative sense, especially in Rahner's Christology, it is the view that God's presence in Christ is simply the presence of God in the appearance of a man rather than through a genuine human subjectivity. *See* p. 108.

Mystery, God as: the reality of God as incomprehensible, present to every finite spirit in the latter's openness to the infinite, and bestowed upon humankind in the new creation and absolute nearness of grace. The divine mystery is called *absolute* because it is an intrinsic characteristic of the divine infinity, not a provisional state of human consciousness at a stage of development. The divine mystery is called *holy* because in evoking the transcendence of human freedom and love, as well as the establishment of all things in being, God alone is the focus of human adoration. *See* pp. 39f., 44ff.

Mysticism: interior meeting and union with the divine infinity who sustains all creation. *See* pp. 142, 166.

Natural law: a term designating the tradition in ethics that asserts morality to be a work of reason, not mere will, and moral obligation to be what reason can explain by asking about the permanent basic structure of the human being, called human nature. *See* pp. 171f.

Nature, human: the basic structures of the human person forming the boundary and channel within which the exercise of freedom in creative love will be effective and so objectively good, outside of which the exercise of freedom in refusal to love will be destructive and so evil; the concept has narrower or larger content depending on the natural-law ethician's understanding of person and freedom. *See* pp. 173ff.

Nicaea, first Council of: ecumenical council of the Church in 325 which responded to Arianism and declared that the Son was not a creature but "of one substance" (*homoousios*) with the Father. *See* p. 109.

Obediential potency: a capacity which is open to fulfillment, yet meaningful even if fulfillment is not granted. For Rahner, human nature as such is obediential potency for the self-communication of God. *See* pp. 72f.

Ontic: a mode of conceptualizing reality through basic categories or paradigms drawn from the impersonal world of things; contrasted with ontological. *See* p. 9.

Ontological: a mode of conceptualizing reality through basic categories or paradigms drawn from the personal world of conscious and free human existence; contrasted with ontic. *See* p. 9.

Original Church (early or primitive Church): *Urkirche,* perhaps better translated as the early Church or the apostolic Church, the Christian community during the formative years from Pentecost until the close of the New Testament period (about A.D. 110). *See* p. 126; also *Foundations,* pp. 335–42.

Parousia: from the Greek word for "presence." As a technical term, it refers to Christ's Second Coming at the time of the world's end. *See* p. 162.

Person, human: traditional term for the human self as an individual rational being of unique value. The modern notion of "person" indicates the spiritual structure of our being: that permanent transcendence through knowledge and love whereby a human subject possesses itself in a conscious, free relationship to other persons, to reality as a whole, and to God as the context of reality. *See* pp. 19f.

Person, divine: the classical notion of "person" was elaborated within the history of Catholic dogma to distinguish the threefold aspect of God's self-communication within the history of salvation: The Origin of the fullness of being (God as unoriginate Origin, as Father); the Self-Manifestation of this plenitude (God as Word, as Son); the Outpouring of this plenitude in the transformation of the human person (God as Holy Spirit). These three aspects of salvation history are God's self-communication, and consequently, they are found within the divine interiority or the "nature" of God. Rahner distinguishes insistently between the modern sense of person (self-presence and self-possession in knowledge and love) and this theologically elaborated notion of person which indicates the three, mutually different ways in which the divine nature exists (three "distinct ways of subsistence"). *See* p. 68.

Petrine office (or Petrine ministry or function): an activity fostering unity in the Church similar to the pastoral (John 21:15–19) and inspirational (Luke 22:32) work of Simon Peter in the New Testament. Recently, Catholic scholars have suggested the term "Petrine office" as useful to identify the biblical roots of what later developed into the ministry of popes who are described as successors of St. Peter. *See* p. 134.

Phenomenology: a careful description of basic human experiences. More technically, a mode of reflection which seeks to read the basic structures of reality in the given contents of consciousness. *See* p. 41.

Prayer: loving response to God's mysterious presence, whether liturgical or private or as a dimension of daily living. *See* p. 151.

Primeval revelation: the God-given orientation, from the beginning of time, of human beings as free subjects toward intimacy with God. *See* pp. 80, 88.

Prophet: an original bearer of a revealed communication from God; one in whom the self-interpretation of God's address to humanity takes place in word and in deed. *See* pp. 85, 87.

Providence: God's guidance of the world's reality and of the course of human affairs toward their perfection. Thus, the plan God's knowledge (knowing all things) and will (holy and loving, mightily sustaining and directing all things) have for the created world. *See* pp. 47, 82, 85.

Redemption: the event in which the real guilt incurred by human acts, guilt from which we cannot escape by ourselves, is removed by the deed of God; the process by which God overcomes the power of sin and brings sinners back into communion with God's own life. *See* pp. 51f., 58ff.

Religion: all that comprises the relations of human beings with Mystery, the Holy, the Sacred. *See* pp. 82f., 138, 143.

Resurrection of Jesus Christ: Jesus Christ in his whole reality, and therefore also in his body, has been saved and raised from his death on the cross to life with God in glory. In this way God the Father set his seal of approval upon the life and teaching of Jesus. *See* pp. 97ff.

Revelation, natural: God's self-disclosure to the world inasmuch as God is the cause of the world's being. *See* p. 80.

Revelation, supernatural: God's self-disclosure to the world inasmuch as God promises God's own life to the world as its future. *See* p. 80.

Revelation, history of: the historical objectification and self-interpretation of God's self-communication to humanity in its world. *See* pp. 79ff.

Revelation, universal transcendental: the supernaturally elevated, unreflexive human experience of movement and orientation toward the immediacy and closeness of God; it is coextensive with the history of the world, although not identical with that history. *See* pp. 13, 87.

Revelation, special categorical: the permanently valid self-interpretation of God's transcendental self-communication to humanity, thematizing the universal categorical history of this self-communication. This "official" history of revelation is what Christians understand by the Old and New Testament history. *See* pp. 86, 88.

Sacrament: an act in which the Church expresses God's unfailing pledge of grace and applies it to a decisive moment of personal religious life. *See* pp. 143ff.

Salvation: the healing and fulfillment of human life through God's self-communication in grace; also, the condition of being removed by God from a spiritually perilous situation. *See* pp. 59, 61f., 65.

Salvation, history of: God's grace at work in history; God's self-communication present within and beneath history and leading individual and world history to a fulfillment of meaning and life. *See* pp. 27, 80, 83ff.

Salvation, general or universal history of: the self-communication of God (grace and revelation, both explicit and implicit) which exists throughout our world, fallen and yet called to life with God, and which thus permeates all of history. *See* pp. 13, 83ff.

Salvation, special history of: a segment of the history of salvation can be special in different ways: by reason of its importance to us or by reason of its proximity to the fulfillment of salvation history, Jesus Christ. In the second sense the Old Testament records a special salvation history. In the first sense, for Asians, the saving history and story of Buddha might be a special segment of salvation history. The Christ event and the subsequent history of its unfolding throughout the world is called ''the last times,'' ''the special advent of the Kingdom of God,'' because Christian faith believes it is the unique line of a history which is saving and toward which all the history of salvation leads. *See* pp. 83ff.

Self-communication, God's: God's free, personal gift of self as the innermost principle of human existence; God's act of giving God's own life away to creatures, over and above creation and providence. *See* pp. 65ff.

Sin, original: the condition of being graceless, or spiritually and morally bound, as a result of the sins of others, not one's own sins. *See* pp. 58ff., 81.

Sin, personal: an orientation, attitude or action which involves rejection of God's love and false love of a creature, due to the misuse of one's own freedom. *See* pp. 54ff.

Sin of the world: the power inherent in the accumulated sins committed down through history and constituting a situation or context for each person's freedom. *See* pp. 59f.

Subjectivity: human existence inasmuch as it experiences itself as conscious, free, and responsible self or subject in the midst of and vis-à-vis a world of objects. Since our human subjectivity is always shared with other human subjects in the world, Rahner also speaks of the intersubjectivity of human existence. *See* pp. 5f., 19f.

Supernatural existential: the initial effect of the permeation of our entire existence by the gratuitous divine self-communication. The supernatural existential is present even prior to human response to God's self-offer. *See* pp. 13, 71ff., 181.

Transcendental: pertaining to that dimension of human experience which entails the unthematic awareness of the wholeness of being itself, implicitly present in ordinary knowledge and freedom as their constant background and goal. *See* pp. 23f., 123; also **Categorical.**

Transcendence in human experience: the characteristic dynamism of the human spirit, whether in knowledge or in love or in freedom, to "move beyond" any particular or finite being toward a context or horizon which gives it final coherence and value. *See* pp. 5f., 9, 19ff., 141f.

Transcendent, God as: God as "wholly other." The characteristic of the divine reality whereby God is always and infinitely beyond anything finite. It is because God is utterly transcendent that God can be pervasively *immanent* in all things, more present to each thing than it is to itself. *See* pp. 42f.

Trinity, economic: God as he is present and reveals himself as Father, Son, and Holy Spirit in the history, or economy, of salvation. *See* pp. 68, 79; also **Person, divine.**

Trinity, immanent: God as he exists eternally in himself as Father, Son, and Holy Spirit. *See* pp. 68, 79; also **Person, divine.**

Universal salvific will of God: God's free offer of himself as saving grace to all men and women. "God wills all persons to be saved and to come to the knowledge of the truth" (1 Timothy 2:4). *See* pp. 62, 70, 82, 98f., 101ff., 112f.

Utopia: classically, any state or situation of ideal perfection; as used by Rahner, it means this-worldly planning achieved by human ingenuity and freedom. *See* pp. 163ff.